Holding Tight to the

Book 1 - Essential Qualities of a Believer

Kaushar Tai

Published in the UK by Aksaa

Edited and produced by Beacon Books and Media Ltd

www.beaconbooks.net

ISBN: 978-1-916955-79-0 Paperback

Cataloguing-in-Publication record for this book is available from the British Library

CONTENTS

Preface

This book was inspired by a colleague who, after attending several of my workshops, encouraged me to compile the content into a book so that others could benefit. Much of what you will read comes from the various courses, talks, and workshops I've delivered to Muslim audiences across the UK, covering topics such as Leadership, Positive Parenting, Cultural Competency, Islamic Personal Development, Marriage, Business Ethics, Mindfulness, Stress Management, Chaplaincy, and Employability Skills.

Though I initially struggled to begin writing, the opportunity arose when I was asked to prepare transcripts for my colleagues Mohammad Yusuf Bashforth and Junaid Rahim, with whom I co-founded the *Two White Muslims* YouTube channel. These transcripts formed the foundation of this book.

A central theme of my teachings has always been the importance of developing good character and drawing closer to Allah^{SWT}. I was deeply impacted by the Hadith of the 'Bankrupt' — where the Prophet (peace be upon him) warns that despite one's prayers, fasting, and zakah, wronging others through slander, injustice, and harm may result in severe consequences on the Day of Judgment. While many lectures focus on *Huququl-Allah* (the rights of Allah), I felt there was insufficient emphasis on *Huququl-Ibad* (the rights of people), which is equally vital for our success in the Hereafter.

The Quran reminds us of the gravity of that Day: *"On that Day a man will flee from his brother, his mother and his father, his wife and his children; each one will have enough concern for themselves to make them indifferent to others."* **(Quran 80:34-37)**

Ultimately, while acts of worship are essential, they must be accompanied by righteous conduct towards others — kindness, patience, forgiveness, and justice. Rights owed to Allah^{SWT} may be forgiven through sincere repentance, but rights owed to people require us to seek their forgiveness directly.

My workshops have aimed to help individuals become more self-aware, to reflect on their conduct, and to uphold the highest moral standards in their dealings with others. Allah^{SWT} has given us countless blessings, and in return, asks only that we be just, compassionate, and mindful of our responsibilities to others.

I pray that this book serves as a helpful reminder of our duties toward *Huququl-Ibad*. Any benefit from this work is solely by the grace of Allah^{SWT}, and any mistakes are my own. I welcome your feedback for correction and ask for your forgiveness and the forgiveness of Allah^{SWT}.

Kaushar Tai

Dedication

I dedicate this book first and foremost to my beloved family and friends. To my dear parents, Mahmood Kassambhai Tai (Guard) and Sugrabibi Tai, for their unwavering care, love, and compassion; to my wife Anisa, for her patience, generosity, and constant support and her sacrifices and encouragement throughout this journey.

I am deeply grateful to my teachers and scholars for their guidance, knowledge, and mentorship, which gave me the confidence to embark on this work. Finally, I extend my heartfelt thanks to all the participants of the various programmes I have delivered in the UK and abroad — their enthusiasm and thoughtful questions have been a constant source of inspiration for this publication.

Acknowledgements

I am deeply grateful to everyone who has contributed to this book in any capacity. In particular, I would like to express my sincere appreciation to Declan Henry and Mahmood Patel for their constructive feedback and valuable suggestions.

Special thanks to Imam Osman Shiekh for carefully verifying the authenticity of the interpretations of the Qur'an and Hadith throughout the work. I am also indebted to Junaid Rahim, Mohammad Yusuf Bashforth, and Reverend Mike Gartland for their thorough review of the grammar, structure, and overall sequence of the book.

About the Author

Kaushar Tai is a seasoned Management and Training Consultant and the Director of Aksaa Management and Training Consultancy, based in Dewsbury, UK. With over two decades of experience across healthcare, social care, and management, Kaushar has developed and delivered training programmes that empower individuals and communities with the tools to lead, serve, and grow - both spiritually and professionally.

Specialising in leadership, personal development, and cultural competency, Kaushar's work bridges the gap between faith and practice. His training reaches Muslim and non-Muslim audiences alike, and he is particularly known for delivering Islamic Cultural Awareness programmes to public sector professionals, including those in health, education, and civil service.

His workshops on Positive Parenting, Marriage, and Islamic Leadership are widely respected for their practical, faith-rooted approach. Kaushar's work reflects a deep commitment to Islamic values, social cohesion, and the belief that holding tightly to the rope of Allah is both a personal and collective calling.

Note on Honorific Abbreviations and Superscript Usage

Throughout this book, standard Islamic honorifics appear in abbreviated superscript form after sacred names to maintain readability while observing reverence. Readers are encouraged to recite the full phrases silently or aloud as an act of remembrance.

SWT (سُبْحَانَهُ وَتَعَالَىٰ): Subḥānahu wa Taʿālā – Glorified and Exalted is He. Used after the name of Allah.

P (صَلَّىٰ ٱللَّهُ عَلَيْهِ وَسَلَّمَ): Ṣallā Allāhu ʿalayhi wa-sallam - Peace be upon him. Used after the name of the Prophet Muhammad.

RA (رضي الله عنه / عنها / عنهم): Raḍiyallāhu ʿanhu/ʿanhā/ʿanhum – May Allah be pleased with him/her/them. Used after the names of the Prophet's Companions.

AS (عليه السلام): ʿAlayhi al-Salām – Upon him be peace – Used after the names of other Prophets or honoured figures.

FOREWORD

by Sheikh Osman

Imam, Hospital Chaplain and Founder of Islamic Nikah Services UK

The Quran and Sunnah have been documented from the early days of Islam. The stringent reporting criteria developed by memorisers and commentators of sacred text ensured that core source materials were not tampered with but preserved and conveyed to future generations intact.

Islamic scripture has been easily accessible not only to scholars but to all people. This has not resulted in a dilution of teachings. If anything, the dynamism of Islamic teachings has enabled the faith to rise effectively to address the challenges of each era, protect it from corruption, safeguard core values, and, over time, sustain internal and external academic discourse, dialogue and scrutiny.

By sharing insights, wisdom and practical experiences in this field, Kaushar demonstrates, in his unique way, how the Quran and Sunnah remain relevant to our lives today. This is another link to the golden chain of transmitting beneficial religious knowledge. Imagine the multiplier impact of this on the lives of so many others!

Kaushar has a rare quality of incisiveness that helps him navigate cultural and parochial sensitivities with ease. He can penetrate traditionally conservative communities without causing offence. His nuanced approach has secured engagement and endorsement from over 100 Masjids and community organisations across the UK, whose leadership have gladly hosted his educational programmes.

Kaushar's conversational style of writing inspires and engages the reader while challenging commonly held assumptions. Kaushar compels us to think with an open mind. His interactive style of dialogue has enabled academics and lay people to get an authentic experience of Islam and Muslims.

Kaushar has a genuine interest in matters affecting wider society and Muslims. He promotes adoption and fostering nationally and engenders solidarity among Muslims by facilitating dialogue between scholars holding differing opinions on matters such as moon-sighting and Eid unification. His passion for inter-faith work has opened many minds to the beauty of our faith and helped nurture within Muslims a healthy appreciation of the diversity of religious practices and denominations found in the UK.

I have known Kaushar since 2005, when we combined efforts to deliver Islam Awareness courses. Since then, other personal development courses on leadership, bereavement, fostering and adoption, health and social care, chaplaincy, marriage and relationships have also been delivered. Over 36,000 participants from statutory agencies and voluntary sector organisations have benefited from the courses Kaushar and his team have delivered so far.

What you have in your hands is the result of dedication, research and genuine effort to gather relevant quotes from the Quran and Sunnah in one place. His narrative provides useful context for the quotes and serves as handy reference points for seekers of knowledge and tutors alike.

Kaushar benefits from a pool of experienced scholars and over 50 male and female co-facilitators who help deliver such courses. Many facilitators are themselves Reverts and bring fresh perspectives to the discussions. The sterling efforts of his skilled facilitators and admin team have added value and enhanced the satisfaction of attendees at his events.

It's a privilege and an honour to be asked to pen a few words by way of a foreword to this publication. I attribute Kaushar's success in the field of learning to his sincerity, humility, charm and generosity of spirit, all backed by Divine Providence.

I hereby commend this and future publications and invite you to also benefit from all the initiatives Kaushar has a hand in.

Sheikh Osman

June 2025

Introduction

I begin this book in the name of Almighty Allah — the Most Gracious, the Most Merciful — whose blessings are countless, whose mercy is infinite, and whose worship is the essence of our faith.

All praise is due to Allah. We seek His help and forgiveness and seek refuge in Him from the evils within ourselves and from our wrong actions. Whoever Allah guides, none can misguide; and whoever He leaves astray, none can guide. I bear witness that there is no deity worthy of worship except Allah, alone without partner, and that Muhammad (peace be upon him) is His servant and messenger.

This book has been written solely to seek the pleasure of Allah (SWT), and it is only by His grace and mercy that it has reached completion. I pray Allah accepts this humble effort and counts it as *sadaqah jariyah* for me — an investment for the Hereafter, where only our deeds will serve as currency.

The book focuses on manners, etiquette, and moral conduct — drawing upon the teachings of the Qur'an and Sunnah. Each topic stands independently, though certain verses or hadiths may be repeated where relevant.

The first section discusses *purification of the soul* and our duties towards others (*Huququl-Ibad*), providing guidance on how to avoid harming others and how to uphold good character. Life is short, and we must strive to remain steadfast in our faith to succeed both in this world and the next. Allah has allowed us to enjoy the blessings of life, but within the boundaries He has set, as our Prophet (peace be upon him) taught us to pray:

"O our Lord! Grant us good in this world and good in the Hereafter, and save us from the punishment of the Fire." (Bukhari & Muslim)

Every action, word, and interaction is recorded, and we are held accountable. Sadly, though many of us know what is required to enter Jannah, few act upon that knowledge. In today's world of trials and tribulations, Muslims need to be even more steadfast than before. Across the globe, from Palestine to Kashmir, from Yemen to Syria, from the West to the East, and North to the South, the Muslim Ummah faces great hardship. Many scholars attribute this to weak *imaan* and disobedience to Allah's commands. As Allah says:

"Indeed, Allah will not change the condition of a people until they change what is in themselves." (Qur'an 13:11)

If this book brings you closer to Allah, increases your mindfulness, and helps you become more observant, then its purpose has been fulfilled — and all credit belongs to Allah alone. Any errors or shortcomings in this work are mine alone, and I ask for your forgiveness and for Allah's pardon. Please do not hesitate to inform me of any mistakes so they may be corrected in future editions, Insha Allah.

May Allah fill our hearts with His light, draw us closer to Him, accept our worship, and bless the entire Muslim Ummah. I humbly request your *duas* for myself, my family, and the Ummah.

There is no copyright on this publication, as its content is drawn from the Quran, Hadith, and the wisdom of our scholars. You are welcome to share, reproduce, or use excerpts freely. Many Scholars have used separate chapters for their Khutba's, please feel free to continue to do so. As a courtesy, I would appreciate being informed of any reproductions, to help understand its impact and improve future efforts, Insha Allah.

Kaushar Tai

1.Beliefs & Theology

(Aqeedah)

Who is Allah?

"Say, 'He is Allah, [who is] One, Allah, the Eternal Refuge. He neither begets nor is born, nor is there to Him any equivalent.'"

Quran 112:1-4

"Allah, the Most High, says, 'I am as My servant thinks I am. I am with him when he remembers Me. If he comes closer to Me by a hand's span, I come closer to him by an arm's length. If he comes to Me walking, I go to him at speed.'"

Bukhari and Muslim

Who is Allah?

Islam emphasises that Allah is not a human-like figure but is transcendent, existing beyond the confines of time, space, or human limitations. Allah is the proper name of the One True God, and this name can refer to no one else. The term "Allah" has no plural or gender, highlighting its uniqueness compared to the word "god," which can be pluralised (gods) or made feminine (goddess). While every language typically has words for "God" or divine beings, "Allah" stands alone as a term exclusive to the Almighty in Islam.

A common misconception among non-Muslims is that Muslims worship a deity distinct from the God of Christians and Jews. This is incorrect. "Allah" is simply the Arabic term for "God," and Muslims believe in the same singular, universal God worshipped by Jews and Christians. However, the three faiths differ in their understanding of God's nature. For instance, Muslims, like Jews, reject the Christian doctrines of the Trinity and Divine Incarnation. Despite these theological differences, Islam teaches that there is only one God, shared by all monotheistic traditions. Islam further emphasises that other religions have, to varying degrees, distorted the pure belief in God by incorporating human ideas into divine teachings.

In Islam, Allah is the Almighty, the Creator, and the Sustainer of the universe. He is entirely unique, incomparable, and beyond human likeness. When Prophet Muhammad[P] was asked about Allah, Allah Himself revealed the response in Surah Al-Ikhlas (Chapter 112), which encapsulates the essence of monotheism: *"Say, 'He is Allah, [who is] One, Allah, the Eternal Refuge. He neither begets nor is born, nor is there to Him any equivalent.'"* **Quran 112:1-4.**

Some critics allege that Allah in Islam is stern and harsh, demanding absolute obedience without compassion. This could not be further from the truth. Each of the Quran's 114 chapters, except one, begins with the verse, *"In the name of Allah, the Most Gracious, the Most Merciful."*

At the same time, Allah is Just. This balance between mercy and justice ensures that wrongdoers and sinners face appropriate consequences, while the pious are rewarded. Those who suffer in their pursuit of Allah's favour and those who oppress others are not treated equally, as justice demands accountability. The belief in an afterlife provides a moral framework, motivating people to live virtuously and seek righteousness.

Islam also rejects any anthropomorphism or favouritism in God's nature. Allah is not characterised in human terms or seen as partial to individuals or groups based on wealth, power, or race. All humans are created equal, and Allah's favour is granted solely based on piety and virtue. Concepts such as God resting, wrestling, or being envious of humanity are considered blasphemous from the Islamic perspective, as they conflict with the belief in God's perfection and transcendence.

The Creator is fundamentally different from creation. If Allah^{SWT} shared the nature of His creation, He would be temporal and dependent, which contradicts His eternal, self-sufficient nature. As the Eternal, He exists without dependence on anything outside Himself, making Him everlasting and limitless.

In Islamic theology, Allah is central to the belief system and is described as being beyond human comprehension, free from any deficiencies or imperfections.

The Quran offers profound insight into the nature of Allah, describing Him with names and attributes that reflect His greatness, mercy, and justice.

What Does Allah Say About Himself?

In the Quran, Allah speaks extensively about His nature, attributes, and relationship with His creation. These self-descriptions help believers understand and connect with Him. Allah introduces Himself in verses such as:

- **In Surah Al-Ikhlas, Allah^{SWT} says:** *"Say, 'He is Allah, [Who is] One, Allah, the Eternal Refuge. He neither begets nor is born, nor is there to Him any equivalent.'"* **Quran 112:1-4.**

- This passage establishes Allah's oneness, eternal nature, and uniqueness.

- **In Surah Al-Baqarah, Allah^{SWT} says in Ayat-ul-Kursi (The Throne Verse):** *"Allah! There is no deity except Him, the Ever-Living, the Sustainer of [all] existence. Neither drowsiness overtakes Him nor sleep. To Him belongs whatever is in the Heavens and whatever is on the Earth."* **Quran 2:255.** This verse highlights Allah's sovereignty, power, and self-sustaining nature.

Allah also repeatedly describes His mercy and compassion. One of the most frequently recited verses in the Quran is: *"In the name of Allah, the Most Gracious, the Most Merciful"* (*Bismillah-ir-Rahman-ir-Raheem*), emphasising that Allah's nature is deeply rooted in mercy and grace.

In many verses, Allah calls attention to His role as the Creator and Sustainer: *"Indeed, your Lord is Allah, who created the heavens and the Earth in six days and then established Himself above the Throne. He covers the night with the day, chasing it rapidly; and [He created] the sun, the moon, and the stars, subjected by His command. Unquestionably, His is the creation and the command; blessed is Allah, Lord of the worlds."* **Quran 7:54.**

What Does Prophet Muhammad[P] Say About Allah?

The Prophet[P] as the final Messenger of Allah, dedicated his life to teaching humanity about the Creator. His teachings, encapsulated in the *Sunnah* (his sayings, actions, and approvals), complement the Quran's descriptions of Allah.

The Prophet[P] emphasised Allah's mercy, justice, and closeness to His servants. One of the most profound hadiths (narrations) that demonstrate Allah's mercy is: *"Allah has written mercy upon Himself: 'My mercy prevails over My wrath.'"* **Bukhari and Muslim.**

The Prophet[P] also taught that Allah is closer to His creation than they might think:

"Allah, the Most High, says, 'I am as My servant thinks I am. I am with him when he remembers Me. If he comes closer to Me by a hand's span, I come closer to him by an arm's length. If he comes to Me walking, I go to him at speed.'" **Bukhari and Muslim.** In another hadith, the Prophet *said, "Verily, Allah is more merciful to His servants than a mother is to her child."* **Muslim.**

These sayings highlight Allah's infinite mercy, love, and readiness to forgive those who turn to Him sincerely.

How Does Allah Wish Us to Worship Him?

Allah commands humanity to worship Him alone, without associating any partners with Him. This principle is central to Islam and is known as **Tawheed** (the oneness of Allah). Worship in Islam encompasses not only acts of devotion, such as prayer, fasting, and charity, but also living a righteous and ethical life guided by Allah. The following are the ways to worship Allah[SWT]:

1. **Sincerity in Worship:** Worship must be directed solely toward Allah. The Qur'an states: *"And they were not commanded except to worship Allah, [being] sincere to Him in religion, inclining to truth, and to establish prayer and to give Zakah. And that is the correct religion."* **Quran 98:5.**

2. **Following the Prophet's Example:** The Prophet[p] taught that acts of worship must align with his teachings, ensuring they are neither excessive nor innovative. He, peace be upon him, *said, "Pray as you have seen me pray."* **Bukhari.**

3. **Gratitude and Remembrance:** Allah desires that we remember Him frequently and express gratitude. The Quran states: *"So remember Me; I will remember you. And be grateful to Me and do not deny Me."* **Quran 2:152.**

4. **Avoiding Shirk (Association of Partners with Allah):** Allah[SWT] says in the Quran: *"Indeed, Allah does not forgive association with Him, but He forgives what is less than that for whom He wills."* **Quran 4:48.** Worshipping Allah involves purity of faith and avoiding idolatry in all forms.

The Attributes of Allah

The Quran and *Sunnah* describe Allah through His **99 Names and Attributes**, known as *Asma'ul Husna* (The Most Beautiful Names of Allah). These names offer insight into Allah's nature. Key attributes include:

1. **Ar-Rahman (The Most Gracious) and Ar-Raheem (The Most Merciful):** Allah's mercy is boundless, encompassing all His creation.

2. **Al-Khaliq (The Creator):** Allah is the originator of everything that exists.

3. **Al-Adl (The Just):** Allah ensures perfect justice in this world and the Hereafter.

4. **Al-Aleem (The All-Knowing):** Allah's knowledge is infinite, encompassing all that was, is, and will be.

5. **Al-Ghaffaar (The Constant Forgiver):** Allah forgives sins repeatedly for those who repent.

6. **Al-Wadud (The Loving):** Allah's love for His creation is unconditional and eternal.

Allah's Mercy and Compassion

Allah's mercy (*Rahmah*) is one of His defining attributes. In a famous hadith, the Prophet[p] *said, "Allah divided mercy into one hundred parts. He kept ninety-nine parts and sent down one part to the Earth. It is because of this one part that creatures are merciful to one another..."* **Bukhari.**

This mercy is evident in the natural world and in Allah's willingness to forgive sinners who sincerely repent. The Quran reassures believers of His compassion: *"Say, 'O My servants who have transgressed against themselves [by sinning], do not despair of the mercy of Allah. Indeed, Allah forgives all sins. Indeed, it is He who is the Forgiving, the Merciful.'"* **Quran 39:53.**

Understanding Tawheed

Tawheed is the essence of Islamic belief, meaning the affirmation of Allah's oneness. It has three main aspects:

1. **Tawheed Ar-Rububiyyah (Oneness of Lordship):** Recognising Allah as the sole Creator, Sustainer, and Controller of the universe.

2. **Tawheed Al-Uluhiyyah (Oneness of Worship):** Devoting all acts of worship exclusively to Allah.

3. **Tawheed Al-Asma wa Sifat (Oneness of Names and Attributes):** Affirming Allah's names and attributes as described in the Qur'an and *Sunnah* without likening them to creation.

Living with the Knowledge of Allah

Understanding Allah and His attributes guides Muslims to live purposefully in this temporary world. Recognising His mercy encourages repentance, while His justice instils accountability. Acknowledging Allah's sovereignty fosters humility and gratitude.

To succeed, humans must:

- **Worship Allah sincerely** and avoid shirk.
- **Follow the guidance** of the Quran and the Prophet[P].
- **Seek Allah's mercy and forgiveness** while striving to fulfil obligations like prayer, fasting, and charity.
- **Reflect on Allah's attributes** to cultivate qualities such as patience, compassion, and gratitude.

Ultimately, this life is a test, and believers are called to prepare for the eternal Hereafter by aligning their lives with the will of Allah. As the Quran reminds us: *"And I did not create the jinn and mankind except to worship Me."* **Quran 51:56.** By worshipping Allah with sincerity and adhering to Tawheed, believers secure their ultimate purpose and eternal success.

Why is Allah beyond Human Comprehension?

Allah is beyond human comprehension because He is entirely unlike His creation and exists outside the limitations of time, space, and physical dimensions. This transcendence is a cornerstone of Islamic theology, emphasising that the Creator's essence and nature are far greater than anything the human mind can fully grasp. Several reasons and Quranic principles explain why Allah is beyond human understanding:

1. Allah's Uniqueness and Oneness

As mentioned earlier, Allah's uniqueness is highlighted in the Quran: *"Say, 'He is Allah, [Who is] One, Allah, the Eternal Refuge. He neither begets nor is born, nor is there to Him any equivalent.'"* **Quran Surah Al-Ikhlas 112:1-4.**

This declaration establishes that Allah is unlike anything in existence. Humans comprehend through comparison and analogy, but Allah has no parallel, making His essence incomparable and beyond the scope of human reasoning.

2. Limitations of Human Intellect

Human beings are finite creatures, confined by their senses, experiences, and intellectual capacity. In contrast, Allah is infinite, eternal, and boundless. The Quran states: *"Vision perceives Him not, but He perceives [all] vision; and He is the Subtle, the Acquainted."* **Quran 6:103.**

While humans can understand some aspects of Allah through His attributes and actions as described in the Quran, His whole nature is far beyond human understanding. For instance, humans cannot grasp the concept of eternity or existence without dependence, which are intrinsic to Allah.

3. Allah's Transcendence

The Quran repeatedly emphasises Allah's transcendence: *"There is nothing like unto Him, and He is the Hearing, the Seeing."* **Quran 42:11.**

Allah's transcendence (in Arabic, *Tanzeeh*) means that He is free from human-like qualities, physical forms, or limitations. Since human comprehension relies on observable phenomena, it cannot encompass Allah, who exists outside these realms.

4. Allah's Infinite Knowledge and Power

Allah's knowledge and power surpass human understanding. Allah[SWT] says: *"And they encompass not a thing of His knowledge except for what He wills."* **Quran 2:255.**

Humans have limited knowledge, whereas Allah's knowledge is infinite, covering everything in the past, present, and future, as well as what is visible and hidden. Such vastness is incomprehensible to the human mind.

5. Allah Is Not Dependent on Creation

All created beings depend on time, space, and physicality for their existence, but Allah is completely self-sufficient and independent. Allah[SWT] says: *"Allah is the Creator of all things, and He is, over all things, Disposer of affairs."* **Quran 39:62.**

If Allah were dependent on His creation, He would cease to be God. His nature as the Sustainer and Creator of everything separates Him from any limitations or dependencies.

6. The Creator-creation Distinction

Allah is the Creator, while humans are His creation. The Quran reminds believers: *"Does He who created not know, while He is the Subtle, the Acquainted?"* **Quran 67:14.**

The creation cannot fully comprehend the Creator, just as an invention cannot fully understand its inventor. This distinction emphasises Allah's supreme position above all existence.

7. Allah's Mercy in Remaining Beyond Comprehension

If Allah were fully comprehensible, He would be limited to human understanding, diminishing His divinity. His incomprehensibility is a mercy, preserving His majesty and safeguarding humanity from attempting to reduce Him to finite concepts.

8. Allah's Attributes Point to His Majesty

While humans cannot comprehend Allah's essence, they can understand aspects of His greatness through His attributes, such as:

- **Al-Khaliq (The Creator):** Allah created everything from nothing.
- **Al-Qadir (The All-Powerful):** Allah's power has no limits.

- **Al-Aleem (The All-Knowing):** Allah's knowledge encompasses all things.

Even these attributes, although understood conceptually, point to qualities that transcend human experience.

9. The Test of Faith

Human inability to comprehend Allah also serves as a test of faith. Believers are called to trust in Allah's wisdom and submit to His will, even without fully understanding His nature. The Quran emphasises this reliance:

"And place your trust in the Ever-Living One who does not die." **Quran 25:58.**

Conclusion

Allah's incomprehensibility underscores His majesty, power, and uniqueness. This divine transcendence ensures that no human effort or imagination can limit or define Him. While humans are unable to grasp Allah's essence fully, they can connect with Him through worship, reflection on His signs, and reliance on His guidance. The Quran encapsulates this beautifully as mentioned: *"And He is the Most High, the Most Great."* Quran **2:255.**

May Allah[SWT] grant us the ability to appreciate and understand Him as He perfectly describes Himself, and also to worship Him alone as He wants us to worship Him. Ameen.

The Three Levels of Religious Practice - Islam, *Imaan*, and Ihsan

"The 'true' servants of the Most Compassionate are those who walk on the earth humbly, and when the foolish address them 'improperly', they only respond with peace."

Quran 25:63

"The most beloved of you to Allah are those who have the best manners."

Bukhari

The three levels of religious practice in Islam, as expressed in the famous hadith of Jibreel, are **Islam,** the outward submission to the will of Allah; *Imaan*, the faith; and Ihsaan, the spiritual excellence. Texts from the Quran, *Sunnah*, and classical scholarly works are cited to distinguish these three levels of our religion. We will examine this crucial aspect of the Islamic faith.

In Islamic terminology, **"Muslim"** and **"Mumin"** refer to different levels of faith and practice. Understanding the distinction and the steps to elevate from one to the other can be deeply insightful.

In the famous hadith of Jibreel, Umar ibn al-Khattab reported: *"We were sitting with the Messenger of Allahpbuh a man appeared with very white clothes and very black hair. There were no signs of travel on him, and we did not recognise him. He sat in front of the Prophet, rested his knees against his, and placed his hands on his thighs. The man said, "O Muhammad, tell me about Islam." The Prophet said, "Islam is to testify there is no God but Allah and Muhammad is the Messenger of Allah, to establish prayer, to give charity, to fast the month of Ramadan, and to perform pilgrimage to the House if a way is possible." The man said, "You have spoken truthfully." We were surprised that he asked him and said he was truthful. He said, "Tell me about faith." The Prophet said, "Faith is to believe in Allah, His angels, His Books, His Messengers, the Last Day, and to believe in providence, its good and its harm." The man said, "You have spoken truthfully. Tell me about excellence." The Prophet said, "Excellence is to worship Allah as if you see Him, for if you do not see Him, He surely sees you." The man said, "Tell me about the final hour." The Prophet said, "The one asked does not know more than the one asking." The man said, "Tell me about its signs." The Prophet said, "The slave-girl will give birth to her mistress, and you will see barefoot, naked, and dependent shepherds compete in the construction of tall buildings." Then, the man returned, and I remained. The Prophet said to me, "O Umar, do you know who he was?" I said, "Allah and His Messenger know best." The Prophet said, "Verily, he was Gabriel who came to teach you your religion."* **Muslim.**

The Prophet[P] informed the believers around him that the man in the white garment was, in fact, the Angel Jibreel, who had come to teach them their religion. This hadith makes us understand the difference between what a Muslim is and what a Mumin is. Being a Muslim is the foundation of Islam, and anyone who enters upon the faith of Islam becomes a Muslim, but it is the beginning of the road. For every one of us, there is a journey to be made in life, from Islam to *Imaan* and then to Ihsan. We begin this process by taking steps towards growth and development, and Islam provides us with a clear path.

We must note that the terms "Mumin" and "Muslim" have also been used synonymously; however, it is essential to differentiate between the two. As the Prophet[P] *said, "Islam is outward, and Imaan is in the heart."* **Musnad Ahmad.**

Definitions of Muslim and Mumin

Muslim

A Muslim is someone who submits to the will of Allah by following the Five Pillars of Islam, which are: the declaration of faith (Shahada), prayer (Salah), fasting during *Ramadan* (Sawm), almsgiving (Zakat), and pilgrimage to Makkah (*Hajj*). The term "Muslim" emphasises the outward actions and the basic requirements of being part of the Islamic community.

Mumin

A Mumin is someone who has reached a higher level of faith, characterised by an inner conviction and sincere devotion to Allah[SWT]. The term "Mumin" refers to a true believer who not only practices the outward rituals but also embodies the deeper spiritual and moral principles of Islam.

***Imaan* (Faith)** in Islam is a comprehensive term that signifies a firm belief in Allah, His angels, His books, His prophets, the Day of Judgment, and divine predestination. It goes beyond mere intellectual acceptance. It encompasses heartfelt conviction, spiritual certainty, and the manifestation of that belief through righteous actions. Below is a breakdown to understand *Imaan* more clearly:

1. **Belief in Allah:** Recognising and affirming the oneness of Allah, His attributes, and His right to be worshipped exclusively.

2. **Belief in Angels:** Accepting the existence of angels, created by Allah, who perform various duties and act as messengers between Allah and His prophets.

3. **Belief in Divine Books:** Believing in all the holy books revealed by Allah, including the Quran, Torah, Psalms, and Gospel, acknowledging them as sources of guidance.

4. **Belief in Prophets:** Recognising and honouring all the prophets sent by Allah[SWT] to guide humanity, with Muhammad[P] being the final prophet.

5. **Belief in the Day of Judgment:** Having faith in the eventual resurrection, judgment, and afterlife, where individuals will be held accountable for their actions and inaction.

6. **Belief in Qadar (Divine Predestination):** Accepting that everything happens according to Allah's will and wisdom, encompassing both good and bad aspects of life.

Elevating from Muslim to Mumin

The transition from being a Muslim to becoming a Mumin involves deepening one's faith and embodying the teachings of Islam in every aspect of life. Some ways to achieve this, supported by examples from the Hadith are:

1. **Strengthening Faith (*Imaan*)**

   Knowledge (Ilm): Deepen your understanding of Islamic teachings by studying the Quran, Hadith, and other Islamic sciences. Knowledge is the foundation of faith. Seeking knowledge enables one to differentiate between what is right and wrong. This is why the Prophet[P] *said,* "Seeking knowledge is an obligation upon every Muslim." **Sunan Ibn Majah.**

   Reflection (Tafakkur): Reflect on the signs of Allah in the universe and within oneself. Contemplation strengthens the heart's connection to Allah.

   Sincerity (Ikhlas): Ensure that all acts of worship and good deeds are done solely for the sake of Allah, free from any form of showing off or seeking approval from others. The Prophet[P] *said, "Islam is to be sincere." The companions asked, "To whom?" He replied, "To Allah, His Book, His prophet, the* ones in authority over you and the general public." **Muslim, Tirmidhi.** The Prophet[P] also *said, "O God! Make my inside better than my outside, and make my outside (also) righteous."* **Tirmidhi.** This shows the importance of our inner reality.

Having Sincerity in Worship: It is narrated by Abu Huraira[RA] that the Prophet Muhammad[P] *said, "Verily, Allah does not look at your appearance or wealth, but rather He looks at your hearts and actions."* **Muslim.** This means that the sincerity and intention behind acts of worship are what elevate a person from merely practising Islam to truly embodying it.

2. **Practising *Taqwa* (Piety)**

Consciousness of Allah: Maintain a constant awareness of Allah in all actions and decisions. *Taqwa* involves being mindful of what pleases and displeases Allah.

Avoiding Sins: Stay away from both major and minor sins. Repent sincerely and immediately if any sin is committed.

Performing Obligatory Acts: Consistently perform the five daily prayers, fasting during *Ramadan*, paying zakat, and performing *Hajj* if able. Fulfilling these obligations is a testament to genuine faith.

3. **Developing Good Character (Akhlaq)**

Truthfulness (Sidq): Be truthful in speech and actions. Honesty is a key trait of a believer.

Patience (Sabr): Exhibit patience in times of difficulty and restraint in times of anger. In a hadith narrated by Anas ibn Malik RA, the Prophet[P] *said, "The greatest reward comes with the greatest trial. When Allah loves a people, He tests them. Whoever accepts that, wins His pleasure, but whoever is discontent with that, earns His wrath"* **Sunan Ibn Majah.** Patience and acceptance of trials with a positive attitude reflect a deep and resilient faith.

Gratitude (Shukr): Be grateful to Allah for all blessings and show appreciation in actions and words.

Allah[SWT] has bestowed countless blessings upon us. He has endowed us with the gifts of sight and hearing, intellect, health, wealth, and family. He has even subjected everything in the universe to us: the sun, the moon, the stars, the *Heavens*, the Earth, and many countless things, as Allah[SWT] states in the Quran:

"If you tried to number Allah's blessings, you could never count them." **Quran 16:18.** As believers, we need to focus on things we simply cannot live without and be grateful to Allah[SWT] for everything that we have. Allah[SWT] says: *"So which of the favours of your Lord would you deny?"* **Quran 55:13.**

Humility (Tawaadhu): Maintain humility, acknowledging one's dependence on Allah and treating others with respect and kindness. Allah[SWT] says in the Quran: *"The 'true' servants of the Most Compassionate are those who walk on the earth humbly, and when the foolish address them 'improperly', they only respond with peace."* **Quran 25:63** The Prophet[P] *said, "The most beloved of you to Allah are those who have the best manners."* **Bukhari.** Good character, including honesty, kindness, and humility, is the hallmark of a true believer.

4. **Acts of Charity and Service**

The Prophet[P] *said, "He is not a believer whose stomach is filled while his neighbour goes hungry."* **Sunan An-Nasai.** True faith involves concern and active support for others, particularly those in need.

The Prophet[P] *said, "The most beloved people to Allah[SWT] are those who are most beneficial to people. The most beloved deed to Allah is to make a Muslim happy, or to remove one of his troubles, or to forgive his debt, or to feed his hunger. That I walk with a brother regarding a need is more beloved to me than that I seclude myself in this mosque in Madina for a month. Whoever swallows his anger, then Allah[SWT] will conceal his faults. Whoever suppresses his rage, even though he could fulfil his anger if he wished, then Allah[SWT] will secure his heart on the Day of Resurrection. Whoever walks with his brother regarding a need until he secures it for him, then Allah[SWT] will make his footing firm across the bridge on the day when the footings are shaken."* **Tabarani, Albani.**

5. **Maintaining Trust and Avoiding Harm**

The Prophet[P] *said, "The Muslim is the one from whose tongue and hand the people are safe, and the believer is the one who is trusted with the lives and wealth of the people."* **Tirmidhi.** Trustworthiness and ensuring others feel safe from any harm are key traits of a Mumin.

These two states, the outer Islam and the inner Islam of the heart, come together to describe the complete Mumin.

A Muslim could be in a state of Islam, i.e., a Muslim but not yet in a state of *Imaan*, or a Mumin, because the outer actions are those of a Muslim only, such as prayers, fasting, and *Hajj*. Maybe what is hidden in the heart is disbelief or doubt. This is a perilous situation to be in, one that the hypocrite often finds himself in. However, it does not make a person a hypocrite if they are sincere and at the beginning of their growth journey. The remedy for this is to acquire knowledge, as it will erase doubts and bring certainty.

This Quranic verse addressed to the Prophet explains the difference between the two stages. Allah[SWT] says: *"The Bedouins say, 'We have believed', Say (Oh Muhammad), 'You have not yet believed, say instead we have submitted', for faith has not yet entered your hearts."* **Quran 49:14.**

This verse was revealed in response to certain Bedouins who had recently outwardly accepted Islam. They claimed to have fully believed (i.e., had complete faith), but their actions and attitudes did not reflect a deep, sincere commitment to the faith.

Allah instructs the Prophet[P] to correct them, saying that they should instead say, "We have submitted," acknowledging that they have accepted Islam outwardly. The reason for this correction is that true faith (*Imaan*) had not yet fully taken root in their hearts; their belief was more superficial and had not reached the level of deep conviction and spiritual maturity.

It highlights the importance of sincere faith that permeates the heart and reflects in a person's actions and behaviour. It also serves as a reminder that Islam is not just about external conformity, but about developing a genuine, internal connection with God. In essence, the verse calls for self-reflection, urging believers to move beyond mere outward submission and strive towards true, heartfelt belief.

In another hadith, narrated by Abdullah ibn Abbas RA, the Prophet[P] took him behind him on his mount and began to teach him the words: *"O young boy! I will teach you some words: Be mindful of Allah, and He will preserve you. Be mindful of Allah, and you will find Him in front of you. If you ask, ask of Allah; if you seek help, seek help from Allah. Know that if the people were to gather together to benefit you with something, they would not benefit you except with something that Allah has already prescribed for you, and if they gather together to harm you with something, they would not harm you except with something that Allah has already prescribed for you. The pens have been lifted, and the pages have dried."* **Tirmidhi.**

This hadith, narrated by Abdullah ibn Abbas[RA] and recorded by Tirmidhi, provides profound guidance on the principles of faith, reliance, and the nature of destiny in Islam.

Allah talks about having belief and turning that into action because that is how Muslims become Mumin. It is all about action. It's about practising what we know. However, before we can practice what we know, we have to seek to understand. That does not mean we should stop seeking to understand and never start practising. Instead, these two things happen simultaneously as we learn and act.

The Mumin actualises that knowledge by living it day to day and trying their best. It's never about being perfect and never making mistakes. Allah knows us better than anyone, and hence, He is the Most Compassionate.

Ihsan is the highest level of the believer

In the Hadith of Jibreel, the Prophet[P] said that Ihsan is a state in which the believer behaves as though he sees Allah, even though he cannot. This means that we should act as though we are constantly in a state of awareness. Being aware that Allah is watching us and seeing everything we do and say is what every Muslim should strive towards. Ihsan is a level that transcends the normal level of a Mumin because the person is constantly in a state of remembering Allah.

When we consistently practice daily prayer rituals, thoughtfully focused, we become stronger and more confident. Our belief in ourselves grows, allowing us to achieve anything we set our minds to. Our connection and trust in Allah deepens, making us even stronger.

Anyone can go from being a Muslim to a Mumin by simply acting upon the knowledge that they have. And anyone can go from being a Mumin to a Muhsin by practising and continually striving to master themselves. Personal growth and development are keys to attaining paradise, as the Messenger of Allah[P] said, *"Indeed, I have been sent in order to perfect honourable character."*

The journey from being a Muslim (one who submits to Allah) to becoming a Mumin (a true believer) and then reaching the level of Ihsan (excellence in worship) is a process of deepening faith, improving character, and perfecting one's worship.

Elevating from Mumin to Muhsin – Ihsan Level

A *Muhsin* is the most pleasing person to Allah[SWT], who practices a high level of *Taqwa* (God-consciousness), has true inner peace, and sincerely wants to attain *Jannath-ul-Firdaus*. A *Muhsin* is one who is constantly striving not to make a single decision, including intention, to commit sins or give in to shortcomings, so that they can attain the ultimate pleasure of Allah SW). They realise that every choice they make, no matter how big or small, is either going to get them closer to Allah[SWT] or away from Allah[SWT].

The Prophet[P] said, *"Allah says: 'Whoever takes a close friend of Mine as an enemy, I declare war on him. My slave does not draw closer to Me by anything more beloved to Me than that which I have made obligatory upon him, and My slave continues to draw closer to Me by doing Nawaafil (optional) deeds until I love him, and if I love him I will be his hearing with which he hears, his vision with which he sees, his hand with which he strikes and his foot with which he walks. If he were to ask of Me, I would surely give to him; if he were to seek refuge with Me, I would surely grant him refuge. I do not hesitate about anything that I want to do, as I hesitate to take the soul of a believer, for he hates death and I hate to hurt him."* **Bukhari.**

This hadith highlights the way to become a close friend of Allah[SWT], reaching the level of Ihsan. This hadith also highlights that the best way to get closer to Allah[SWT] is by doing what is obligatory, i.e., the *Wajib*(s).

Hence, every *Wajib* is the most loved action to Allah[SWT]. Therefore, a *Muhsin* performs the *Wajib*(s) and continues to draw closer to Allah[SWT] by doing the *Nawaafil,* which are *Mustahab* (desirable), the recommended actions.

This highest level of faith is where one worships Allah as if they see Him. It involves perfecting one's worship and actions to achieve excellence, as follows:

1. **Perfecting Worship**
   - **Khushu (Concentration):** Develop deep concentration and humility in prayers. Understand the meanings of what is recited and maintain focus on Allah.
   - **Regular Supererogatory Prayers (Nawaafil):** In addition to obligatory prayers, regularly perform additional prayers, such as Tahajjud (night prayer) and Dhuha (forenoon prayer).
   - **Quran Recitation and Memorisation:** Regularly recite, memorise, and ponder over the meanings of the Quran. Implement its teachings in daily life.

2. **Enhancing Spirituality**
   - **Dhikr (Remembrance of Allah):** Engage in constant remembrance of Allah through various forms of dhikr. This keeps the heart connected to Allah.

- **Dua (Supplication):** Frequently make sincere supplications to Allah, asking for guidance, forgiveness, and the strength to achieve Ihsan.
- **Muraqabah (Self-Accountability):** Regularly take account of your actions, seeking to improve and rectify any shortcomings.

3. **Excellence in Character:**
   - **Altruism (Eethaar):** Prefer others over oneself in matters of goodness and charity.
   - **Compassion (Rahmah):** Show mercy and compassion towards all of Allah's creations.
   - **Forgiveness (Afw):** Forgive others for their mistakes and wrongdoings, seeking Allah's forgiveness in return.

4. **Seeking Allah's Pleasure:**
   - **Intention (Niyyah):** Ensure that every action, whether religious or mundane, is done to seek Allah's pleasure.
   - **Contentment (Ridha):** Develop contentment with Allah's decree and trust in His wisdom in all aspects of life.
   - **Love for Allah and His Messenger:** Cultivate a deep love for Allah and the Prophet Muhammad[P] by following the *Sunnah* and striving to emulate the Prophet's character.

Becoming a Mumin from being a Muslim and reaching the level of Ihsan is a continuous journey of self-improvement, spiritual growth, and sincere devotion. It involves deepening one's faith, enhancing the quality of worship, developing excellent character, and maintaining a constant awareness of Allah's presence. Through persistent effort, sincere intention, and Allah's guidance, one can strive to achieve these lofty spiritual states.

May Allah[SWT] grant us the Taufiq to strive toward reaching the level of Ihsan and remaining steadfast to maintain it.

The Purpose of Life in Islam

"I have only created jinns and humans that they may worship Me."

Quran 51:56

"How wonderful the affair of the believer is! Indeed, all of his affairs are good for him. This is for no one but the believer. If something good happens to him, he is grateful to Allah, which is good for him. And if something bad happens to him, he has patience, which is good for him."

Muslim

What is the purpose of our life? Why did Allah^SWT create us? This is an important question every human being should ask themselves.

Why are we born? What is the object of our existence, what is the wisdom behind the creation of man and this tremendous universe? What are we supposed to do in this life?

Think about these questions. Islam has the answer to every question we ask.

Some people argue that there is no proof of any divine origin, no proof that there is a God, and no proof that this universe has come about through any divine purpose. Some people believe this way, and they suggest that perhaps this world came into existence by chance. The Big Bang and this entire great world, with all its orchestration, just came together. They argue that life lacks a definite purpose and that there is no evidence, either through logic or science, to prove the existence of a God, a purpose, or any divine reason behind this world.

Islam provides clear and concise answers to these questions. Allah says: *"Verily! In the creation of the Heavens and the Earth, and in the alternation of night and day, there are indeed signs for men of understanding, who remember Allah standing, sitting, and lying down on their sides, and contemplate the creation of the Heavens and the Earth, (and conclude), "Our Lord! You have not created all this without purpose, glory to You! Grant us salvation from the torment of the Fire."* **Quran 3:190-191.**

In this verse, Allah^SWT clearly mentions to us, first drawing our attention to the creation of our own being. The various postures of the human body and the diverse attitudes of people. He draws our attention to the *Heavens*. The alternation of night and day. The sky, the stars, the constellations. And then He says to us that He has not created all of this for any foolish purpose! Because when you see the design of it, you know that the design of it is compelling and very precise. And something compelling and precise that is beyond our own calculation and imagination cannot be foolish. It cannot be just thrown together.

In essence, the purpose of creation for all men and women for all times has been just one: "To know and worship Allah". Allah^{SWT} says, *"I have only created jinns and humans that they may worship Me."* **Quran 51:56.**

Allah is self-sustaining and has Angels that worship Him nonstop. So why does Allah command humans and Jinn to worship him? If we say that Allah is in no need of anything from us, yet He commands us to worship Him, then is this not a contradiction?

As Muslims, we understand that Allah is far above His creation insofar as He is not dependent on any part of it. Quite simply, it is out of His mercy that He has created us. Allah^{SWT} commands certain things and forbids other things. It is not Allah who benefits from the commands He gives us; we are the ones who benefit.

When Allah commands us to abstain from eating pork, blood, and animals found dead, or if He forbids the drinking of alcohol, it is not Allah who benefits from this if we obey, nor is He harmed if we disobey. We are the ones who suffer from disobeying Him, and we are the ones who benefit from obeying. This applies to anything that Allah commands us to do and anything He commands us to avoid.

In a hadith Qudsi, which is a revelation from Allah expressed in the Prophet's^P words, we learn the following: Allah's Messenger^P once said that Allah^{SWT} *said,*

"O My servants, I have made oppression unlawful for Me and unlawful for you, so do not commit oppression against one another.

O My servants, all of you are liable to err except those whom I guide on the right path, so seek the proper guidance from Me so that I may direct you to the right path.

O My servants, all of you are hungry and needy except those whom I feed, so ask for food from Me, so that I may feed you.

O My servants, all of you are naked except those whom I provide garments, so ask for clothes from Me, so that I should clothe you.

O My servants, you commit error night and day, and I am there to pardon your sins, so ask pardon from Me so that I may grant you pardon.

O My servants, you can neither do Me any harm nor any good.

O My servants, even if the first in creation among you and the last in creation among you and even the whole of human race of yours and that of Jinns, even, become God-conscious like the heart of the most God-conscious person among you, that would add nothing to My power.

O My servants, even if the first in creation among you and the last in creation among you and the whole human race of yours and that of the Jinns too in unison become the most wicked like the heart of a single person, that would take nothing of My power.

O My servants, even if the first in creation among you and the last in creation among you and the whole human race of yours and that of Jinns also all stand in one plain ground and you ask Me and I confer upon every person what he asks for, it would not in any way cause any loss to Me any more than that which is lost to the ocean by dipping a needle in it.

O My servants, it is but your deeds that I reckon up for you and then recompense you for, so let him who finds good, praise Allah; and let him who finds other than that, blame no one but himself." **Muslim**

Here we learn from this hadith that Allah forbids what is harmful and enjoins on us what is beneficial. If we study prohibitions closely and use available science, it is easy to see that actions and things Islam prohibits are harmful. Allah forbids what is harmful and enjoins on us what is beneficial. Allah^SWT also expresses his power and might, and that He is very merciful.

Were Allah not merciful and only intended to serve Himself, we would find some commands that were beneficial to Him only and harmful to us. We find no such commands in any part of the Quran or in anything that the Prophet Muhammad^P has commanded us.

Allah^SWT says: *"Those who follow the Messenger, the unlettered Prophet, whom they find mentioned in their own scriptures, in the Torah and the Gospel; for he commands them what is just and forbids them what is evil; he allows them as lawful what is good and pure and prohibits them from what is bad and impure; he releases them from their heavy burdens and from the yokes that are upon them. So, it is those who believe in im, honour him, help him, and follow the light that is sent down with him, who will prosper."* **Quran 7:157.**

Allah created us out of His mercy. He created good and evil and gave us the ability to choose between right and wrong, knowing full well that some of us would choose what is harmful to us and some would follow His guidance. He will reward us for choosing good and following His guidance and punish us for harming ourselves by choosing evil.

Part of this guidance involves recognising all the incredible blessings that He has created alongside us, enabling us to lead a beneficial life.

Allah^{SWT} says: *"All in the Heavens and the earth entreat Him for their needs; a new, mighty task engages Him each day."* **Quran 55:29.** This means Allah^{SWT} is continuously and endlessly functioning in this universe and creating countless new things with new and yet new forms and designs and qualities, He is giving death to one and life to another, exalting one and debasing another, causing one to recover and another to remain ill, rescuing a drowning one and drowning a floating one. He provides sustenance to countless creatures in various ways. His world never remains in the same state; it changes every moment, and its Creator arranges it in a new state and fashion every time, which is different from every previous form and fashion and state.

Allah^{SWT} has given us everything we need to sustain this life, but more importantly, He has shown us the way to achieve something even more incredible, the chance to live in eternity in Paradise in His glorious presence.

To achieve Paradise, it is necessary to remain in close contact with Him regularly as much as we can, and if possible, at all times of the day and night. Hence comes the necessity of prayer and piety. We do ourselves a great disservice if we miss this opportunity.

Allah alone deserves to be worshipped. Allah^{SWT} says: *"He it is Who has brought you into being, and has given you hearing and sight and has given you hearts to think and understand. How seldom do you give thanks."* **Quran 67:23.**

This verse means that Allah has made us human, not cattle. We were not meant to follow blindly whatever error and deviation we find prevailing in the world, without considering for a moment whether the way we had adopted was right or wrong. We have not been given these ears that we may refuse to listen to the one who tries to distinguish right from wrong for us and may persist in whatever false notions we already have in our minds. We have not been given these eyes that we may follow others like the blind and may not bother to see whether the signs scattered around us in the world testify to the unity of God, which the Messenger^p is preaching, or whether the system of the universe is Godless, or is being run by many gods simultaneously.

Likewise, we have not been given this knowledge and intelligence, so we may give up thinking and understanding to others and adopt every crooked way that has been enforced by someone in the world, without using our intellect to determine whether it is right or wrong. Allah^{SWT} has blessed us with knowledge and intelligence, sight and hearing, so that we may recognise the truth. Still, we are being ungrateful to Him in that we employ these faculties for every other object than the one for which they had been granted.

The purpose of our creation was not only to offer prayer and fast in the month of *Ramadan*, give Zakat, and go for *Hajj*. Rather, these are the duties that we must do. Our purpose as a whole is to be conscious, express gratitude, and sincerely worship our Lord, Allah Al Mighty.

When we fulfil such a noble duty, our hearts find tranquillity and peace, and no calamity that befalls us, which comes from Allah in the first place, will be seen as a bad thing or as a problem in our lives. There will be no worries that occupy our minds. We will feel at ease with what Allah has ordained for us for we have established a sincere relationship with our Lord, who created everything that we need, who controls everything that we are so worried about, who provides for all our needs for which we strive day and night seeking our worldly provision when it is Him who is the Owner of all these.

The Prophet[P] *said, "How wonderful the affair of the believer is! Indeed, all of his affairs are good for him. This is for no one but the believer. If something good happens to him, he is grateful to Allah, which is good for him. And if something bad happens to him, he has patience, which is good for him."* **Muslim.**

Alhamdulillah, God has favoured us and me and made you realise His blessings, and given us the determination to fulfil our purpose before it is too late. Among the greatest blessings that Allah grants to His slaves are the opportunity and ability.

Allah[SWT] has given us the ability to know and understand only a few of His blessings and the purpose of our existence. He has also provided us with many opportunities day in and day out in which we can submit these blessings for servitude, obedience, and worship only and sincerely to Him.

Islam teaches that life is a test or trial designed to reveal an individual's true nature. Consequently, death is not perceived as an end but rather as the commencement of the final and everlasting life in the Hereafter. Before entering either Heaven or Hell, there must be a Day of Judgment, where individuals confront their true selves, gaining awareness of their nature and understanding the consequences of their actions on Earth. Each person's reward or punishment is determined based on their attitude, appreciation, and efforts during their lifetime on earth. No one is held accountable for the actions or beliefs of others, and individuals are not judged for what they were unaware of or incapable of doing.

In essence, life is an examination, and death is a period of rest following the test. This phase can be either easy for the faithful or challenging for the wicked. Reward and punishment are proportionate to each person, with Allah being the Final Judge. The purpose of life, therefore, according to Islamic teachings, can be summarised as follows:

1.   Life on Earth is a test.

2. The life in the grave is a resting or waiting place before the Day of Judgment.
3. The Day of Judgment brings clarity regarding the individual's fate based on their desires and actions.
4. The Permanent or Afterlife is spent either in luxurious splendour or miserable punishment.

For Muslims, this understanding shapes their purpose, acknowledging that Allah creates them and will undergo a period in the material world before death and the subsequent judgment. The Muslim's ultimate purpose is to surrender, submit, and obey in purity and peace to Allah, following His orders as outlined in the Holy Quran and through the teachings of the Prophet Muhammad[P]. This includes beliefs in the oneness of Allah, ritualistic prayers, charity, fasting in *Ramadan*, and pilgrimage to Mecca.

In contrast, for a disbeliever, life's purpose often revolves around accumulating wealth and power, as well as indulging in worldly pleasures. However, Islam asserts that such pursuits hold no value in the grave, on the Day of Judgment, or in the Next Life. The purpose of life, as understood by a believing Muslim, can be succinctly expressed as "Obey God."

The belief in the Big Bang Theory

The astronomer Edwin Hubble observed distant galaxies using an extremely powerful telescope. He made two mind-boggling discoveries. First, Hubble figured out that the Milky Way isn't the only galaxy. He realised that faint, cloud-like objects in the night sky were other galaxies far, far away. The Milky Way is just one of billions of galaxies. Hubble also discovered that the galaxies are constantly moving away from each other. In other words, the universe is expanding. The most notable aspect we know about it is that it is continually expanding. A few years later, Belgian astronomer Georges Lemaître used Hubble's remarkable discoveries to propose an answer to a crucial astronomical question: How did the universe begin?

If the universe is constantly expanding, then it must have been smaller in the past. And long, long ago, it was much smaller. That means billions of years ago, everything in the universe was contained in a tiny ball that exploded! Wow! This breakthrough idea later became known as the Big Bang! The Big Bang was the moment 13.8 billion years ago when the universe began as a tiny, dense fireball that exploded. Most astronomers use the Big Bang theory to explain the origin of the universe. However, what caused this explosion in the first place remains a mystery. Since the Big Bang, the universe has been expanding.

There is no contradiction in the Quran with these scientific findings. Allah[SWT] says: *"The Heavens and the earth were joined together as one unit before We clove them asunder"* **Quran 21:30.** Following this big explosion, Allah says in the Quran: *"Then He* turned to the Heaven while it was all smoke. He said to the Heaven and the Earth: "Come (into being), willingly or unwillingly." They said, "Here we come (into being) in willing obedience." **Quran 41:11.**

The Quran further states that Allah created the sun, the moon, and the planets, each with its distinct course or orbit. Allah^SWT says: *"It is He Who created the night and the day, and the sun and the moon; all (the celestial bodies) swim along, each in its rounded course."* **Quran 21:33.**

With regards to the expansion of the Universe, Allah^SWT says: *"The Heavens, We have built them with power. And verily, We are expanding it."* **Quran 51:47.** This means **that** Allah^SWT has given human beings signs that they can reflect on and ponder the creation of Allah. The scientists who discovered the Big Bang were not a coincidence. Allah^SWT willed it like this so that we can come closer to understanding the existence of Allah and the purpose behind its creation.

In conclusion, the sole purpose and salvation for Muslims lie in obeying God. Understanding the Creator, expressing gratitude, and worshipping Him without partners are integral aspects of this purpose. Learning about the Messengers, Prophets, and the word of God is crucial for individuals seeking truth with an open heart and an open mind. Embracing this message with sincerity and seeking guidance from Allah is the key to realising one's true purpose in life.

May Allah^SWT grant us the *taufiq* to truly understand our purpose in life so that we submit only to Him in this world and reap the rewards in the Hereafter.

Al-Qadr – Preordainment

"Indeed, all things We created with predestination."

Quran 54:49

"Be mindful of Allah and He will protect you. Be mindful of Allah and you will find Him before you. If you ask, ask from Allah. If you seek help, seek help from Allah. Know that if the nations gather together to benefit you, they will not benefit you unless Allah has decreed it for you. And if the nations gather together to harm you, they will not harm you unless Allah has decreed it for you. The pens have been lifted and the pages have dried."

Tirmidhi

The Concept of Preordainment in Islam

One of the fundamental beliefs in Islam is the concept of "Al-Qadr". The word "Qadr" in Arabic is translated as "destiny" or "fate" in English. It also means divine foreordained or predestination. Believing in Qadr is one of the six articles of faith, known as *Imaan*. When a believer sincerely believes in the Divine Decree, they are affirming that everything that happens in life comes from Allah^{SWT}, whether good or bad. The belief is that Allah^{SWT} willed it to happen. Allah^{SWT} is all-powerful, all-knowing, and knows what is good and what is bad. He Almighty determines, decides, and Wills everything in the universe according to His Power and Wisdom. Allah^{SWT} says in the Quran, *"Indeed, all things We created with predestination."* **Quran 54:49.**

The topic of Divine Decree will never fully be understood and comprehended by humans, as this concept deals with the essence of God's Power and Will, which is beyond what our finite minds can comprehend. Anyone who believes in the divine decree and rests his case with Allah^{SWT} in all matters is truly a believer in Islam.

Allah^{SWT} has revealed in the Quran that He created angels from light, the Jinn from fire, and the first human, namely Adam^{AS}, from dust. He bestowed free will to the Jinn and Humans, but not to the Angels, who fulfil all commandments of Allah^{SWT}. Humans were the last of the three creations.

After the creation of Adam^{AS}, Allah^{SWT} ordered the Angels to prostrate to him, and they all did, as they were created only to obey, except Shaytaan, who refused, as he considered himself loftier than Adam^{AS}. This is the first example of free will.

We learn from the scriptures that as Shaytaan was cast out of Paradise due to his disobedience, he also caused Adam^AS and Hawa^AS to disobey Allah^SWT, thus leading to their removal from Paradise. This is the second example of free will. However, Allah^SWT does not compel or induce anyone while they have free will. Allah^SWT says in the Quran: *"The Angels prostrated themselves all of them together. Except for Shaytaan, he refused to be among the prostrators. God said, 'O Shaytaan! What is your reason for not being among the prostrators? 'Shaytaan said, 'I am not the one to prostrate myself to a human being, whom You created from sounding clay of altered black smooth mud.' God said, 'Then get out from here for verily you are an outcast or cursed one. Verily, the curse shall be upon you till the Day of Resurrection."* **Quran 15:30–5.**

Allah^SWT allowed Shaytaan and his soldiers to commit mischief and attempt to divert Human beings away from fulfilling Allah's commandments, but at the same time gave humankind a clear warning and guidance regarding Shaytaan's fall and his plot to misguide man. Allah^SWT says: *"And [mention] when We said to the angels, 'Prostrate to Adam,' and they prostrated, except for Iblees/Shaytaan. He was of the jinn and departed from the command of his Lord. Then will you take him and his descendants as allies, other than Me, while they are your enemies? Wretched it is for the wrongdoers as an exchange."* **Quran 18:50.** In another verse, Allah^SWT says: *"Verily, We showed him (human) the way, whether he be grateful or ungrateful."* **Quran 76:3.**

Allah^SWT sent a succession of Prophets in order to guide mankind, while Shaytaan was busy at work to turn people away from the remembrance and obedience to Allah.

Allah^SWT, who is All-Knowing and All-Wise, knows what we have done in the past, what we are doing in the present, and what we will do in the future. In fact, this is in the knowledge of Allah, even before the time of our birth.

The provision, life span, deeds, and ultimate fate in the Hereafter of every human being are written by the angels as soon as the soul is blown into the foetus. Our destiny was decreed for us even before we were born.

The Prophet^P *said, "The creation of each one of you is in his mother's womb for forty days or nights, then as a clot for a similar period, then as a piece of flesh for a similar period, then the angel is sent to it to announce four decrees. He writes his provision, his life span, his deeds, and whether he is blessed or damned. Then, he breathes the soul into it. Verily, one of you acts with the deeds of the people of Paradise until he is not but an arm's length away from it, yet the decree overtakes him, he acts with the deeds of the people of Hellfire and thus enters Hellfire. And one of you acts with the deeds of the people of Hellfire until he is not but an arm's length away from it, yet the decree overtakes him, he acts with the deeds of the people of Paradise and thus enters it."* **Bukhari and Muslim.**

We are set upon a path, with our fate ahead of us, as soon as we enter this world. Yet our will and our actions are meaningful because, by Allah's will, they are the causes of changing course. Since Allah[SWT] is in control of destiny, the only way to secure a good fate is to appeal to Allah[SWT] through worship, prayer, and good deeds. We have no control over ourselves. The beloved Prophet[P] *said, "Be mindful of Allah and He will protect you. Be mindful of Allah and you will find Him before you. If you ask, ask from Allah. If you seek help, seek help from Allah. Know that if the nations gather together to benefit you, they will not benefit you unless Allah has decreed it for you. And if the nations gather together to harm you, they will not harm you unless Allah has decreed it for you. The pens have been lifted and the pages have dried."* **Tirmidhi.**

Despite our fate already being written, we are required to take action by being mindful of Allah[SWT] and doing good and fulfilling His command. This hadith emphasises that everything happens by the will of Allah, despite Allah[SWT] not being pleased with everything that occurs.

Some people may argue that if one is destined to Hell or Heaven, then where is the free will in this? The answer to that is simple. The fact that it is written does not mean we are aware of it. It only means that Allah[SWT] is aware of what we will do, but is not compelling us to do it.

There are important aspects to the belief in the divine decree:

1. **Allah[SWT] is all-knowing**
   The belief that Allah[SWT] is Knowledgeable of all things and events. It is He who instigates and controls the universe and all that happens within and outside it, whether major or minor, at all times and all places. Allah's foreknowledge is infallible and complete. As Allah[SWT] says: *"And with Him are the keys of the unseen; none knows them except Him. And He knows what is on the land and in the sea. Not a leaf falls but He knows it. And no grain is there within the darkness of the Earth and no moist or dry [thing] but that it is [written] in a clear record"* **Quran 6:59.**

2. **Allah[SWT] has recorded everything in the preserved table**
   The belief that Allah[SWT] has recorded everything from the beginning of time to the Day of Judgment in a Tablet He has kept is known as the *Lawh Al-Mahfooth* (The Preserved Tablet). What happens to a person is all known to Allah[SWT], including a person's lifespan, the *rizq* (sustenance) they will receive, the deeds they commit, whether they will be happy or sad, and the time of a person's death is all written and recorded in this Tablet. In fact, Allah[SWT] has recorded all matters pertaining to His creation fifty thousand years before He created the *Heaven*s and

earth. Allah^{SWT} says: *"Do you not know that Allah^{SWT} knows what is in the Heaven and Earth? Indeed, that is in a Record. Indeed that, for Allah, is easy."* **Quran 22:70.**

3. Nothing occurs without the Will of Allah^{SWT}

The belief that nothing can occur without the Will and Power of Allah^{SWT}, whether this would be from the action of Allah^{SWT} or the actions of human beings. Nothing happens randomly; the Almighty has planned everything. As Allah^{SWT} says: *"And your Lord creates what He Wills and Chooses..."* **Quran 28:68.** A Muslim acknowledges that whatever has afflicted him was meant to afflict him and could not have been avoided or prevented. On the other hand, whatever has not afflicted him was not meant to afflict him, and he can prevent nothing unless Allah^{SWT} has willed it.

4. Allah^{SWT} created everything

The belief that Allah^{SWT} is the creator and originator of all things. Allah^{SWT} says: *"...and has created each thing and determined it with [precise] determination."* **Quran 25:2.** Whilst Allah^{SWT} has predestined everything, He has bestowed on every human being the free will to make his or her own decisions. It is the choice of his creation to do good or bad in life. To undertake good deeds and fulfil Allah's commandments and earn his pleasure, or commit sins and earn His displeasure. However, just because each person's choices are known to Allah^{SWT} beforehand, it does not mean that they will not be held accountable on the Day of Judgment for all decisions they make and actions they take. Allah^{SWT} forces nothing upon anyone. It is important to note that Allah^{SWT} will not hold anyone accountable for things that are out of their control, or for things they cannot do.

It is pretty clear that we have a choice between doing good and evil, and we will be judged accordingly. However, a good doer without *Imaan* (faith) will receive the reward in this world but not in the Hereafter. As Allah^{SWT} says: *"Whoever desires the harvest of the Hereafter – We increase for him in his harvest. And whoever desires the harvest of this world – We give him thereof, but there is not for him in the Hereafter any share."* **Quran 42:20.**

So, from this, we learn that we are given guidance from the Quran and the *Sunnah* of our beloved Prophet^p as well as the freedom to choose. It is totally up to us how we conduct ourselves. We must be aware that we reap the consequences of our own choices. The fact that our choices and fate are written before birth only indicates that Allah^{SWT} is the Knower of all things.

Allah^{SWT} is All-Just, All-Wise, and He tests humanity according to their strength and what their soul can bear. A Muslim acknowledges the fact that whatever difficulties they are facing are from Allah[SWT] as a way of testing and determining which of His slaves are obedient and which are not; who can bear challenges with patience, trust, and rely on Allah[SWT] and who cannot. However, no one will be sent any calamity or difficulty that they cannot bear. Allah[SWT] says: *"God does not burden any human being with more than he is well able to bear."* **Quran 2:286.**

A Muslim acknowledges that whatever befalls him or her is in accordance with Allah's Will and Plan, whether or not they understand and accept this or not. A Muslim puts his trust and reliance on Allah[SWT], as Allah[SWT] acts in accordance with His wisdom in all matters. A believer simply needs to affirm that Allah[SWT] is All-Loving and that He loves His servants more than their parents, and be mindful that whatever Allah[SWT] does, He has a good motive. A believer always assumes good and does not lose faith. As the Prophet[P] *said, "How wonderful the affair of the believer is! Indeed, all of his affairs are good for him. This is for the believer alone. If something good happens to him, he is grateful to Allah, which is good for him. And if something bad happens to him, he has patience, which is good for him."* **Muslim.**

Those who believe in the divine decree have truly grasped the purpose of life, and they will enjoy good mental health knowing that Allah[SWT] is All-Knowing and has good in store for us. The heart and mind will be at peace, and the believer is content in the heart and acknowledges that nothing happens without a purpose. A believer is confident that whatever afflicted him could not have escaped him, and whatever missed him could not have reached him, as Allah[SWT] is in complete control of all happenings and events, and he predestines everything.

The Quran and *Sunnah* are clear in expressing the moral responsibility of humankind. Allah[SWT] *said, "Each soul is responsible for its own actions; no soul will bear the burden of another. You will all return to your Lord in the end, and He will tell you the truth about your differences."* **Quran 6:164.**

This is the whole purpose of life; the great test culminating on the Day of Judgment would not make sense unless the judgment was just and meaningful. Hence, Allah[SWT] delegated free will to humankind to be used in the service of good. Our will is "free will" in the sense that we are not forced to do what we do. We are rewarded or punished in the Hereafter based upon what we did with our God-given will.

The essence of the matter is that good deeds lead to a good ending, and evil deeds lead to an evil ending. The Prophet[P] *said, "Good works protect from evil fates. Charity in secret extinguishes the wrath of the Lord; maintaining family ties increases one's lifespan; and every good deed is considered a form of charity. The people of good in the world are the people of good in the Hereafter, and the people of evil in the world are the people of evil in the Hereafter. And the first to enter Paradise are the people of good."* **Tabarani.**

The Prophet[P] also *said, "There is no Muslim on the earth who calls upon Allah in supplication but that Allah will grant it to him or divert some evil away from him, so long as he does not ask for something sinful or cut off family ties"*. **Tirmidhi.** The Prophet[P] himself supplicated to Allah[SWT] for protection from an evil fate, recognising that it is Allah[SWT] alone who holds the power over the Decree. Hepbuh supplicated: *"O Allah, guide me among those You have guided, secure me among those You have secured, protect me among those You have protected, bless me in what You have given me, and save me from the evil You have decreed. Verily, You alone decree, and none can issue decree over You. Indeed, he cannot be humiliated by anyone who is protected by You. Blessed are You, our Lord, the Almighty."* **Tirmidhi.**

Accepting a calamity that Allah[SWT] has decreed is one of the most challenging tests we face in life. Once a calamity occurs, we should accept that it has happened and Allah[SWT] is aware of it, then take any appropriate action. We should not dwell on the past by repeating the events in our minds over and over in despair. It serves no purpose. The beloved Prophet[P] *said, "If something befalls you, then do not say, 'If only I had done something else.' Rather say, 'Allah[SWT] has decreed what He wills.' Verily, the phrase 'if only' opens the way for the work of Shaytaan."* **Muslim.**

Accepting the decree after the fact, however, does not imply that we should not learn from our mistakes and negative experiences. As our beloved Prophet[P] said, *"The believer is not stung twice from the same hole."* **Bukhari.** We learn from this that we should not make the same mistake twice, nor should we allow a negative experience to repeat itself if it can be prevented. A mistake is usually a learning curve.

With this understanding, it is only Allah[SWT] upon whom we totally depend to bring these good causes about. Every action we intend in the future should be qualified as only occurring under the will of Allah[SWT], because we know by our will and ability alone it will not happen. Allah[SWT] says: *"Do not say of anything, 'I will do that tomorrow,' without adding, 'God willing – i.e., Insha Allah."* **Quran 18:23-24.** The actions and causes, without the will of Allah[SWT] to support them, are essentially nothing, yet they are still necessary for bringing about a good fate. Action is always prescribed for the believers about the decree, both before it comes to be and after it is fulfilled.

May Allah[SWT] grant us, all believers and non-believers, the *taufiq* to fully comprehend this important article of belief and guide us to fulfil the free choice that we have correctly; a way that is pleasing to Allah[SWT] and that which will ultimately take us to *Jannah* Insha Allah.

The concept of Jihad in Islam

"... enjoin good and forbid evil."

Quran 3:104

"The best Jihad is saying a word of truth in the court of a tyrant ruler."

Abu Dawud

The word "Jihad" has been in frequent use in the Western press over the past several years, explained directly or subtly, to mean holy war. As a matter of fact, the term "holy war" was coined in Europe during the Crusades, meaning the war against Muslims. It does not have a counterpart in the Islamic glossary, and Jihad is certainly not its translation.

On my Islam awareness courses that I deliver as part of cultural competency training, I ask my non-Muslim participants what they understand by the term Jihad. Eighty per cent of the participants who attend put their hand up to say "holy war".

The Arabic word "jihad" means "struggling" or "striving" and applies to any effort exerted by anyone. In this sense, a student struggles and strives to get an education and pass course work; an employee strives to fulfil their role and maintain good relations with their employer; a surgeon seeks to assist his patient as best as he can, a believer struggling to get up early in the morning to pray the *fajr* prayer, and so on. Jihad can be carried out through speech, the pen, lobbying, picketing, or the Quran by inviting people to the message of Islam.

Since Islam is not confined to the boundaries of the individual but extends to the welfare of society and humanity in general, an individual cannot keep themselves in isolation from what happens in their community or the world at large, hence the Quranic injunction to the Islamic nation to take as a duty "to enjoin good and forbid evil." **Quran 3:104.**

Islam allows the use of force as a last resort to bring about the greater good or peace. Every country believes in maintaining an Army to keep the peace and provide protection and security to its people. The same is true in Islam. There are strict parameters laid down, however, in Divine Law should force be used. Allah says in the Quran: "And fight in the way of God those that fight you, but do not transgress, for indeed God does not like the transgressors. **Quran 2:190.** This verse forms the basis of all Islamic laws relating to fighting, i.e., you are allowed to fight those who fight you, but not to oppress those who have done you no harm.

In another verse, Allah says: "Allah does not prohibit you from showing kindness and being just with those who do not fight you nor have driven you out of your homes. Indeed, Allah loves those who are just." **Quran 60: 8.** This verse further explains that, not only is fighting innocent civilians forbidden, but Muslims are ordered to be kind and just with those who did not harm them.

The Prophet[P] gave specific guidelines should force be used. These were summarised by Abu Bakar, may Allah be pleased with him. He stated: "Do not dishonour a treaty. Do not mutilate the dead. Do not kill women. Do not kill children. Do not kill the old. Do not kill those without weapons. Do not kill those engaged in worship (priests, rabbis etc.) Do not cut down trees. Do not burn crops. Do not poison the wells of your enemies. Fight only those who come at you." This means fighting only as a last resort and only for the greater good of society.

The Prophet[P] referred to battle as a "minor jihad" in comparison to the struggle against the evil of one's soul, which he described as the "superior jihad". Therefore, military action is a subset of jihad, not its entirety. That was what the Prophet[P] emphasised to his companions when returning from a military campaign; he told them, "This day we have returned from the minor jihad (war) to the major jihad (self-control and betterment)."

Jihad is not a declaration of war against other religions and certainly not against Christians and Jews, as some media and political circles want it to be perceived. Islam does not fight other religions. Christians and Jews are considered as fellow inheritors of the Abrahamic traditions by Muslims, worshipping the same God and following the tradition of Abraham[P]. In fact, the Prophet[P] *said,* "The best Jihad is saying a word of truth in the court of a tyrant ruler". **Abu Dawud**

We must acknowledge again, for the sake of honesty, that historically, all traditions —Muslim, Christian, Jewish, and others —have had their lapses in honestly following the valued ideals of their religions or philosophies. We all make mistakes, and we continue to do so. Muslims are no exception, and time and again, religion was exploited by ambitious tyrants or violated by ignorant mobs. This is no reflection on religion, but it highlights how desperately humanity needs better education, a more enduring concern for human dignity, rights, and freedom, and a vigilant pursuit of justice, even at the cost of curbing political and economic greed.

What does Islam say about Terrorism?

Islam is a religion of mercy and does not permit terrorism. Allah[SWT] says in the Quran: "God does not forbid you from showing kindness and dealing justly with those who have not fought you about religion and have not driven you out of your homes. God loves just dealers." **Quran 60:8.** In another verse, Allah[SWT] says: "If anyone killed a person not in retaliation for murder or to spread mischief in the land, it would be as if he killed the whole of humanity. And likewise, if anyone saved a life, it would be as if he saved the whole of humanity." **Quran 5:32.**

Islamic teachings make it clear that acts of inciting terror, the wholesale destruction of buildings and properties, the bombing and maiming of innocent men, women, and children are all forbidden and detestable acts according to Islam. When individual Muslims commit an act of terrorism, they are guilty of violating the laws of Islam. With regard to suicide bombings, there is no concept of this in the teachings of Islam, and it is considered to be a major sin.

The only situations where fighting is allowed is in self-defence. Aggression is always prohibited. From the entire Quran, a tiny percentage discusses "war". Fighting was only justified when the believers in the time of the Prophet[P] had to face hostile opposition because of their religious views, and were in many cases forced to fight to save their lives. The bulk of the Quran focuses on worshipping God, leading a righteous life and attaining salvation in the Hereafter.

In fact, aggression is forbidden, and fighting is only permitted in self-defence. Allah[SWT] repeats, "do not aggress, "multiple times and only if attacked, is one allowed to fight back, and when the perpetrators refrain from fighting and offer one peace, the believers are told to stop fighting.

There are several verses in the Quran that can be misinterpreted and have been misinterpreted by extremist groups to justify their terrorist mission. Sadly, some young people are groomed and radicalised to commit atrocities against innocent people, thinking they are doing the right thing and that Allah will be pleased with them. This is far from the truth. Allah says in the Quran: "Whoever kills a soul... it is as if he had slain mankind entirely. And whoever saves one - it is as if he had saved mankind entirely." **Quran 5:32**

To understand the verse of the Quran fully, one needs to simply complete the sentence, or read the preceding or following verse, and it becomes evident that the verse in no way promotes violence.

The Quran is a message to the whole of humanity that repeats 114 times, "In the Name of God the Most Compassionate the Most Merciful." It instructs believers to show goodness to those who do evil (41:34), to speak words of peace to those who are hostile (25:63), to call to the way of God with wisdom and beautiful sayings (16:125), to treat peaceful non-Muslims with the utmost kindness and justice (60:8), to be the best of people towards other people (3:110), and to respect freedom of religion (2:256, 10:99).

There is simply no plausible way to understand the Quran in a manner befitting of mercy, compassion and peace. Any sincere and reasonable person looking at these passages must necessarily recognise that the Quran stands for mercy, not for destruction and violence.

To insist on characterising the religion as inherently violent is to play right into the hands of extremists on both sides who wish to incite hatred and perpetuate war.

The Media

Islamophobia is at its peak due to the negative portrayal of Islam in the media and what some misguided Muslims have done in the name of Islam, but which has no basis in Islam. Fear and mistrust are rife and have come about due to misunderstandings and not having enough knowledge about Islam and Muslims. The primary source of information for many people is what they receive from the media. I learnt this only too well from the 25,000 or so who attended my Islam Awareness Courses since 2004.

'Islamic Terrorism', 'Muslim fundamentalists', women being oppressed and forced to wear the veil, 'forced marriages' and 'terror plots' are some of the terms associated with Islam and Muslims. This brings fear to the general population and creates a greater divide between Muslims and non-Muslims. Only those who research further to seek the truth about Islam are enlightened about the religion, and studies show that approximately 5000 people embrace Islam in the UK every year. Four times as many women as men.

When the caricatures of the Prophet Mohammad[P] were published in the Danish newspapers, it touched a nerve within every Muslim. The two primary sources of knowledge that Muslims follow in religious matters are the Quran and the *Sunnah*, i.e., the Prophet's teachings and sayings, as well as following his example. When Non-Muslims remark negatively about someone who is so highly regarded by Muslims, Muslims all over the world become outraged.

Having said this, there is no excuse whatsoever for Muslims to counter this with equal negativity, threat of violence or terrorism. The Prophet[P] was very often persecuted and ill-treated himself during his lifetime, and at no point did he react in a negative way. This peaceful existence was one of the main reasons Islam spread so quickly.

God sent the Prophet as a mercy to mankind. When non-Muslims learn about the *seerah* (the study of the Prophet's life), they come to know how kind, generous, forgiving, helpful, supportive, and charitable he was.

The media need to draw a line between what is termed freedom of expression and inciting racial and religious hatred by the way they write, using insensitive language and misrepresenting Islam and Muslims.

Some politicians have also begun to use terms that are not only insensitive but also abusive. This shows a lack of knowledge of Islam on their part. These unchallenged comments create further division in society and help the young introduce political Islam to counter this. Some words such as 'Islamic Terrorism', 'Muslim extremism', 'Islamic fundamentalism and 'Jihadists' need to be challenged. This sort of language is bringing greater division, mistrust, and misunderstanding. Perhaps when the dust settles and more academic and scientific research is done, there needs to be an effort made to find solutions to the real causes of extremism and terrorism. Only then can people responsible take effective measures to prevent future occurrences. Also, the term "Extremist Muslim" is misused. There is no such thing as an extremist Muslim and a Moderate Muslim, and there is no basis in the religion of Islam, just as there is no extreme Christian or Jew and a Moderate Christian or Jew. A Muslim is a Muslim. One can say they are observant or practising Muslims and non-observant or non-practising Muslims.

What is Radicalisation and its possible causes?

The government's Prevent Duty Guidance defines radicalisation as "the process by which a person comes to support terrorism and extremist ideologies associated with terrorist groups".

There has been no clear link or exact cause identified for someone becoming radicalised. It could be a multiple of factors. Some suggestions include: those experiencing an identity or personal crisis and individual sociopsychological factors; Individuals with feelings of unmet aspirations or a sense of injustice; people with a need for adventure or excitement; social and political factors; individuals who feel socially isolated, and possibly, suffering from depression; Those who have a history of criminal behaviour; culture and identity crisis; trauma; radicalisers and groomers at play misusing the verses of the Quran; the lack of integration and racism leading some Muslims feeling excluded from the society; the role of social media.

It is far too easy for analysts who are not Muslim to focus on the small part of the extremist threat that a few misguided Muslims pose to non-Muslims in the West demonize one of the world's great religions, and to drift into Islamophobia, blaming a faith for patterns of violence that are driven by a tiny fraction of the world's Muslims.

Those who purport to violence and terrorism do not represent Islam and are only a tiny percentage of the total 1.7 billion Muslims in the World.

Britain has always held a high position in striving towards equality, peace, and justice, and is seen as respectful of other people's faith. This is the reason why we have Mosques, Gurdwaras, Temples and Synagogues, and people are freely able to practice their faith.

All faiths and people of no faith have so much in common. There is a need to dwell more on these commonalities rather than the small differences that exist among communities.

May Allah[SWT] grant us the correct understanding of our *deen*, to understand Jihad in its proper context, and to challenge violent extremist views.

Scientific Facts in the Quran

"We will show them Our signs in the universe and in their own selves, until it becomes manifest to them that this (the Quran) is the truth"

Quran 41:53

As believers, we are required to reflect and ponder the verses of the Quran and scientific discoveries.

The relationship between the Quran and science is of considerable interest, especially for those who see the correlation between the two as evidence of the Quran's divine origin. As believers, we are required to reflect and ponder the verses of the Quran and scientific discoveries. As Allah[SWT] says: *"We will show them Our signs in the universe and in their own selves, until it becomes manifest to them that this (the Quran) is the truth"* **Quran; 41:53.**

Based on this Quranic verse, Allah[SWT] exhorts Muslims to observe and study the universe to find some of His signs. For this reason, many verses of the Quran invite Muslims to study nature and seek knowledge, which has been interpreted as encouragement for scientific inquiry.

Many examples show that the Quran anticipated scientific discoveries that were made much later. Below are some examples.

1. Embryology

- **The Quranic Verse:** *"We created man from a drop of fluid, then placed it in a safe place. Then We made the drop into a clinging clot and made the clot into a lump, and the lump into bones, and We clothed the bones with flesh, then developed it into another creation. So blessed be Allah, the best of creators."* (Quran 23:13-14)

- **Scientific Explanation:** Modern embryology has discovered that human development indeed begins from a drop of fluid (sperm), which fertilises the ovum to form a zygote. This zygote implants itself in the uterus wall (a safe place), then develops into a blastocyst and further differentiates into various tissues, including bones and flesh.

2. Mountains as Stabilisers

- **The Quranic Verse:** *"Have We not made the earth a resting place? And the mountains as stakes?"* (Quran 78:6-7)

- **Scientific Explanation:** Geology has found that mountains have deep roots and act like stakes or pegs, helping to stabilise the Earth's crust. This understanding emerged through the concept of plate tectonics, which explains the balancing role of mountains in stabilising the Earth's crust.

3. Expansion of the Universe

- **The Quranic Verse:** *"And the Heaven We constructed with strength, and indeed, We are [its] expander."* (Quran 51:47)

- **Scientific Explanation:** The concept of an expanding universe was first proposed in the 20th century, along with the Big Bang theory. Observations by Edwin Hubble demonstrated that galaxies are moving away from each other, indicating that the universe is expanding.

4. Barrier Between Seas

- **The Quranic Verse:** *"He released the two seas, meeting side by side; between them is a barrier [so] neither of them transgresses."* (Quran 55:19-20)

- **Scientific Explanation:** Oceanography has found that when different seas meet, a physical barrier forms between them due to differences in salinity, temperature, and density. This results in distinct layers that do not mix immediately.

5. Human Fingertips

- **The Quranic Verse:** *"Yes, We are able to reconstruct his fingertips."* (Quran 75:4)

- **Scientific Explanation:** This verse is often associated with the unique nature of fingerprints, which are now used for identification because they are distinct to each individual and remain unchanged throughout a person's lifetime.

6. Iron as a Material

- **The Quranic Verse:** *"And We sent down iron, in which is strong material, as well as many benefits for mankind..."* (Quran 57:25)

- **Scientific Explanation:** The phrase "sent down" is intriguing because modern science indicates that iron is not native to Earth. It is believed to have come from supernova explosions and meteorites that bombarded the early Earth, thus "sent down" from outer space.

7. Protective Atmosphere

- **The Quranic Verse:** *"And We made the sky a protected ceiling, but they, from its signs, are turning away."* (Quran 21:32)

- **Scientific Explanation:** Earth's atmosphere acts as a protective layer, shielding life from harmful solar radiation and preventing the planet from extreme temperatures.

8. Ocean Depths and Internal Waves

- **The Quranic Verse:** *"Or [they are] like the darknesses within a vast deep ocean, which is covered by waves, above which are waves, above which are clouds..."* (Quran 24:40)

- **Scientific Explanation:** Marine science has discovered that there are internal waves beneath the ocean's surface, which can be compared to surface waves. These internal waves occur at the density boundaries between different layers of water.

9. The Role of Water in Life

- **The Quranic Verse:** *"And We made from water every living thing. Then will they not believe?"* (Quran 21:30)

- **Scientific Explanation:** Modern biology recognises that water is essential for all forms of life. Cells are composed mainly of water, and it is necessary for the biochemical processes that sustain life.

10. The Development of Human Senses

- **The Quranic Verse:** *"It is He who produced for you hearing and vision and hearts; little are you grateful."* (Quran 23:78)

- **Scientific Explanation:** The development of the human senses is a complex process that involves the differentiation of cells and the formation of organs, starting from the embryonic stage and continuing after birth.

11. Sun Moving in Orbit

- **The Quranic Verse:** *"And it is He who created the night and the day and the sun and the moon; all [heavenly bodies] in an orbit are swimming"* (Quran, 21:33).

- **Scientific Explanation:** Although it was only a widespread belief in the 20th century amongst astronomers, today it is a well-established fact that the Sun, the Moon, and all the other bodies in the Universe are moving in an orbit and constantly moving, not stationary as commonly thought before.

12. Pain Receptors

- **The Quranic Verse:** *"We shall send those who reject our revelations to the (hell) fire. When their skins have been burned away, We shall replace them with new ones so that they may continue to feel the pain: God is almighty, all-wise"* (Quran, 4:56).

- **Scientific Explanation:** For a long time, it was thought that the sense of feeling and pain was dependent on the brain. However, it has been discovered that pain receptors are present in the skin. Without these pain receptors, a person would not be able to feel pain.

13. Frontal Lobe

- **The Quranic Verse:** *"No indeed! if he does not stop, We will seize him by the forehead, his lying, sinful forehead"* (Quran, 96:15-16).

- **Scientific Explanation:** This verse refers to Abu Jahl, a cruel and oppressive tribal leader during the time of the Prophet Muhammad[P]. Allah revealed this verse to warn him. Modern research into anatomy suggests that the prefrontal area of the human brain is involved in planning, aggression, and motivation. So, it is the part of our brain which is responsible for lying. The mention of the forehead is specific and intentional, and it is another scientific fact stated in the Quran.

14. Climatology

- **The Quranic Verse:** *"And We send the fertilizing winds and send down water from the sky providing it for you to drink and you are not maintainers of its resources."* (Quran, 15:22).

- **Scientific Explanation:** This verse illustrates how the water is moved from the ocean to the land through the combination of evaporation and wind. The ocean loses water to the air when the water evaporates and turns into water vapour (steam). If the air over the ocean didn't move, the ocean water would reabsorb much of the steam. Thus, the water is sent down from the sky, providing it for us to drink, and as Allah says, "... and you are not maintainers of its resources", it is only Allah.

15. Astronomy

- **The Quranic Verse:** *"It is not for the sun to overtake the moon, nor does the night outstrip the day, but each, in an orbit, is swimming."* (Quran, 36:40).

- **Scientific Explanation:** This verse, when examined through the lens of modern science, aligns with our understanding of the orderly and predictable movements of celestial bodies. The sun and moon follow their orbits, and the cycles of day and night are a direct result of Earth's rotation. Modern astronomy confirms that celestial bodies, including the sun and moon, follow specific orbits. The sun orbits the centre of the Milky Way galaxy, while the moon orbits the Earth. This aligns with the Quranic description of each body moving within its orbit.

16. Prohibition of Pork

- **The Quranic Verse:** *"Prohibited to you are dead animals, blood, the flesh of swine, and that which has been dedicated to other than Allah..."* (Quran, 5:3). There are other verses that prohibit the consumption of Pig.

- **Scientific Explanation:** Science has identified several health concerns related to the consumption of pork, which can be seen as corroborating the wisdom behind the prohibition of eating pork. Some of the parasites and diseases that are harmful include Trichinella spiralis, which causes trichinosis, a disease that leads to symptoms such as diarrhoea, abdominal pain, fever, and muscle pain; Taeniasis, Pork tapeworm that can infect humans, leading to taeniasis, which may cause digestive problems and, in severe cases, cysticercosis, affecting the brain and other tissues; Hepatitis E. Pigs are a known reservoir for Hepatitis E virus, which can be transmitted to humans through the consumption of undercooked pork, leading to liver disease.

17. Formation of Clouds

- **The Quranic Verse:** *"Do you not see that Allah gently drives the clouds, then joins them together, piling them up into masses, from which you see raindrops come forth? And He sends down from the sky mountains 'of clouds' loaded with hail, pouring it on whoever He wills and averting it from whoever He wills."* (Quran 24:43).

- **Scientific Explanation:** This is an accurate description of how the winds push small clouds, and the ones that are near each other amalgamate. Then, a vertical updraft occurs, and the upper part of the cloud expands upward in the sky. As a result, different parts of the cloud are raised to divergent points and look as if many clouds are piled on top of each other (stacking). This study only took place in the past two centuries.

18. Internal Waves in the Ocean

- **The Quranic Verse:** *"....like darknesses within an unfathomable sea which is covered by waves, upon which are waves, over which are clouds - darknesses, some of them upon others. When one puts out his hand [therein], he can hardly see it...."* (Quran, 24:40).

- **Scientific Explanation:** Oceanographers, while studying water bodies, discovered that the long-held belief that waves only occur on the ocean's surface is incorrect. In reality, the waves are present internally underneath the surface of the water and are created when the lower part of the oceanic body faces an obstacle. This barrier creates a disturbance in the water body, leading to oscillation.

20. Fasting in the Month of *Ramadan*

- **The Quranic Verse:** *"O you who have believed, decreed upon you is fasting as it was decreed upon those before you that you may become righteous."* (Quran, 2:183).

- **Scientific Explanation:** Many scientific benefits support the holistic wisdom of fasting as prescribed in Islam. Some of these benefits include **Improved Metabolic Health**: fasting can enhance insulin sensitivity and lower blood sugar levels, thereby reducing the risk of type 2 diabetes. **Weight Management**: Fasting helps reduce body fat and improve weight control by limiting calorie intake and promoting fat burning. **Cellular Repair**: Fasting triggers autophagy, a process in which cells remove damaged components and regenerate, thereby protecting against diseases such as cancer. **Reduced Inflammation**: Fasting has been shown to decrease markers of inflammation, which is linked to various chronic conditions. **Enhanced Brain Function**: Fasting supports brain health by promoting the production of brain-derived neurotrophic factors and reducing oxidative stress. **Improved Heart Health**: Fasting can improve heart health by reducing risk factors such as blood pressure, cholesterol levels, and triglycerides.

21. The benefits of Wudhu

- **The Quranic Verse:** *"O you who have believed, when you rise to [perform] prayer, wash your faces and your forearms to the elbows and wipe over your heads and wash your feet to the ankles..."* (Quran, 5:6).

- **Scientific Explanation:** The Scientific benefits of wudhu are many. The main ones are: **Hygiene and Cleanliness**: Regular washing of the hands, face, and feet helps remove dirt, bacteria, and other impurities, contributing to overall cleanliness and reducing the risk of infections; **Skin Health**: The frequent washing involved in wudhu helps to keep the skin clean and hydrated, reducing the likelihood of skin conditions such as acne and dermatitis; **Circulation Improvement**: The act of washing various parts of the body with water can improve blood circulation, as the massage-like motions during ablution stimulate blood flow; **Stress Relief and Relaxation**: The ritual of wudhu involves a repetitive, mindful process that can induce a state of calm and relaxation, reducing stress levels; **Enhanced Mental Focus**: The practice of wudhu helps in mental preparation and focus for prayer, providing a break from daily activities and promoting mindfulness; **Prevention of Illness**: Regularly washing hands and face can prevent the spread of germs and decrease the incidence of respiratory and gastrointestinal infections.

These examples show how the above verses mentioned in the Quran align with modern scientific understanding.

May Allah[SWT] grant us the Taufiq to reflect, ponder, and understand that there is always wisdom in following the Quran and *Sunnah,* in that not only does this benefit us, but also that Allah[SWT] will reward us for fulfilling His prohibitions and commandments.

The 99 Names of Allah and Their Significance

"He is Allah, besides Whom there is no god, the Knower of the unseen and the seen. He is the Most Compassionate, the Most Merciful."

Quran 59:22-24

The 99 Names are titles that describe Allah's perfect qualities, such as His mercy, power, knowledge, justice, and majesty. These names are derived from divine revelation and are mentioned throughout the Quran and Sunnah.

The 99 Names of Allah—also known as *Asma'ul Husna* (أسماء الله الحسنى)—are attributes and descriptions of God mentioned in the Qur'an and Hadith. Each of these names represents a distinct quality or attribute of Allah[SWT], and together they help Muslims understand the nature of their Creator.

The 99 Names are titles that describe Allah's perfect qualities, such as His mercy, power, knowledge, justice, and majesty. These names are derived from divine revelation and are mentioned throughout the Quran and *Sunnah*.

Spiritual Benefits

- **Understanding Allah:** Each name reveals a distinct divine trait, deepening love, awe, and trust in Allah (e.g., *Ar-Rahman* – The Most Merciful, *Al-Adl* – The Just).
- **Enhancing Worship:** Muslims use these names in supplications, following Quranic guidance for meaningful prayers.

- **Moral Guidance:** The names serve as ethical models. While Allah's attributes are absolute, believers strive to embody qualities such as mercy (*Ar-Rahman*), justice (*Al-Adl*), and forgiveness (*Al-Ghaffar*) in their lives.

- **Source of Comfort:** In times of difficulty, names such as *Al-Latif* (The Subtle) and *Al-Wakeel* (The Trustee) offer reassurance of Allah's care and support.

- **Path to Paradise:** The Prophet[P] promised Paradise for those who learn, understand, and live by these names.

The 99 Names:

1. Ar-Rahman (الرحمن) – The Most Merciful

Allah's mercy encompasses all creation. He showers blessings on both believers and non-believers. In our lives, remembering Ar-Rahman helps us recognise Allah's endless grace, even when we falter, and reminds us to show compassion to others.

2. Ar-Rahim (الرحيم) – The Most Compassionate

Ar-Rahim signifies special mercy reserved for believers. It reminds us that after hardship, Allah's tender care awaits us, encouraging hope and trust in His forgiveness.

3. Al-Malik (الملك) – The King and Owner of Dominion

Allah owns everything in the universe. Recognising Him as Al-Malik instils humility and detachment from worldly possessions, recognising that everything ultimately belongs to Him.

4. Al-Quddus (القدوس) – The Absolutely Pure

Allah is free from all imperfections. Reflecting on Al-Quddus inspires us to purify our hearts, actions, and intentions, as we strive for sincerity and integrity.

5. As-Salam (السلام) – The Source of Peace and Safety

Allah is the giver of peace and safety. When we remember As-Salam, we find solace in His protection and seek to spread peace among others.

6. Al-Mu'min (المؤمن) – The Giver of Faith and Security

Allah grants security and faith to hearts. This name reassures us that true safety comes from trusting Allah, even in turbulent times.

7. Al-Muhaymin (المهيمن) – The Guardian, The Witness, The Overseer

Allah oversees and guards everything. Recognising Al-Muhaymin helps us trust in His perfect awareness and strive to be mindful of our deeds.

8. Al-Aziz (العزيز) – The Almighty

Allah is all-powerful and undefeatable. Remembering Al-Aziz encourages us to rely on His strength and not fear worldly challenges.

9. Al-Jabbar (الجبار) – The Compeller, The Restorer

Allah mends broken hearts and enforces His will. When we feel broken or helpless, Al-Jabbar's remembrance brings comfort and healing.

10. Al-Mutakabbir (المتكبر) – The Supreme, The Majestic

Only Allah possesses true greatness. Contemplating Al-Mutakabbir humbles us and reminds us to avoid arrogance.

11. Al-Khaliq (الخالق) – The Creator, The Maker

Allah creates from nothing with wisdom and precision. This deepens our awe of nature and inspires gratitude for life itself.

12. Al-Bari (البارئ) – The Evolver

Allah creates all living beings with unique forms and functions. It teaches us to respect the diversity and complexity of His creation.

13. Al-Musawwir (المصور) – The Fashioner

Allah shapes every creation uniquely. Remembering Al-Musawwir nurtures self-acceptance and appreciation for the uniqueness in others.

14. Al-Ghaffar (الغفار) – The Constant Forgiver

Allah repeatedly forgives. Knowing Al-Ghaffar motivates us to seek forgiveness and forgive others continually.

15. Al-Qahhar (القهار) – The All-Subduer

Allah's power can humble the mightiest. Reflecting on Al-Qahhar instils awe, guiding us to submit to His will.

16. Al-Wahhab (الوهاب) – The Supreme Bestower

Allah gives freely without expecting return. Remembering Al-Wahhab reminds us to be generous and grateful.

17. Ar-Razzaq (الرزاق) – The Provider

Allah sustains all creatures. Trusting Ar-Razzaq alleviates anxiety about sustenance and teaches contentment.

18. Al-Fattah (الفتاح) – The Opener, The Judge

Allah opens doors and resolves matters. Calling upon Al-Fattah gives hope in difficult situations, seeking His guidance.

19. Al-`Alim (العليم) – The All-Knowing

Allah's knowledge encompasses all. Reflecting on Al-`Alim encourages us to seek knowledge and act with awareness of His omniscience.

20. Al-Qabid (القابض) – The Withholder

Allah restricts provisions or situations wisely. Trusting Al-Qabid helps us accept trials with patience.

21. Al-Basit (الباسط) – The Extender

Allah extends mercy, provision, and ease. Recognising Al-Basit inspires us to remain hopeful and generous.

22. Al-Khafid (الخافض) – The Abaser

Allah lowers whom He wills. It reminds us that status is fleeting and that we should remain humble.

23. Ar-Rafi' (الرافع) – The Exalter

Allah elevates whom He wills. Trusting Ar-Rafi' encourages us to seek spiritual elevation rather than worldly rank.

24. Al-Mu'izz (المعز) – The Honor-Giver

Allah grants dignity and honour. Remembering Al-Mu'izz inspires us to seek honour through good character.

25. Al-Mudhill (المذل) – The Dishonorer

Allah can disgrace the arrogant. Reflecting on Al-Mudhill teaches humility and respect for others.

26. As-Sami' (السميع) – The All-Hearing

Allah hears all supplications. Knowing As-Sami' strengthens our prayer and sincerity.

27. Al-Basir (البصير) – The All-Seeing

Allah sees everything. Remembering Al-Basir helps us act righteously, knowing nothing escapes His sight.

28. Al-Hakam (الحكم) – The Impartial Judge

Allah judges with perfect justice. Trusting Al-Hakam eases our hearts when faced with injustice.

29. Al-`Adl (العدل) – The Utterly Just

Allah never wrongs anyone. Reflecting on Al-`Adl encourages us to practice fairness.

30. Al-Latif (اللطيف) – The Subtle One, The Most Gentle

Allah works in subtle, unseen ways. Recognising Al-Latif comforts us in trials, knowing help may come unexpectedly.

31. Al-Khabir (الخبير) – The All-Aware

Allah knows the inner secrets. Awareness of Al-Khabir fosters self-reflection and sincerity.

32. Al-Halim (الحليم) – The Most Forbearing

Allah is patient with our shortcomings. Reflecting on Al-Halim teaches us the importance of patience and tolerance.

33. Al-Azim (العظيم) – The Magnificent, The Infinite

Allah's greatness surpasses all. Remembering Al-Azim fills the heart with awe and humility.

34. Al-Ghafur (الغفور) – The Great Forgiver

Allah forgives extensively. Calling on Al-Ghafur gives hope for redemption.

35. Ash-Shakur (الشكور) – The Most Appreciative

Allah rewards our small efforts abundantly. Knowing Ash-Shakur encourages gratefulness and good deeds.

36. Al-Aliyy (العلي) – The Most High

Allah is exalted above all. Reflecting on Al-Aliyy centres our focus on divine, not worldly, elevation.

37. Al-Kabir (الكبير) – The Most Great

Allah's greatness is absolute. Remembering Al-Kabir humbles us and reduces attachment to status.

38. Al-Hafiz (الحفيظ) – The Preserver

Allah safeguards everything. Trusting Al-Hafiz brings peace of mind in times of uncertainty.

39. Al-Muqit (المقيت) – The Sustainer

Allah maintains all existence. Recognising Al-Muqit cultivates reliance on His provision.

40. Al-Hasib (الحسيب) – The Reckoner

Allah takes perfect account. Awareness of Al-Hasib encourages accountability and integrity.

41. Al-Jalil (الجليل) – The Majestic

Allah possesses infinite majesty. Reflecting on Al-Jalil invites reverence and deep respect.

42. Al-Karim (الكريم) – The Most Generous, The Most Esteemed

Allah's generosity knows no bounds. Remembering Al-Karim inspires generosity and gratitude.

43. Ar-Raqib (الرقيب) – The Watchful

Allah watches over us always. Being mindful of Ar-Raqib guides us toward righteous behaviour.

44. Al-Mujib (المجيب) – The Responsive One

Allah answers prayers. Trusting Al-Mujib inspires sincere and hopeful supplication.

45. Al-Wasi' (الواسع) – The All-Encompassing, the Boundless

Allah's mercy and knowledge are vast. Reflecting on Al-Wasi' expands our sense of hope.

46. Al-Hakim (الحكيم) – The All-Wise

Allah's wisdom governs all. Trusting Al-Hakim helps us accept what we do not understand.

47. Al-Wadud (الودود) – The Most Loving

Allah's love is pure and unconditional. Remembering Al-Wadud nourishes our hearts with love and inspires us to love others sincerely.

48. Al-Majid (المجيد) – The Glorious, The Most Honourable

Allah's glory is unparalleled. Reflecting on Al-Majid fills our hearts with awe and reverence.

49. Al-Ba'ith (الباعث) – The Infuser of New Life

Allah will resurrect all. Belief in Al-Ba'ith strengthens faith in the Hereafter and the concept of accountability.

50. Ash-Shahid (الشهيد) – The All Observing Witnessing Everything

Allah witnesses all actions. Awareness of Ash-Shahid fosters honesty and mindfulness.

51. Al-Haqq (الحق) – The Absolute Truth

Allah is the ultimate reality. Reflecting on Al-Haqq guides us to seek truth and justice.

52. Al-Wakil (الوكيل) – The Trustee

Allah manages all affairs. Trusting Al-Wakil brings peace and reduces anxiety.

53. Al-Qawiyy (القوي) – The All-Strong

Allah's strength is limitless. Remembering Al-Qawiyy inspires confidence in His support.

54. Al-Matin (المتين) – The Firm One

Allah's power never falters. Trust in Al-Matin strengthens our resilience in times of trial.

55. Al-Waliyy (الولي) – The Protecting Associate

Allah is the ally of believers. Reflecting on Al-Waliyy reassures us of His constant support.

56. Al-Hamid (الحميد) – The Praiseworthy

All praise belongs to Allah. Remembering Al-Hamid cultivates gratitude and praise in all circumstances.

57. Al-Muhsi (المحصي) – The All-Enumerating, The Counter

Allah records everything precisely. Awareness of Al-Muhsi encourages accountability.

58. Al-Mubdi' (المبدئ) – The Originator, The Initiator

Allah initiates creation from nothing. Reflecting on Al-Mubdi' inspires awe for His creative power.

59. Al-Mueed (المعيد) – The Restorer, The Reinstater

Allah restores life after death. Trusting Al-Mueed strengthens belief in resurrection.

60. Al-Muhyi (المحيي) – The Giver of Life

Allah grants life to all. Reflecting on Al-Muhyi deepens gratitude for life.

61. Al-Mumit (المميت) – The Creator of Death

Allah determines life and death. Awareness of Al-Mumit reminds us of our mortality and responsibility.

62. Al-Hayy (الحي) – The Ever-Living

Allah never dies. Remembering Al-Hayy reassures us of His eternal care.

63. Al-Qayyum (القَيوم) – The Sustainer, The Self-Subsisting

Allah sustains everything. Trusting Al-Qayyum reinforces complete reliance on Him.

64. Al-Wajid (الواجد) – The Perceiver

Allah lacks nothing and perceives everything. Reflecting on Al-Wajid encourages contentment and self-sufficiency.

65. Al-Majid (الماجد) – The Glorious, The Most Noble

Allah's nobility and glory are boundless. Remembering Al-Majid elevates our sense of divine grandeur.

66. Al-Wahid (الواحد) – The One

Allah is uniquely One. Contemplating Al-Wahid deepens Tawheed (monotheism) and the unity of faith.

67. As-Samad (الصمد) – The Self-Sufficient, The Impenetrable

Allah needs nothing; everything depends on Him. Reflecting on As-Samad strengthens dependence solely on Allah.

68. Al-Qadir (القادر) – The Omnipotent

Allah is capable of all things. Remembering Al-Qadir inspires hope in impossibilities.

69. Al-Muqtadir (المقتدر) – The Creator of All Power

Allah's control is absolute. Trusting Al-Muqtadir fosters submission to His will.

70. Al-Muqaddim (المقدم) – The Expediter

Allah brings forward whom He wills. Reflecting on Al-Muqaddim fosters gratitude for the opportunities it presents.

71. Al-Mu'akhkhir (المؤخر) – The Delayer

Allah delays matters wisely. Awareness of Al-Mu'akhkhir teaches patience and trust in divine timing.

72. Al-Awwal (الأول) – The First

Allah exists before everything. Reflecting on Al-Awwal reinforces faith in His eternal nature.

73. Al-Akhir (الأخر) – The Last

Allah remains after all else ends. Remembering Al-Akhir emphasises focus on eternal life.

74. Az-Zahir (الظاهر) – The Manifest

Allah's signs are apparent. Reflecting on Az-Zahir strengthens our recognition of His presence.

75. Al-Batin (الباطن) – The Hidden One, Knower of the Hidden

Allah knows all hidden matters. Trust in Al-Batin encourages inward sincerity.

76. Al-Wali (الوالي) – The Sole Governor

Allah governs all affairs perfectly. Awareness of Al-Wali reassures us of divine governance.

77. Al-Muta'ali (المتعالي) – The Self Exalted

Allah is exalted above all attributes of creation. Reflecting on Al-Muta'ali keeps our worship sincere.

78. Al-Barr (البر) – The Source of All Goodness

Allah's goodness is perfect. Remembering Al-Barr nurtures benevolence in our conduct.

79. At-Tawwab (التواب) – The Ever-Accepter of Repentance

Allah forgives those who repent. Trusting At-Tawwab encourages constant return to Him.

80. Al-Muntaqim (المنتقم) – The Avenger

Allah avenges the wronged. Remembering Al-Muntaqim reminds us that ultimate justice belongs to Allah.

81. Al-'Afuww (العفو) – The Supreme Pardoner

Allah erases sins. Reflecting on Al-'Afuww invites sincere repentance and forgiveness from others.

82. Ar-Ra'uf (الرؤوف) – The Most Kind

Allah is exceedingly compassionate. Remembering Ar-Ra'uf teaches gentleness and empathy.

83. Malik-ul-Mulk (مالك الملك) – Master of the Kingdom, Owner of the Dominion

Allah owns the dominion entirely. Reflecting on Malik-ul-Mulk reduces attachment to material life.

84. Dhul-Jalali Wal-Ikram (ذو الجلال و الإكرام) – Lord of Glory and Honour, Lord of Majesty and Generosity

Allah is majestic and generous. Reflecting on this name inspires awe and reverence.

85. Al-Muqsit (المقسط) – The Just One

Allah establishes justice perfectly. Remembering Al-Muqsit inspires fairness and equity.

86. Al-Jami' (الجامع) – The Gatherer, the Uniter

Allah gathers all on the Day of Judgment. Reflecting on Al-Jami' reminds us of the importance of accountability and unity.

87. Al-Ghaniyy (الغني) – The Self-Sufficient, The Wealthy

Allah needs nothing. Trusting Al-Ghaniyy fosters contentment and gratitude.

88. Al-Mughni (المغني) – The Enricher

Allah enriches whom He wills. Reflecting on Al-Mughni encourages gratitude for provisions.

89. Al-Mani' (المانع) – The Withholder

Allah prevents harm as wisdom dictates. Trusting Al-Mani' teaches us that not receiving is sometimes mercy.

90. Ad-Darr (الضار) – The Distresser

Allah allows hardship for wisdom. Remembering Ad-Darr encourages patience during trials.

91. An-Nafi' (النافع) – The Propitious, the Benefactor

Allah benefits whom He wills. Trusting An-Nafi' encourages hope and trust in His plan.

92. An-Nur (النور) – The Light

Allah illuminates hearts and guides. Reflecting on An-Nur inspires a desire to seek knowledge and clarity.

93. Al-Hadi (الهادي) – The Guide

Allah guides hearts to the truth. Remembering Al-Hadi inspires us to seek His guidance in all our affairs.

94. Al-Badi (البديع) – The Incomparable Originator

Allah's creativity is matchless. Reflecting on Al-Badi inspires awe in the beauty of creation.

95. Al-Baqi (الباقي) – The Everlasting

Allah is eternal. Trusting Al-Baqi shifts focus to eternal values.

96. Al-Warith (الوارث) – The Inheritor, The Heir

Allah inherits all after creation ceases. Reflecting on Al-Warith reminds us of the temporariness of life.

97. Ar-Rashid (الرشيد) – The Guide, Infallible Teacher and Knower

Allah guides to the

 right path. Remembering Ar-Rashid encourages us to seek wisdom and make the right choices.

98. As-Sabur (الصبور) – The Patient One

Allah is patient with creation. Reflecting on As-Sabur encourages perseverance in the face of trials.

99. Al-Majid (المجيد) – The Glorious One

Allah is infinitely glorious. Remembering Al-Majid inspires a continual sense of praise and awe.

Final Thoughts

The 99 Names of Allah are not just titles; they are a comprehensive map of divine perfection, offering insight into who Allah is and how He interacts with His creation. They guide Muslims in their faith, worship, ethics, and personal development. Allah says: *"He is Allah, besides Whom there is no god, the Knower of the unseen and the seen. He is the Most Compassionate, the Most Merciful."* **Quran 59:22-24.**

The 99 Names of Allah are not mere titles but a profound reflection of divine perfection. They shape a Muslim's faith, worship, character, and spiritual journey.

2. Worship & Rituals (Ibadah & Fiqh)

"Without doubt, in the remembrance of Allah do hearts find contentment."

Quran 13:28

"The closest a person is to His Lord is when he is in prostration."

Bukhari

The Importance of Salah

Despite salah being the most important act of worship for us believers and being the second pillar of Islam, it is a sad fact that many Muslims do not pray. The purpose of *Salah* is to put ourselves in touch with Allah; to strengthen our relationship with Him; and to be grateful for all of His blessings. Just as the body requires physical needs such as food and water, the soul has spiritual needs. *Salah* is the submission to the Creator, reminding us of the purpose of life. The soul can only be nourished through acts of worship, the most important of which is Salah. One can be very healthy, physically, but spiritually, we are dead if we do not pray salah. How worrying is that!

Salah enriches the soul, and yet man is forgetful, especially with our busy lifestyles. Prayer satisfies our spiritual needs and puts us in contact with our Creator. This gives the soul peace and contentment.

We all go through trials and tribulations —the problems that befall us, the challenges that we face in our everyday lives. We get engrossed in our worldly life, and then, five times a day, we take a short break from it to help bring us calm, peace, and tranquillity while submitting to our Creator. Without a doubt, it relieves our daily stresses. Allah[SWT] says: "Without doubt, in the remembrance of Allah do hearts find contentment." **Quran 13:28**

With salah, we have direct communication with Allah[SWT], and as our beloved Prophet[P] said, "The closest a person is to His Lord is when he is in prostration." **Bukhari.** The Arabic word for prayer, *as-salah,* is derived from the Arabic word meaning "connection." We connect with Allah[SWT] in this special meeting five times a day. The Prophet[P] said, "When any one of you stands to pray, he is communicating with his Lord, so let him pay attention to how he speaks to Him." **Bukhari.**

In another hadith, our beloved Prophet[P] told us that salah is the key to Paradise. He said, "The key to Paradise is prayer; the key to prayer is *Wudu* (ablution)." **Ahmad.** So, the act of *wudhu* in itself is worship, but also the water we apply to our bodies helps us to be physically and spiritually cleansed before we prepare to be in front of Allah[SWT].

Prayer is the second most important pillar of Islam, and is the most regular compulsory action in a Muslim's life. We fast for just one month every year; we give *Zakah* once a year; and *Hajj* is only performed once in a lifetime. However, prayer is the one act that must be fulfilled five times a day, regardless of the circumstance. In fact, Allah[SWT] did not exempt the Muslims from praying even during the battle! He says: "Guard strictly your (habit of) prayers... If you fear (an enemy), pray on foot, or riding." **Quran 2:238.**

If this is the case in the time of war, then what about peace? We are required to pray until we reach *sakaraatul maut* – the last pangs of death. Unless one is mentally unstable, of course, then it is not obligatory.

Abu Huraira reported: The Messenger of Allah, peace and blessings be upon him, said, *"The first action for which a servant of Allah^{SWT} will be held accountable on the Day of Resurrection will be his prayers. If they are in order, he will have prospered and succeeded. If they are lacking, he will have failed and lost. Suppose there is something defective in his obligatory prayers. In that case, the Almighty Lord will say: See if my servant has any voluntary prayers that can complete what is insufficient in his obligatory prayers. The rest of his deeds will be judged the same way."* **Tirmidhi.** Therefore, we pray the compulsory prayer and the voluntary prayers to help compensate for any discrepancies in the obligatory prayer. *Subhan-Allah!* We are truly so blessed! So, it is recommended that we perform all the *Sunnah* and as many voluntary prayers as possible. We know it does not take long.

We should also be aware that *Salah* is what makes us believers, so we should be very careful to pray all our Salah. Our beloved Prophet^P said, *"Between faith and unbelief is abandoning the prayer."* **Muslim.** Similarly, Hepbuh *said, "The comparison of one who remembers Allah^{SWT} and one who does not, is like that of the living and the dead."* **Bukhari.** This is a warning from our beloved Prophet, differentiating between those who perform prayer and those who do not.

Benefits of Salah

Protection against evil

Man was created weak, and without seeking help from Allah, it will be impossible to refrain from evil. Allah^{SWT} says: "Verily, prayer restrains (oneself) from shameful and unjust deeds..." **Quran 29:45.**

There is no doubt that the one who stands before Allah^{SWT} willingly will be different from the one who does not. How can one continue to commit the same sins if one is standing before Allah^{SWT} 5 times a day?

By realising Allah's greatness and dependence on our Lord, man is humbled and rids us from pride and arrogance. In prayer, the Muslim places the highest part of his body and the source of his intellect, his head, on the ground and says, *"How perfect is my Lord, the Most High."* Humbleness is one of the qualities which Allah^{SWT} has associated with success. He says, "Successful indeed are the believers, who are humble in their prayers." **Quran 23:1-2.** Of course, this can only be achieved when one understands what one is reciting and concentrates with humility.

Salah washes away sins

Everyone commits sins and everyone is expected to sin; however, Allah[SWT] has provided, in prayer, a way to wipe out those sins. Allah[SWT] says: *"And perform prayer... surely the good deeds remove the evil deeds."* **Quran 11:114**.

In a hadith narrated by Abu Huraira wherein he *said,* I heard Allah's Messenger[P] saying: *"If there was a river at the door of any one of you and he took a bath in it five times a day, would you notice any dirt on him?"* They said, *"Not a trace of dirt would be left."* The Prophet[P] added, *"That is the example of the five prayers with which Allah blots out (cancels) evil deeds."* **Bukhari.**

Numerous trials and problems surround man. Once we focus on strengthening our relationship with our Lord, He, who is All-Powerful, will fix our worldly problems. As our scholars say, whoever reinforces their relationship with Allah, Allah[SWT] will strengthen their relationship with the creation. As Allah[SWT] says: *"Seek help in patience and prayer."* **Quran 2:153.**

Prayer unites the *Ummah*

When the prayer is performed in congregation, it fosters brotherhood, equality, and humility among Muslims. The worshippers stand in rows, shoulder to shoulder, without any distinction of race, nationality, colour, wealth, family or status, and all pray together as one body. This act of unity helps demolish all barriers which stand between men.

The Prophet[P] said, *"Prayer in congregation is better than praying alone by twenty-seven degrees."* **Bukhari.** Attending the *Masjid* means we meet people from the neighbourhood regularly, thereby practising community cohesion and creating love for one another. We greet and say Salaams to each other regularly, and never feel lonely, but part of the Ummah of the Prophet[P].

For those who abandon prayer, there is a grave warning from Allah. Allah[SWT] says: *"O Mankind, what has deceived you concerning your Lord, the Most Generous?"* **Quran 82:06.**

By not praying, you are actually disobeying our Creator. This is a very serious matter, as the whole purpose of our existence is to worship Allah, yet we are disobeying our Creator every day by not praying. This is a grave mistake. Allah[SWT] says: *"Then, there has succeeded them a generation who have given up prayer and have followed their* *desires. So, they will be thrown into Hell. Except those who repent and believe, and work righteousness."* **Quran 19:59-60.** Allah states: *"(The people in Hell will be asked:) What has caused you to enter Hell? They will say: We were not of those who used to pray…"* **Quran 74:42-43.** For those who do not pray, I urge you to make a start!

By not praying, you are being ungrateful. Refusing Allah's invitation as your Creator to establish this close relationship with Him is the ultimate ingratitude. Allah^{SWT} created you and gave you everything. Allah^{SWT} says: *"It is He who has created you and endowed you with hearing and seeing and hearts, little are you grateful."* **Quran 67:23.**

The Prophet's feet would sometimes swell because he would stand in prayer for lengthy periods. When asked about this, he would reply, *"Should I not be a grateful servant of my Lord?"*

What excuse will you give to your Creator on the Day of Judgement when we will all stand before Him to account? Allah^{SWT} has blessed us with 24 hours, and yet Allah^{SWT} only asked that we spend a small percentage of that day for prayer.

The Prophet^P said, *"On the Day of Resurrection the feet of the son of Adam will not move away till he is questioned about five matters: on what he spent his life; in doing what he made his youth pass away; where he acquired his property, and on what he spent it; and what he did regarding what he knew."* **Tirmidhi.**

The person who had no connection with Allah^{SWT} helplessly seeks other means to look for calmness, contentment, and peace, but it will be nowhere to be found. Their searches will be in vain, as they wander aimlessly.

Allah^{SWT} says: *"And whoever turns away from My remembrance - indeed for him is a life of hardship. And We will raise him on the Day of Resurrection, blind. He will say, "My Lord, why have you raised me blind while I was (once) seeing?" (Allah) will say, "Thus did Our signs come to you, and you forgot (disregarded) them; and thus, will you, this Day, be forgotten."* **Quran 20:124-6.**

We must remember that Allah^{SWT} does not need our prayers. Allah^{SWT} does not need anything from anyone. He is the Almighty and all-powerful, yet merciful and forgiving. It is we who need Him.

Allah^{SWT} says: "Give thanks to Allah, and whoever gives thanks, it is only for his own soul's good, and whoever is ungrateful, surely Allah is free of all needs, Worthy of all praise." **Quran 31:12.**

When we do not establish prayer in our lives, we are toying with disbelief.

People may make excuses such as "I have no time" or "I'm too busy at work or studying." This is pure deception. When you make time for your prayers and prioritise them in life, Allah^SWT will bless your time, making you more effective, efficient, and successful. Allah^SWT says in the Quran: "Surely, the prayers are made obligatory for the believers at their prescribed times." **Quran 4:103.** No matter how busy you are, make time for Salah. It doesn't take long, and you will be more productive and energised afterwards.

Contemplate this *hadith*. The Prophet^P *said,* "If they knew the merits of the 'Isha and Fajr prayers, they would come to them (in the mosque) even if they had to crawl." **Bukhari.** What excuse do we honestly have when we face our Lord on that difficult Day?

Although we primarily offer salah because it is a religious duty. However, science has also enabled us to see the physical benefits. Therefore, in addition to all the religious and spiritual benefits, salat also comes with physical benefits. Such as:

Improved Body Posture

When we are in the standing position, about to begin the salat, with our feet evenly apart and our body firm and upright, the hands are placed in a position that aligns the spine and maintains balance. The head is slightly lowered, with the gaze directed downwards, allowing the body to remain grounded yet relaxed. In this posture, both the brain and the body are at ease. When performed regularly throughout the day, this position contributes to improved posture and physical alignment.

Secretion of Glands

In the state of *qiyaam* in which we recite *Surah Fatiha* that contains almost all the long vowels, the sound vibrations of which, when produced, give the signal to the mind to increase the secretion of glands like the pituitary gland and the thyroid gland, in addition to increasing the condition of the lungs. Thus, reciting Surah Al-Fatiha during the *qiyaam* part helps improve the function of the glands and lungs.

Stretches the Body

In the state of ruku, we bend to the knees while keeping the back and the hands straight. This posture of offering prayers is one of the best ways to stretch the body without overexertion. When we are in such a posture, the back, thighs, and calves of a person become fully stretched, and blood flow to the upper part of the body also improves. This posture also helps engage the core, as well as the abdominal muscles, and serves as a crunch exercise. Therefore, as a result of this posture, a person stretches their body five times a day, which also helps strengthen the core.

Abs Control

The *Sajdah* posture of salat can help significantly in controlling the belly from expanding and accumulating fat. The knees and both feet are on the ground, while the head is lowered in a way that applies gentle pressure to the abdominal muscles, strengthening them. This position helps control abs, and performing it five times a day is a good form of exercise.

Blood Flow

People have blood pressure problems due to issues with blood flow. They have either too much blood flowing to a particular part of the body or very little blood flowing to a specific part. To avoid such a blood flow problem that can lead to blood pressure issues, all the postures in salat help regulate blood flow to all parts of the body. The *qiyaam* position helps maintain normal blood flow, the *ruku* posture directs blood flow to the upper part of the body, while in the state of *tashahhud*, blood flow is also directed to the lower part of the body. Therefore, all the movements in salat can help regulate the blood flow to all parts of the body. Researchers also assert that the varying motions in prostration help improve cerebral (brain) circulation and reduce the risk of ischemic brain disease.

Cleanliness

As we need to be in a pure state of cleanliness, we perform Wudu before every prayer, which helps clean the outer surface of the body, which is the best thing that can happen for the skin. Therefore, the general state of cleanliness in all the areas of the body leads to the skin staying healthy and a person feeling fresh, energised and lively.

The losers are those people who, despite knowing that *Salah* is an obligatory act of worship, are denying themselves not only the spiritual and physical benefits but are bringing displeasure to Allah^{SWT} and the consequences of which we will only know on the day of Judgment.

Life is all about ups and downs, and there will undoubtedly be times when your *imaan* will dip. When this happens, you may not be praying on time or giving up altogether. We, human beings, are fallible, and we need something to boost our *Imaan* and get back on track.

However, when you take even baby steps towards getting back to normality and improving yourself, and you have the sincere intention of giving up sin and start striving to increase your *Imaan* after a lull, then Allah^{SWT} will definitely run towards you in achieving this. The Messenger of Allah pbuh*said,* "Allah^{SWT} says: "..Whoever draws close to me by the length of a hand, I will draw close to him by the length of an arm. Whoever draws close to me by the length of an arm, I will draw close to him by the length of a fathom. Whoever comes to me walking, I will come to him running. Whoever meets me with enough sins to fill the Earth, not associating any idols with me, I will meet him with as much forgiveness." **Muslim.** This means we should never lose hope in Allah. If you wish to rectify yourself, then this is enough motivation from Allah^{SWT} to return to Him. The best way to do so is to start praying your salah if you have given up.

Our *Imaan* fluctuates according to our life circumstances and situations. Everyone is different and handles difficulties and problems in their own unique way. There are situations that occur in our lives, such as the loss of a loved one or a bad accident, or when we are nearing death, when our hearts are softened and full of *Imaan*, just as they are when we are fasting in the month of *Ramadan*, when the Shayateen are tied. Then there are other times when we are so engrossed in worldly affairs that our heart becomes devoid of the much-needed *Imaan*.

When our imaan is low, we must take measures to restore it. We should be aware of the things that decrease our imaan in order to avoid them and those that increase our *Imaan* to embrace them. One of the best ways to do this is to never neglect your Salah.

Salaah is like oxygen. Your quality and concentration may be reduced, and your enthusiasm for prayer may be at an all-time low, but never give up altogether. Just as we need air to breathe and survive, *Salaah* is what we need to nourish our souls. This means all five daily prayers – fajr and isha included, because there is a hadith narrated by Abu Hurairah wherein the Prophet^P *said,* "No prayer is more burdensome to the hypocrites than the fajr (dawn) prayer and the Isha (night) prayer; and if they knew their merits, they would come to them even if they had to crawl to do so." **Bukhari and Muslim.** *Subhan-Allah!* Just imagine we would attempt to crawl to pray to our salah, if we knew the benefits, and yet if we do not pray, we are inadvertently committing sin. We certainly do not want to be those described as hypocrites. Therefore, never lose hope – strive to get back to what you used to be. It is alright to feel low, but do not get disillusioned and get led by the Shaytan, who will discourage you from praying.

We are very close to Allah^{SWT} when we pray. The Prophet^P *said,* "The closest the slave will draw to his Lord is when he is performing *sujood* (prostrating)". **Muslim.** So never abandon prayer, no matter what!

It is through prayer that a Muslim individual seeks closeness to the Creator and attains inner peace and tranquillity, and Allah^{SWT} knows best His creation. Thus, He says in the Quran: "Verily, man was created impatient, irritable when evil touches him and niggardly when good touches him. Except for those devoted to prayer, those who remain constant in their prayers..." **Quran 70:19-23.**

We see many people who appear very successful and happy, yet they do not practice their faith and do not pray their salah. Do you really think they are happy and content? Not according to our *deen.* They are, in fact, in a dangerous illusion.

Allah^{SWT} says: "Whoever works righteousness — whether male or female — while he (or she) is a true believer (of Islamic Monotheism) verily, to him We will give a good life (in this world with respect, contentment and lawful provision), and We shall pay them certainly a reward in proportion to the best of what they used to do (i.e., Paradise in the Hereafter)." **Quran 16:97. So**, the successful ones are those who are righteous and a believer; and one can only be a believer if one prays their salah. Let us be reminded once again of what our beloved Prophet Muhammad^P *said*, "Between faith and unbelief is abandoning the prayer." **Muslim.**

My brothers and sisters, let us make every effort to perform our five daily prayers; otherwise, we not only miss out on the spiritual and physical benefits of prayer, but we will also be among the losers on the Day of Judgement.

May Allah^{SWT} grant us the *taufiq* never to miss our obligatory acts of worship and help us resist *shaytan,* whose job it is to divert us from the straight path.

Khushu - Elevating your *Salah* to the level of Servitude

"Successful indeed are the believers: those who are humble in their prayer."

Quran 23:1-2

"The first thing to be lifted from this ummah will be khushu, until you will not find anyone with khushu."

Tabarani

Salah is the second of the five pillars of Islam. It is one of the greatest acts of worship. It is an act in which the believer shuts off the world around him to converse directly with Allah[SWT], displaying his complete servitude to Him.

Salah was the *Sunnah* of every Prophet through which they honoured Allah[SWT] and sought His assistance. It is one of the best ways to remember Him, become close to Him, and erase our many sins. It is also Islam's criterion, distinguishing the believers from the disbelievers, and it is a *Nur'* (light) that will come to our rescue in the grave and on the Day of Resurrection.   Our beloved Prophet[P] described salah as the 'joy' of his life. Yet sadly, many of us today consider the same salah an inconvenience. Instead of 'wanting' to pray, we feel like we 'have' to pray.

How, then, can we become like our beloved Prophet[P] and learn to experience a similar joy? How can we derive peace and serenity in and from our salah? How can we make salah the lifeline that it is, helping us overcome the trials and uncertainties that the Ummah is facing? And how can we train ourselves to perform this lofty act with complete humility and concentration with *Khushu*? Let us explore this.

What is Khushu?

Khushu is one of the actions of the heart. Khushu refers to the heart that stands with complete humility, lowliness, and full concentration towards Allah. In essence, Khushu resides within the heart and is manifested through the limbs and organs. With khushu, our heart softens, becomes still, and humbles itself to its Lord. Our heart submits and focuses on Allah[SWT] to such an extent that everything else retreats into insignificance. Our limbs and organs then follow the heart, and they too are humbled.

Our beloved Prophet[P] *said, "There is a lump of flesh in the body: if it is sound, the whole body will be sound but if it is corrupt, the whole body will be corrupt. Truly, it is the heart."* **Bukhari.** If the heart is corrupted by negligence or insinuating whispers from Shaytan, the worship of the body's faculties will also be corrupt.

A humble heart results in the humbling of the ears, eyes, head, and face. This is why the Prophet[P] would say in his ruku: *"My hearing, sight, mind, bones, and nerves are humbled to You."* **Muslim.** Thus, our hearing submits to Allah, and we only listen to what He has permitted. Our eyes do not glance at the haram. Every part of our body, both interior and exterior, humbles itself and obeys its Creator.

Khushu extinguishes the 'fires' of lust and desire and illuminates our hearts with the 'light' of Allah's Greatness and Might. We become fully aware that Allah[SWT] is looking at us, and this fills our hearts with His reverence. In other words, Khushu means calmness, serenity, tranquillity, dignity, and humility. What makes a person have this khushu is fear of Allah and the knowledge that He is always watching.

The Importance of Khushu in Salah

Salah is the key to our success in this world and the next. However, if we neglect this crucial aspect, we will lose it, and we will be unable to pursue the path that leads to the good in both this life and the next. The poor quality of salah is akin to not reaping the full benefits of a powerful life management tool given to us by our Creator. Undoubtedly, when our salah is in good condition, we will notice that all the other life affairs also naturally fall into their proper places with ease. Times of ease become more joyful, and times of difficulties become easy, or at the very least become bearable. Allah[SWT] says: *"Successful indeed are the believers: those who are humble in their prayer."* **Quran 23:1-2.** Here, Allah[SWT] describes the qualities of successful believers as those who are humble.

Ibn Kathir explained this verse thus: *"Khushu in ṣalah is only attained by the one who has completely emptied his heart for it, who fully occupies himself for it and does not pay attention to anything else besides it, and who prioritises it over everything else. At that point, it becomes a source of comfort and intense joy."*
Khushu is so important for us today that the Prophet[P] stated, *"The first thing to be lifted from this Ummah will be khushu, until you will not find anyone with khushu."* **(Tabarani)** If our salah feels like a chore, it is because there is an absence of khushu in our salah. Once we experience khushu, our salah will transform into a source of comfort and joy. It will become something we continuously seek pleasure in and cannot live without.

The Prophet[P] *said, "And if he stands to pray and praises Allah, extols Him and glorifies Him with what He is most deserving of; and* ***shows wholehearted devotion to Allah,*** he will revert to being sin-free (as pure) as he was on the day his mother gave birth to him." **Muslim.** Amr Abasah[RA] states that he heard this from the Prophet more than seven times. In another hadith, Uqbah b. Amir[RA] heard the Messenger of Allah[P] say:

"If any Muslim performs wuḍu, and does so properly, then stands and performs two rakah of prayer in which he focuses with his heart as well as his face [i.e. is not physically distracted], Paradise is guaranteed for him." **Muslim**

The Prophet[P] also said, "Five prayers which Allah has made obligatory. Whoever does Wudu properly for them, prays them on time, does ruku properly and has perfect khushoo, it is a promise from Allah that he will be forgiven, but whoever does not do this, has no such promise – if Allah wishes, He will forgive him, and if He wishes, He will punish him." **Abu Dawood.** This shows the great importance of Khushu in our salah.

Khushu is of Two Kinds. The first is the khushu of the heart, which involves bringing the full intention and attention of the heart to prayer, accompanied by constant contemplation of what is being recited. The second is the khushu of the body, which consists of the peaceful stillness of the body and avoidance of unnecessary actions, such as yawning, fidgeting, adjusting one's clothes, or looking at a watch, or allowing the eye or mind to be drawn to anything outside the prayer.

The Prophet[P] said, "Allah commands you to offer Salah. When you are offering Salah, do not turn away; for Allah directs His Face towards the face of His praying servant, as long as they do not turn away." **Tirmidhi.**

The main enemy of a believer is the shaytan who will always try his best to disrupt our salah. So, what do we do? Well, we have to fight shaytan and his whispers because he is always busy trying to preoccupy us with thoughts of everything other than Allah[SWT].

The Prophet[P] said, "When the call to prayer is announced, Shaytan takes to his heels and passes wind loudly so that he does not hear the adhan. When the adhan finishes, he comes back. When the iqamah is proclaimed, he takes to his heel (again). When the iqamah finishes, he comes back so that he can obstruct the person's heart with his whispers, saying 'Remember such and such, remember such and such,' things which he did not remember before, to the extent that the person no longer knows how much he has prayed." **Bukhari.**

Uthman Abi al As[RA] came to the Prophet[P] and said, "O Messenger of Allah, indeed Shaytan comes in between me and my salah and my recitation of the Quran and causes me to doubt." The Messenger of Allah[P] told him: "That is a shaytan known as Khinzab. When you feel his presence, seek Allah's protection from him and spit lightly to your left three times." Uthman Abi al As[RA] said, "I did that and then Allah made him go away from me." **Muslim.** We learn from this hadith that we need to say: أَعُوْذُ بِاللّٰهِ مِنَ الشَّيْطَانِ الرَّجِيْمِ and spit lightly to your left three times, as mentioned above in the hadith. We need to continue doing this whenever we feel the Shaytan's presence, not just occasionally. However, avoid spitting during the congregational prayers.

Maintaining composure and stillness throughout prayer is also important, as it is essential for the prayer to be valid. Once, the Prophet[P] entered the mosque and saw a man hastily bowing and prostrating while praying, so he said to him, *"Go back and pray, for you have not prayed."* The man *said, "By the One Who has sent you with the Truth, I cannot do any better than this. Please, teach me."* The Prophet[P] said, *"When you stand up for Salah, say Takbir (Allahu Akbar), and then recite whatever you can of the Quran (what you know by heart). Then bow until you become peacefully still in your bowing, then rise until you are standing up straight. Then prostrate until you are peacefully still in your prostration, then sit up until you are peacefully still in your sitting; and do that throughout your entire Salah."* **Bukhari.** Thus, we must perform our prayer slowly and with tranquillity, giving each part its due attention. We should not rush to the next step, but instead, keep our body steady and calm, allowing each joint and bone to return to its normal position before proceeding to the next action.

How to Attain Khushu

- Prepare mentally and physically for standing before the Supreme Creator.

- Strive to pray in the congregation in the *Masjid*. Aim to arrive early.

- Be punctual with the *Sunnah* and nafl prayers, as they awaken your heart and prepare you for attaining greater khushu in the farḍ prayers.

- Get rid of distractions. Eat and use the bathroom before praying. The Prophet[P] said, *"You should not pray when food is served or when resisting the urge to urinate or defecate."* **Muslim.**

- When we are not praying in the *Masjid*, choose a quiet place to pray, free from noise, motion, and distractions, such as people walking or chatting around you, telephones ringing, or the TV playing in the background, so you can focus on your *Salah* better, and will help you to enter a 'peaceful zone'.

- Stop sinning. Protect yourself from all *ḥaram,* especially your eyes and your tongue. Do not expect yourself to have khushu if you have just watched something *ḥaram*.

- Fight Shayṭan and his whispers. Always be on guard, as Shayṭan wants to destroy your ṣalah. Seek Allah's protection and force yourself to reflect on what you are saying. Say: "A'udhu billahi min ash-shaytan ir-rajim" (I seek refuge in Allah from the accursed devil).

- Memorise and understand the meaning of all that you are saying in the salah. This means learning the translation of everything you are saying in ṣalah and being fully mindful when saying it. Ibn Abbas^RA *said, "Only that which you were mindful of in your ṣalah will be accepted from you."*

- Vary the adhkar and surahs in your salah. This will help you concentrate and focus more.

- Remember death and the Hereafter during and outside of the salah. Imagine you are praying your final prayer. Visualise the stages of the Hereafter in your salah. The Prophet^P said, *"When you stand for your prayer, pray as if you are saying farewell...."* **Ibn Majah.**

- Keep in mind that Allah^SWT responds to you. In salah, you are conversing with your Lord. As you talk to Him, He responds to you. Feel privileged to be in direct conversation with the Lord of the worlds.

- Be calm and lengthen your salah. The journey through salah is remarkable. Each part is a unique milestone, bringing its sweetness and joy. Every action and statement has its form of servitude to Allah. Be calm and do not rush through your salah just to reach the end. Ibn Abbas^RA *said, "Praying two rakah with contemplation is better than praying all night while the heart is heedless."* **Ibn Abbas.**

- Pray with utmost humility as though you are seeing Allah^SWT, and if not, then know that Allah^SWT sees you. When asked by Jibril^AS to define Ihsan, the Prophet^P said, *"That you worship Allah as though you are seeing Him; for if you cannot see Him, He truly sees you"* **Muslim.**

- Go for salah with full presence and concentration. Incline to Allah completely. Focus on Him Alone. If you turn to Him, He will turn to you. If you turn away from Him, He will turn away from you. Achieve this by removing the world from your heart and purifying your heart of desires and doubts.

- Understand the Importance of Salah. Reflect on the significance of *Salah* as the most important act of worship and the primary connection between you and Allah^SWT. Recognising its importance will naturally lead to more reverence and focus during prayer.

- Prepare Mentally and Physically for Salah. This means performing wudhu with mindfulness, realising that it is not just a physical act but a spiritual cleansing. This helps in preparing your mind and body for prayer.

- Wear clean and modest clothing that is comfortable, which will help minimise distractions during Salah.

- If you are not praying in the *Masjid* or congregation, choose a quiet space without distractions, noise, and interruptions.   Remember, the *Masjid* is the best place for men to pray in the congregation.

- Slow down your recitation and movements. Avoid rushing by performing each action and recitation slowly and deliberately. Rushing through the prayer often leads to a loss of focus and mindfulness.

- Pause between each action. Take a moment between the different positions (standing, bowing, prostrating) to reflect and maintain your focus.

- Pray in the state of mindfulness. Try to focus entirely on the present moment during Salah. If your mind starts to wander, gently bring your attention back to the prayer. Remind yourself that you are standing before Allah. Visualise standing before Allah by imagining that you are directly in the presence of Allah, which can help to increase your humility and concentration. The more you practice mindfulness in Salah, the easier it becomes to achieve khushu.

- Have sincerity (Ikhlas). Pray for Allah alone. Ensure that your intention (niyyah) is purely for the sake of Allah and not for showing off or fulfilling a ritual mechanically. Sincerity in intention fosters greater khushu.

- Pray on time and make it a habit to prepare mentally before each Salah. Do not procrastinate. When the time for salah comes, stop what you are doing and prioritise your salah.

- Engage in extra worship. Performing additional nawafil prayers, in addition to the obligatory ones, can help improve concentration and deepen your connection with Allah.

- After every fard salah, engage in dhikr (remembrance of Allah).

- Engage in regular dhikr and Quran recitation outside of Salah. This practice helps in keeping your heart soft and more receptive during prayer.

- Make dua to Allah. Continuously ask Allah in your dua to grant you khushu in your prayers. Sincerely seeking Allah's help is a powerful way to achieve a deeper level of concentration and humility.

- Control your thoughts. Before starting your prayer, seek refuge in Allah from Shaytan by saying, "A'udhu billahi min ash-shaytan ir-rajim" (I seek refuge in Allah from the accursed Shaytan). This can help in reducing distractions and stray thoughts. If distractions occur, acknowledge them but do not dwell on them. Refocus on your recitation and actions.

- Try hard not to yawn during prayer, and if this is not possible, then cover your mouth. The Messenger of Allah[P] said, *"If one of you yawns during salah, let him suppress it as much as he can as Shaytan enters (the mouth)"* **Muslim.**

Khushu is not exclusive to salah. We should continuously remember that Allah sees us, hears us, and knows our thoughts. As Allah[SWT] says: *"And indeed We have created man, and We know whatever thoughts his inner self develops, and We are closer to him than (his) jugular vein."* **Quran 50:16.** This verse implies that Allah's power and knowledge are nearer to him than his jugular vein.

Shaytan will have a greater share of your salah than you when you first try to pray with Khushu. Then you will start competing with him, going back and forth, until you secure half of it. However, don't give up; you must then continue to fight until you can ensure all of your salah. The Prophet[P] said, *"A man returns from his prayer and only a tenth, ninth, eighth, seventh, sixth, fifth, fourth, third or half of it, is recorded for him.*" **(Abu Dawud)**

If you pray salah as it ought to be prayed, fulfilling its conditions and with complete concentration and humility, your heart will become purified. Eventually, your heart will become illuminated. Your *Imaan* will increase. You will incline more to goodness and abhor evil.

Remember, the process of attaining khushu and enjoying salah requires time and effort. It will not happen overnight. Therefore, never give up; keep striving.

May Allah[SWT] bless us with continuous khushu both in and outside of salah. Ameen.

Introduction to the Holy Quran

"We will show them Our signs in the horizons and within themselves until it becomes clear to them that it is the truth. But is it not sufficient concerning your Lord that He is, over all things, a Witness?"

Quran 41:53

The Quran is the actual word of God, not created but revealed by Him through the angel Gabriel to Prophet Muhammad pbuh, over a period of 23 years, beginning in 610 CE, when Prophet Muhammad was 40 years of age, and concluding in 632 CE, the year of his death.

The Holy Quran is the central religious text of Islam. The Quran is written in classical Arabic and is considered by Muslims to be the final revelation of God for the benefit of humanity. It is believed by Muslims to be the actual word of God, not created but revealed by Him through the angel Gabriel to Prophet Muhammad (peace and blessings be upon him), over a period of 23 years, beginning in 610 CE, when Prophet Muhammad was 40 years of age, and concluding in 632 CE, the year of his death.

The Quran consists of over 6500 verses spread across 30 sections. The Quran is divided into 114 chapters. Each chapter, known as *a Surah,* is further divided into verses known as *Aayaat.* The Quranic verses address various aspects of life, including morality, law, and spirituality. The Quran is a timeless source of inspiration, and Muslims strive to follow its teachings in their daily lives. It is recited and memorised by millions of Muslims around the world, and its recitation holds special importance, especially during the month of *Ramadan.*

The Quran addresses all of humanity

The Quran is regarded as a universal and timeless message for all humanity. The Quran explicitly states that its message is meant for all of humanity. For example, in *Surah Al-Anbiya,* chapter 21, verse 107, God says*: "And We have not sent you, [O Muhammad], except as a mercy to the worlds."* This verse emphasises the universal nature of the Prophet Muhammad's mission.

Additionally, in Surah Al-Fussilat, chapter 41 verse 53, God says: *"We will show them Our signs in the horizons and within themselves until it becomes clear to them that it is the truth. But is it not sufficient concerning your Lord that He is, over all things, a Witness?"*

These verses inform us that the Quranic guidance is intended for all humanity, and its teachings are applicable to people from diverse backgrounds and cultures. Muslims are encouraged to share the message of the Quran with others, but the acceptance and understanding of the message are considered matters of personal choice and free will. God makes it clear that no force should be put upon anyone. God says: *"There is no compulsion in religion. The Right Way stands clearly distinguished from the wrong."* Quran chapter 2 verse 256. This verse means that the system of Islam, encompassing belief, morals, and practical conduct, cannot be imposed on anyone by force or compulsion.

Who is the Author of the Quran and responsible for its preservation?

Muslims view the Quran as divine and unaltered scripture. Therefore, the authorship of the Quran is attributed to God, who promises to protect the Quran from the changes and manipulations that occurred in earlier holy texts. God states in *Surah al-Hijr,* chapter 15, verse 9: *"Indeed, it is We who revealed the Quran and indeed, We will be its guardian."* This verse of promise from God is enough to assure us that He will indeed protect the Quran from any change over time. The Quran has remained unaltered over the past 14 centuries.

What is the purpose of the Quran?

The primary purpose of the Quran is to guide individuals and societies in all aspects of life. These include:

Guidance: The Quran serves as a comprehensive guide for Muslims, offering spiritual, ethical, and practical advice for all aspects of life. It provides principles and laws to govern personal conduct, family life, social justice, and other aspects of society.

Spiritual Enlightenment: The Quran is regarded as a source of spiritual nourishment, enabling believers to deepen their connection with God and achieve closeness to Him. It addresses fundamental questions about the purpose of life, the afterlife, and the nature of God.

Preservation of God's Message: The Quran is the final and complete revelation of God's will, confirming and preserving the essential teachings found in earlier scriptures, such as the Torah and the Bible. It is considered a safeguard against human error or intentional alteration to sacred texts that affected previous scriptures.

Legal and Ethical Framework: The Quran contains laws and ethical principles that Muslims are encouraged to follow. It outlines permissible and prohibited actions, social justice principles, and guidelines for moral conduct.

Prophetic Stories: The Quran includes narratives about various Prophets and their communities, providing lessons and examples for believers. These stories are meant to offer moral and spiritual insights.

Unity and Identity: The Quran plays a crucial role in unifying the global Muslim community (*ummah*) by providing a common set of beliefs, values, and practices. It contributes to the formation of a distinctive Muslim identity.

Recitation and Worship: Muslims recite verses from the Quran in their prayers and other acts of worship. The rhythmic and melodic recitation, known as *Tajweed*, is considered a form of worship in its own right.

Overall, the Quran is central to Islamic theology, law, and morality, serving as a comprehensive guide for Muslims seeking to lead a righteous and fulfilling life in accordance with the teachings of Islam.

How is the Quran different from other revelations, the Torah, Psalms of David, and the Gospel?

In Islam, the Quran is regarded as the final and complete revelation from God to humanity, conveyed through the Prophet Muhammad (peace be upon him). While there are similarities between the Quran and other religious scriptures, such as the Torah revealed to Moses, the Psalms of David revealed to David, and the Gospel revealed to Jesus, notable differences exist between these scriptures. These are as follows;

Universal Message: While the previous scriptures are viewed as guidance for specific communities or periods, the Quran is regarded as a universal message for all of humanity, lasting until the end of time. It addresses people of all races, nations, and backgrounds.

Finality of Revelation and Preservation: Muslims believe that the Quran is the last and final revelation, superseding all previous scriptures. It is considered by Muslims to be the culmination and perfection of God's guidance to humanity. Muslims believe that the Quran is perfectly preserved in its original form, without any alteration or corruption since the time of its revelation. This is seen as a distinctive feature not shared by previous scriptures, which Muslims believe have changed over time.

Language: The Quran is written in classical Arabic, and Muslims believe that the linguistic beauty and eloquence of the Quran are unparalleled. The language is considered a miracle, and even though translations exist, the original Arabic is deemed essential to a complete understanding.

Content: While there are similarities in moral teachings, monotheism, and some historical accounts, there are also differences in specific laws, rituals, and theological concepts. For example, the Islamic understanding of the oneness of God (*Tawhid)* and the finality of prophethood in Muhammad (peace be upon him) are emphasised in the Quran.

Prophets: The Quran acknowledges and respects the prophets and messengers mentioned in previous scriptures, such as Adam, Noah, Abraham, Moses, and Jesus (peace be upon them all), but it also provides additional details and corrections to certain narratives found in those earlier scriptures.

This summary reflects the beliefs held by Muslims regarding the Quran's uniqueness. Interfaith dialogue often explores these similarities and differences to foster understanding among different religious communities.

What are the Inspirational verses of the Quran?

Different verses may resonate with individuals differently based on their circumstances and perspectives. Here are a few verses that are often considered inspirational:

1. *Surah Al-Baqarah* (2:286): "Allah does not burden a soul beyond that it can bear..."
2. *Surah Al-Imran* (3:185): "Every soul will taste death, and you will only be given your full compensation on the Day of Resurrection..."
3. *Surah Al-Ankabut* (29:69): "And those who strive for Us - We will surely guide them to Our ways. And indeed, Allah is with the doers of good."
4. *Surah Ash-Sharh* (94:5-6): "For indeed, with hardship [will be] ease. Indeed, with hardship [will be] ease."
5. *Surah Al-Qalam* (68:4): "And indeed, you are of a great moral character."
6. *Surah Al-Hadid* (57:4): "And He is with you wherever you are. And Allah, of what you do, is Seeing."
7. *Surah Al-Mulk* (67:2): "He who created death and life to test you [as to] which of you is best in deed - and He is the Exalted in Might, the Forgiving."

These verses convey messages of hope, resilience, faith, and God's mercy. Interpretations may vary, and it is recommended to seek guidance from knowledgeable scholars to gain a deeper understanding of the context and meaning of Quranic verses.

Verses of the Quran that inspire people and help reflect our status in Creation

Numerous verses in the Quran help inspire us to reflect on the purpose of our creation and the world around us. Below are a few verses from the Quran that have inspired Muslims and non-Muslims alike:

Surah Al-Isra (17:70): *"And We have certainly honoured the children of Adam and carried them on the land and sea and provided for them of the good things and preferred them over much of what We have created, with [definite] preference."* This verse highlights the inherent dignity and honour bestowed upon all human beings.

Surah Al-Hujurat (49:13): *"O mankind, indeed We have created you from a male and female and made you peoples and tribes that you may know one another. Indeed, the most noble of you in the sight of Allah is the most righteous of you. Indeed, Allah is Knowing and Acquainted."* This verse promotes the idea of unity, diversity, and the equality of all people, irrespective of their backgrounds.

Surah Al-Asr (103:1-3): *"By the time, indeed, mankind is in loss, except for those who have believed and done righteous deeds and advised each other to truth and advised each other to patience."* This verse is often appreciated for its concise message about the importance of faith, good deeds, and mutual encouragement in pursuit of truth and patience.

Surah Al-Baqarah (2:286): *"Allah does not burden a soul beyond that it can bear..."*This verse is often cited for its message of hope and resilience, emphasising that difficulties are manageable and that individuals are not burdened beyond their capacity.

Surah Al-Anbya (21:33): *"It is He Who created the night and the day, and the sun and the moon. Each of them is floating in its orbit."* This verse refers to a scientific fact concerning the system of the universe. Scientific discoveries have proved that we live in a vast universe that depends on revolution. The Earth revolves around the sun once a year, the moon revolves around the Earth once per lunar month, and the other planets of the solar system also revolve around the sun, each in its orbit.

Surah Al-Fussilat (41:53): *"We will show them Our signs in the horizons and within themselves until it becomes clear to them that it is the truth. But is it not sufficient concerning your Lord that He is, over all things, a Witness?"* This verse is a promise from God that He will show people His signs in different regions of the *Heaven*s and the Earth and within their own selves so that it may become clear to them and they may understand that the Quran is the truth sent down by Allah.

Surah Al-Muminun (23:12-14) *"And certainly we created man from an extract of clay. Then We placed him as a sperm-drop in a firm lodging (the womb). Then We made the sperm-drop into a clinging clot, then We turned the clot into a lump (of flesh), then We made from the lump bones, then We clothed the bones with flesh; thereafter We developed it into another creation. So Glorious is Allah, the Best of creators".* This verse mentions how God created humans as perfect beings from an insignificant and humble state of sperm. This is the primary state of the embryo, which develops after conception. Then it assumes the form of a lump of flesh, and thereafter, with internal and external organs, gradually takes human shape.

Non-Muslims who were inspired by the Quran and embraced Islam

According to the Independent Newspaper, quoting the Inter-faith think-tank Faith Matters, suggests that in the UK, as many as 5,000 people embrace Islam nationwide each year. The number of people embracing Islam is increasing. This is despite negative media portrayals of Islam and Muslims throughout the world.

Throughout history, there have been individuals from various religious backgrounds who, after studying the Quran or interacting with Muslims, were inspired by the teachings of Islam and eventually embraced the faith. Here are a few examples:

Malcolm X (El-Hajj Malik El-Shabazz): Malcolm X was a prominent American civil rights activist who initially belonged to the Nation of Islam, a group with beliefs divergent from mainstream Islam. However, during his pilgrimage to Mecca in 1964, Malcolm X experienced a transformation and embraced orthodox Islam. He found inspiration in the diverse and inclusive nature of the Muslims he encountered during the pilgrimage.

Yusuf Islam (formerly Cat Stevens): Cat Stevens was a famous British singer-songwriter in the 1960s and 1970s. After a near-death experience in 1976, he began exploring various spiritual paths. Eventually, he embraced Islam and changed his name to Yusuf Islam. Since then, he has been actively involved in philanthropy and promoting Islamic causes.

Dr. Jeffrey Lang: Dr. Jeffrey Lang is an American mathematician and professor who converted to Islam after a thorough study of the Quran. His journey to Islam is documented in his book "Struggling to Surrender: Some Impressions of an American Convert to Islam."

Muhammad Asad (Leopold Weiss): Born Leopold Weiss in Austria, Muhammad Asad was a journalist, traveller, and writer who embraced Islam in 1926. He is known for his translation of the Quran and his influential book, "The Road to Mecca," which details his journey to Islam.

Maryam Jameelah (Margaret Marcus): An American-Jewish woman who converted to Islam, Maryam Jameelah was a prolific writer and scholar. Her writings focused on Islam and the challenges faced by Muslims in the modern world.

Abdullah Quilliam (William Henry Quilliam): As a 19th-century British convert from Christianity to Islam, Abdullah Quilliam is noted for founding England's first Mosque and Islamic Centre in Liverpool.

The journey towards Islam is a personal and spiritual discovery. People may be drawn to Islam for various aspects of the faith and its way of life. It is essential to approach the Quran with an open mind and seek a deeper understanding of the verses within their cultural and historical contexts.

People are drawn to Islam for various reasons, and these individuals find inspiration in the teachings of the Quran, the practical example of the Prophet Muhammad[P], and the welcome that Muslim communities offer to new adherents.

We pray that our efforts are blessed with sincerity of intent, so that those searching for the truth may be rightly guided.

Dua – An important act of Worship

"And whosoever fears Allah and keeps his duty to Him, He will make a way for him to get out (from every difficulty), and He will provide for him from (resources) he never could imagine. And whosoever puts his trust in Allah, then He will suffice for him. Verily, Allah will accomplish His purpose. Indeed, Allah has set a measure for all things".

Quran 65:2-3

"Dua is worship. Your Lord said: call on Me and I will answer you."

Abu Dawud

Dua is truly one of the most important acts of worship that should not be neglected. There is nothing else, other than the *dua* to Allah[SWT], that can directly and regularly shield, protect and arm the believer against the trials and tribulations of this life.

What is Dua

Dua literally means invocation, an act of supplication. The term is derived from an Arabic word meaning to 'call out' or to 'summon', and is regarded as a profound act of worship. The Prophet[p] *said, "Dua is worship. Your Lord said, Call on Me and I will answer you."* **Abu Dawud.** Dua is a noble and spiritual form of worship that enables the believer to appreciate the majesty and eminence of the Creator.

Being a Muslim does not mean that Allah will not test us and put us on trial. We will face challenges and difficulties. There will be times when we will have a bad day at work and disputes with family and friends that will sadden us; we will have emotional breakdowns when we lose our loved ones, and there will be instances when we get saddened and worried due to some other calamity or challenges. However, the believer will turn to his Lord in his time of need and make dua to Allah[SWT].

Allah[SWT] says: *"And whosoever fears Allah and keeps his duty to Him, He will make a way for him to get out (from every difficulty), and He will provide for him from (resources) he never could imagine. And whosoever puts his trust in Allah, then He will suffice for him. Verily, Allah will accomplish His purpose. Indeed, Allah has set a measure for all things".* **Quran 65:2-3.** This is a compelling verse that motivates the believer to ask Allah for all their needs and to have complete trust in Him. Even though the support or help may come from other sources, be mindful that even that will have come through the Mercy of Allah.

In another verse, Allah[SWT] says: *"No disaster strikes except by permission of Allah. And whoever believes in Allah, He will guide his heart. And Allah is Knowing of all things."* **Quran 64:11.** Therefore, Dua is a plea from the very heart of a believer directed towards Allah — the Hearer of all things, the knower of all secrets. It is a confession that emanates from the heart of a believer that he is weak and helpless, and that he cannot achieve anything without Allah's help and aid. It is an implicit affirmation of every single Name and Attribute of Allah, for it affirms that Allah is the Creator, the Sustainer, the Controller of all Affairs, the Hearer, the Seer, the Merciful, the Great, the All-Powerful, the Ever-Capable, and other beautiful names and attributes.

What is the purpose of the Dua?

The believer turns to his Lord to obtain from Him contentment, peace, and serenity, and to seek beneficence that will never be found from other sources. When he turns to the Lord of all lords, and the King of all kings, the One Who is Self-Sufficient from all wants, and Who is Praised at all times, then the Lord answers. Allah[SWT] says. Verily, your Lord has *said, "Call on Me; I will answer your (Prayer): but those who are too arrogant to serve Me will surely find themselves in Hell – in humiliation!"* **Quran 40:60.** Therefore, if one wants to get closer to Allah[SWT], then dua is amongst the greatest acts of worship and one of the best ways to bring a worshipper closer to Allah[SWT].

The Prophet[P] mentioned that Allah descends to the lowest *Heaven* and says: *"Who is calling Me so I can answer him? Who is asking something of Me that I may give it to him."* **Bukhari and Muslim.** In this way, Allah[SWT] is commanding His servants to make *dua* to Him, seek help from Him, and emphasises that whoever is too arrogant to worship Him will enter the Fire of Hell. This means that Allah[SWT] expects believers to make dua in times of both good and bad. In good times, a believer is expected to thank Allah[SWT] for His blessings, praising Him and at times of affliction, beseeching Him for help and protection.

Dua is also one of the best ways for a person to increase *their imaan.* It is a powerful reminder of man's inherent incapability and Allah's unlimited powers. We all know that we have absolutely no control over our destiny, nor do we have the power to benefit ourselves or avert any evil befalling us. This proves that the one making dua sincerely believes that Allah hears his dua and will respond to it.

One of the primary purposes of doing dua is to repent from sins. The worshipper is humiliated in front of His Lord, in a state of fear, submitting himself to the will of Allah, earnestly desiring Allah's help, and asking for forgiveness. The believer will raise his hands, turning to Allah with the best of hopes for gaining rewards from Him, exemplifying the statement of Allah: *"Verily, they used to hasten to do good deeds, and they used to make dua to Us with hope and fear and used to humble themselves before Us."* **Quran 21:90.**

The Messenger of Allah[P] said, *"Ask Allah for His favour. Verily, Allah Almighty loves to be asked and among the best acts of worship is to wait in expectation of relief."* **Tirmidhi.** The Prophet[P] also *said, "The house in which remembrance of Allah is made and the house in which Allah is not remembered are like the living and the dead."* **Muslim.**

When we make *Dua* to Allah[SWT], Allah[SWT] is pleased with us. *Dua* is the most powerful tool that the believer has, yet it is one of the most misunderstood acts of worship. First, we must remember that Allah[SWT] always wants good for you, and will give you whatever He, the Most-Wise, sees as being in your best interest. Secondly, Allah[SWT] does not just answer your *dua* with what you asked for and what you want, but more importantly, with what you need and what is best for you.

If you make *dua* and ask for something which you think is good for you, but it may be bad for you, you do not know that, but Allah[SWT] does, and He will withhold it from you and give you that which is good for you. If you make *dua* and it is not forthcoming immediately, then be patient, do not allow *Shaytaan* to make you believe that Allah[SWT] will not answer your *Dua*. If you begin to have negative thoughts and expectations of Allah[SWT], Allah[SWT] will not give you what you expect.

The Prophet, *said, "There is no Muslim who calls upon his Lord with a dua in which there is no sin or severing of family ties, but Allah[SWT] will give him one of three things: Either He will answer his prayer quickly, or He will store (the reward for) it in the Hereafter, or He will divert an equivalent evil away from him."* They said, *"We will say more dua."* Hepbuh said, *"Allah's bounty is greater."* **Ahmad and Tirmidhi.**

So, three ways Allah[SWT] answers our *Dua*

1. **Yes.** You ask for something, and Allah[SWT] gives it to you immediately. That is awesome. Just be grateful to Allah[SWT] and thank Him.
2. **Yes, but not now.** You ask for something, and Allah[SWT] delays giving it to you because He wants to draw you closer to Him through your desperate need for Him. Only Allah[SWT] can help you. So, do not despair, be patient. Allah[SWT] will avert any evil equivalent to the level of what you ask for.
3. **I have better plans for you.** Allah[SWT] is withholding what you ask for. This is because what you ask for is not good for you, but you are unable to see it. Or He will give you something better on the Day of Judgement.

No doubt, there is wisdom behind Allah's decisions, which may take us years to actually understand and realise that Allah[SWT] saved us from a terrible fate. We often make *dua* for what we want in this world, such as having a better job, a new house, or a car. There is no harm in asking for what is permissible, but more importantly, what we should be asking for, first and foremost, is strong *imaan,* and to be on the right path, because this is your precious asset and a great blessing. If *Imaan* is devoid in the heart, then you have lost everything and nothing is good. No matter how rich and famous you become, it is not going to benefit you in any way.

Also, remember to make dua at times of ease. We should not only beseech Allah when we are in difficulty but also at times of plenty. The Prophet[P] said, *"Remember Allah during times of ease and He will remember you during times of hardship."* **Ahmad.**

Etiquettes of Dua

The manner and procedure of dua should only be taken from the Quran and *Sunnah.* Just as a person cannot use his mind or whims to decide how to pray or fast, so too must he restrain himself to the verses of the Quran and *Sunnah* when it comes to the manner and etiquette of dua.

1. Perform *Wudu*
It is NOT compulsory to perform *Wudu* before making dua. However, performing *Wudu* is a way of purifying yourself and getting into the correct mindset for speaking to Allah[SWT]. Abu Musa Al-Ashari[RA] narrated that the Prophet[P] after the battle of Hunain, called for water, performed *Wudu*, then raised his hands and *said, "O Allah! Forgive Ubaid Abi Amir!"* **Bukhari.**

2. Face the *Qibla*
It is not compulsory to face the *Qibla* while making dua. However, the Prophet[P] would sometimes do so. Abdullah bin Zaid[RA] reported: *"Allah's Messenger[P] went out to this Musalla i.e., the praying place, to offer the prayer of Istisqa (a prayer for rain). He invoked Allah for rain and then faced the Qibla and turned his cloak inside out..."* **Bukhari.**

3. Call upon Allah in a low voice
Allah[SWT] is all-knowing and all-hearing. Allah[SWT] is even aware of our thought processes and what we are thinking before we speak. So, no need to raise your voice or shout, Allah[SWT] can hear you. Abu Musa Al-Ashari[RA] *said, "We were in the company of the Prophet[P] on a journey, and whenever we ascended a high place, we used to say Takbir in a loud voice. The Prophet[P] said, "O people! Be kind to yourselves, for you are not calling upon a deaf or an absent one, but you are supplicating to the All-Hearing, the All-Seeing".* **Bukhari.** Also, Allah[SWT] says: *"Do not recite your prayers too loudly or too silently, but seek a way between."* **Quran 17:110.**

This means that when we are making a private dua, we should remember that Allah[SWT] is as close as our jugular vein through His power and knowledge. As Allah[SWT] says: "*And indeed We have created man, and We know whatever thoughts his inner self develops, and We are closer to him than (his) jugular vein.*" **Quran 50-16.**

There is no need to be loud. Allah[SWT] also says: "*And remember your Lord by your tongue and within yourself, humbly and with fear, without loudness in words, in the morning and in the afternoon, and be not of those who are neglectful.*" **Quran 7: 205**. Whether we are alone in our bedroom, in public, or in the *Masjid*, we need to have a low voice and ensure we do not disturb others.

4. Begin your dua with praising Allah[SWT] and sending salutations to the Prophet[P]

Do not rush into your dua without first praising Allah[SWT] and then sending supplications upon our beloved Prophet[P]. The Prophet[P] *said, "'When any one of you have performed Salah and wants to supplicate, let him begin with praising His Lord and glorifying Him, then send prayers upon the Prophet[P]. Then he may supplicate for whatever he wishes.*" **Tirmidhi.**

You can invoke Allah through His beautiful names. Allah[SWT] says: *"Allah has the Most Beautiful Names. So, call upon Him by them."* **Quran 7:180.** There are many names that you can call upon Allah, but the most commonly used are: *Ar-Rahman: The Most Gracious; Ar-Razzaq: The Provider; Ar-Rahim – The Most Merciful; Al-Ghafur – The Great Forgiver.*

Sending blessings upon the Prophet[P] can be done by reciting: *"Allahumma Baarik Ala Muhammadiw Wa Ala Aali Muhammadin Kamaa Baarakta Ala Ibrahima Wa Ala Aali Ibrahima Inna'ka Hamidum Majid."* The translation of this is: O Allah, let Your Blessings come upon Muhammad[P] and the family of Muhammad[P] as you have blessed Ibrahim and his family.

5. Raise your hands when making dua

Raising our hands to make dua is a *Sunnah* and we are strongly encouraged to do so from the hadith wherein the Prophet[P] *said, "Indeed your Lord - Blessed and Almighty is He - is Shy and Most Generous. He is shy when His servant raises his hands to Him (in dua) to turn them away empty."* **Abu Dawud.** This implies that a person who raises his hand in dua to Allah[SWT] will not be turned away empty.

The Prophet[P] would raise his blessed hands in supplication. As for the specific way the hands should be raised during supplication, this is a matter of personal preference and flexibility. Each individual has a natural inclination towards how they stretch their hands out in need of their Creator, and so slight variations from individual to individual are not uncommon. One can supplicate with the hands separated or joined together;

with them at the level of the chest or the shoulders or even the face, with the arms outstretched or otherwise; and all of these modes are fine. The important thing is to supplicate sincerely with one's heart and realise whom one is asking.

6. The content of the Dua

It is not the length of your dua that matters, but rather the meaning and intentions behind it that are of importance. Aisha[RA] reported that *the Messenger of Allah (pbuh) preferred duas that were few in words but comprehensive in meaning.* **Abu Dawud.** So be concise and clear. The best duas are the duas of the Prophet[P] but it is permissible to say other words according to the specific needs of a person.

7. Have faith that your dua will be accepted and Allah will respond one way or another

Allah[SWT] says: *"And when My slaves ask you (O Muhammad) concerning Me, then (answer them), I am indeed near (to them by My Knowledge). I respond to the invocations of the supplicant when he calls on Me (without any mediator or intercessor). So let them obey Me and believe in Me, so that they may be led aright."* **Quran 2:186.** The Prophet[P] said, *"When you ask, ask of Allah; and when you seek help, seek help from Allah."* **Tirmidhi.** Therefore, have total faith in Allah and consistently ask Allah directly, seeking no intermediary between us and Him.

8. Ask Frequently

Ask frequently and do not lose hope. There is nothing wrong with repeating your requests. Also, remember, Allah's Kingdom is vast, so do not restrict yourself when asking Him for something. Be firm in your asking. For example, do not say: *"Allah forgive me if you wish"*; instead, beg Allah for exactly what you want. The Messenger of Allah[P] said, *"When one of you makes a supplication, he should not say, 'If you wish.' He should be firm in asking and he should have great hope. Allah does not think that anything that He gives is too great."* **Bukhari.**

9. Mention good deeds you have done for the sake of Allah[SWT]

Abdullah bin Umar[RA] narrated: The Prophet[P] said, *"While three men were walking, it started raining and they took shelter in a cave in a mountain. A big rock rolled down from the mountain and closed the mouth of the cave. They said to each other, 'Think of good deeds which you did for Allah's sake only and invoke Allah by giving reference to those deeds so that He may remove this rock from you.'"* **Bukhari.** This is exactly what happened. Each person mentioned their good deeds, and Allah[SWT], on each occasion, slightly moved the rock until all three invoked Allah with their good deeds. Allah[SWT] then granted them relief through the movement of the rock, allowing them to escape.

10. Seek the best times and places

Among the best times is the time just before Fajr, the last third of the night, the last hour of *Jummah* - Friday, when rain is falling, and between the Adhan and Iqamah. Among the best places are mosques in general, and al-*Masjid* al-Haraam in Makkah in particular. Among the situations in which dua is more likely to be answered are when one is mistreated or oppressed, when one is travelling, when one is fasting, when one is in desperate need, and when a Muslim makes dua for his brother in his absence.

Some Duas recommended by the Prophet[P]

There are numerous duas that the Prophet[P] used to recite in his daily life. Below are the selected few:

1. **The best dua for glorifying Allah** - "Allah is free from imperfection and I begin with His praise, as many times as the number of His creatures, in accordance with His Good Pleasure, equal to the weight of His Throne and equal to the ink that may be used in recording the words (for His Praise)." **Muslim.** Transliteration Subhana Allah wa bihamdihi adada khalqihi wa rida nafsihi wa zinata arshihi wa midada kalimatihi. سُبْحَانَ اللهِ وَبِحَمْدِهِ: عَدَدَ خَلْقِهِ، وَرِضَا نَفْسِهِ، وَزِنَةَ عَرْشِهِ، وَمِدَادَ كَلِمَاتِهِ

2. **Best of Dua** - "O our Lord, grant us the best in this life and the best in the next life, and protects us from the punishment of the Fire." **Bukhari and Muslim.** Rabana atina fi dunya hasanatan wa fil akhirati hasanatan wa qina adhaba an-nar. رَبَّنَآ ءَاتِنَا فِى ٱلدُّنْيَا حَسَنَةً وَفِى ٱلْـٔاخِرَةِ حَسَنَةً وَقِنَا عَذَابَ ٱلنَّارِ

3. **Best dua for forgiveness** - "O Allah! You are my Lord. None has the right to be worshiped except You. You created me and I am your servant and I abide by your covenant and promise as best I can. I seek refuge in you from the evil, which I have committed. I acknowledge your favour upon me and I knowledge my sins, so forgive me, for verily none can forgive sin except you." **Bukhari.**

Allahumma anta rabbi la ilaha illa anta khalaqtani wa an abduk wa ana ala ahdika wa wa'dika ma istata'tu, a'udhu bika min sharri ma sana'tu, abou' laka bi ni'matika alaya, wa abou'u bi dhanbi, fa-ghfir li, fa innahu la yaghfiru dhunuba illa anta.

اللَّهُمَّ أَنْتَ رَبِّي لَا إِلَهَ إِلاَّ أَنْتَ خَلَقْتَنِي وَأَنَا عَبْدُكَ وَأَنَا عَلَى عَهْدِكَ وَوَعْدِكَ مَا اسْتَطَعْتُ أَعُوذُ بِكَ مِنْ شَرِّ مَا صَنَعْتُ أَبُوءُ لَكَ بِنِعْمَتِكَ عَلَيَّ وَأَبُوءُ لَكَ بِذَنْبِي فَاغْفِرْ لِي فَإِنَّهُ لَا يَغْفِرُ الذُّنُوبَ إِلاَّ أَنْتَ

4. **Best Dua for Protection** - The Prophet *said,* "He who recites three times every morning and evening: 'In the Name of Allah with Whose Name there is protection against every kind of harm in the earth or in the *Heaven*, and He is the All-Hearing and All- Knowing,' nothing will harm him." **Abu Dawud and Tirmidhi.** Transliteration Bismi Allah alladhi la yadorru ma'a ismihi shay' fil ardi wala fi sama' wa huwa sami'u al alim.

بِسْمِ اللَّهِ الَّذِي لاَ يَضُرُّ مَعَ اسْمِهِ شَىْءٌ فِي الأَرْضِ وَلاَ فِي السَّمَاءِ وَهُوَ السَّمِيعُ الْعَلِيمُ

5. **Best Dua for Depression** - "The supplication of Prophet Yunus[P] when he supplicated, while in the belly of the whale, was: "There is none worthy of worship except You, Glory to You, Indeed, I have been of the transgressors. So indeed, no Muslim man supplicates with it for anything, ever, except Allah responds to him." **Tirmidhi.** Transliteration: La ilaha illa anta subhanaka inni kuntu mina adhalimeen. لاَ إِلَهَ إِلاَّ أَنتَ سُبْحَانَكَ إِنِّى كُنتُ مِنَ الظَّالِمِينَ

6. **Best Dua For Inner Peace** - Abu Musa[RA] reported: The Messenger of Allah said to me: "Shall I not guide you to a treasure from the treasures of *Jannah*?" I *said,* "Yes, O Messenger of Allah!" Thereupon, he[P] *said,* (Recite) 'La hawla wa la quwwata illa billah' "There is no change of a condition nor power except by Allah". **Bukhari and Muslim.** La hawla wa la quwwata illa bi Allah al 'aliyyi al adhim. لاَ حَوْلَ وَلاَ قُوَّةَ إِلاَّ بِاللَّهِ الْعَلِيِّ الْعَظِيمِ

What you need to say in your Dua

Ask Allah for exactly what you want. Consider Allah[SWT] as your closest friend. Talk to Allah[SWT] as if you are having a conversation with Him. Describe to Him what is on your mind. Let Him know how you feel and be very precise in your dua. Ask Allah to bless you in this world and the Hereafter. To ask Allah only for matters of this world is a sign of weakness in one's *Imaan*, as the blessings of the Hereafter are the true blessings. Allah[SWT] says in the Quran: "*......And there are those amongst mankind who say, 'O Allah! Give us in this life and they will have no share of the Hereafter. And there are those who say, 'O Allah! Give us good in this life, and good in the Hereafter, and save us from the Fire of Hell! These shall have a share of what they earned, and Allah is swift in Reckoning".* **Quran 2:200-202.**

When making dua for all the Muslim Ummah who are suffering across the Globe, be specific. Mention that Allah[SWT] helps the people of Syria, Palestine, Yemen, the Rohingya Muslims, the Uyghur Muslims in China, and so on.

When is our Dua not answered?

It is worrying when we turn to Allah^{SWT} and ask for His help and blessings, only to find that our supplication remains unanswered. This is the most saddening moment for a Muslim. Allah^{SWT} has assured us that He responds to our supplications, so why do our duas remain unanswered? There are righteous Muslims who make dua, yet their supplication remains unaccepted for months or even years. Therefore, we need to know why our duas are not accepted. There are several reasons which help us understand this phenomenon.

Showing Impatience

We should be patient and have trust in Allah. The Prophet^P *said, "The dua of anyone of you may be answered (by Allah) as long as he does not show impatience by saying, 'I prayed to Allah but my prayers have not been answered."* **Bukhari.** Therefore, we should not give up making dua.

Earning unlawful income

The Messenger of Allah^P said, *"O people! Allah is Pure and, therefore, accepts only that which is pure. Allah has commanded the believers as He has commanded His Messengers by saying: 'O Messengers! Eat of the good things, and do good deeds.'* **Quran 23:51.** And Allah^{SWT} also *said, 'O you who believe! Eat of the lawful things that We have provided you...'"* **Quran 2:172.** Then the Prophet (pbuh) *mentioned the person who travels for an extended period of time, with his hair dishevelled and covered in dust. He lifts his hand towards the sky and thus makes the supplication: 'My Rubb! My Rubb!' But his food is unlawful, his drink is unlawful, his clothes are unlawful, and his nourishment is unlawful; how can his supplication be accepted?"* **Muslim.** We should always earn income from halal sources; otherwise, our dua will be rejected.

When doubting Allah's response

When we make Dua, we should put our trust in Allah and be sure of Allah's response. Never think of the bad deeds we have committed because Allah is the Oft-Forgiving, Most Merciful. The Prophet^P said, *"Make dua while being certain of the response."* **Tirmidhi.** Do not doubt Allah's response because He will not answer our call when we doubt His response.

Lacking sincerity in our dua and being heedless

When making dua, we should stay focused and be conscious of whom we are calling upon. The Prophet ^{P} said, *"You should know that Allah does not answer the dua that comes from a heedless heart."* **Tirmidhi.** Allah^{SWT} says, *"Call then upon Allah with sincere devotion to Him."* **Quran 40:14.**

Not sending salutations to the Prophet[P]

A dua is not accepted until the blessings and salutations are sent to the Prophet[P] along with it. Umar Ibn Al-Khattaab[RA] said, *"Dua is suspended between Heaven and earth and none of it is taken up until you send blessings upon your Prophet[P]."* **Tirmidhi.**

Making dua conditional

Saying such things as: "O Allah, forgive me if You will or O Allah, have mercy upon me if You will." The person who makes dua has to be resolute in his supplication, striving hard and earnestly repeating his dua. The Prophet[P] *said, "Let not any one of you say, O Allah, forgive me if You will, O Allah, have mercy on me if You will. Let him be resolute in the matter, whilst knowing that no one can compel Allah to do anything."* **Bukhari and Muslim.** Therefore, make dua unconditionally.

Asking Allah for prohibited things

Dua has certain limits, and if one goes beyond these limits, one is transgressing in making Dua. It goes without saying that one should not ask Allah[SWT] things that are prohibited either in this life or in the Hereafter. For example, it is not permissible to supplicate to harm someone, or for something miraculous to happen or for something logically impossible to take place or something against the *Shariah.* Allah[SWT] says in the Quran: *"Call upon your Lord in humility and privately; indeed, He does not like transgressors."* **Quran 7:55.**

Committing Sins

Sin is one of the main reasons why duas are not answered. Therefore, the person who is making dua should hasten to repent and seek forgiveness before he makes dua. Allah tells us that Nooh[P] *said, I said (to them): 'Ask forgiveness from your Lord, verily, He is Oft-Forgiving; He will send rain to you in abundance, And give you increase in wealth and children, and bestow on you gardens and bestow on you rivers."* Quran **71:10-12.** Therefore, when we sin, we should always repent and turn back to Allah; Allah[SWT] is Oft-Forgiving, Most Merciful.

It is not essential that we adhere to all of these points and be free of all that could prevent our duas from being answered. We just need to try hard and ensure we do not do things that prevent our duas from being answered. Allah[SWT] is merciful and forgives our minor mistakes.

Conclusion

If we do not get what we ask for from Allah[SWT], then remember our dua might avert a calamity, an illness, or some other difficulty that was destined for us. We never truly know what is best for us, but Allah[SWT] certainly does, and He always delivers.

May Allah[SWT] guide us to the straight path and enable us to make dua in accordance with His teachings and the examples set by our beloved Prophet ([P]). May Allah[SWT] also grant us the ability to strive to please our Lord at all times and allow us to have full *Yaqeen* in Allah answering our dua and practice patience in His response.

The Virtues of the Istikhara Prayer?

".... Once you make a decision, put your trust in Allah. Surely Allah loves those who trust in Him."

Quran 3:159

"The Messenger of Allah pbuh used to teach his companions to make Istikharah in all things, just as he used to teach them surahs from the Qur'an.

Bukhari

At certain junctures in life, we often find ourselves faced with pivotal decisions that will have a profound impact on our lives or future. These decisions can include choosing a career, getting married, buying a car or a house, relocating, or moving to a foreign land, among others.

Despite considering all the positives and negatives of the choices we have to make and consulting with family, friends, or other experienced, skilled, and qualified people, the task of reaching a sound decision still leaves us doubtful and nervous. This is expected. However, for us believers, *Alhamdulillah*, we can perform Istikhara, a dua that helps us make the right choice and not leave us worried during this crucial time of decision-making.

The word Istikhara originates from the Arabic root word *Khair,* which is an umbrella term connoting all that is good. The word stems from a verb pattern that means 'to seek that which is good' The term Istikhara means 'to look for Allah's Guidance, Wisdom, Support, Supervision, Consultation, Goodness, and Blessings.' Whenever a believer has to make a decision, they should seek Allah's guidance and wisdom. Allah^{SWT} alone knows what is best for us, and there may be good in what we perceive as bad, and bad in what we perceive as good.

Istikharah is a form of prayer that asks Allah to guide us in making a decision, essentially choosing the best of two or more options when a person needs to select just one. The Istikhara Prayer and Dua are done when a decision is to be made in matters which are neither obligatory nor prohibited. This means that a person does not need to seek counsel from Allah to decide whether to go for *Hajj* or not. This is because if a person is financially and physically able to do it, then *Hajj* is obligatory, and we do not have a choice. However, if they need to choose which *Hajj* Agency is best suited for taking them for *Hajj*, then this is quite a valid reason for Istikhara.

Our beloved Prophet[P] used to teach his companions to seek counsel from Allah for every matter. For example, Istikharah was described in a Hadith narrated by Jabir ibn Abdullah Al-Salami, who *said, "The Messenger of Allah[P] used to teach his companions to make Istikharah in all things, just as he used to teach them surahs from the Qur'an.* **Bukhari.** When the Prophet [P] said to make Istikharah in all things, this meant in both major matters and minor ones. This is because even an insignificant matter may have significant consequences.

Therefore, a person should not regard anything as too insignificant, thinking it is small and not pay attention to it, and thus not pray istikhaarah, which in effect rejects praying for guidance concerning it. A person may regard something as insignificant, but doing it or not doing it may lead to great harm. Concerning even an insignificant matter to prove the point, the Prophet[P] *said, "Let one of you ask his Lord even about his shoelace."* This makes it clear that it is a mistake to limit istikhaarah to rare cases or a few issues. Rather, the believers should turn to Allah and seek His guidance in all their affairs.

We are certainly blessed with this powerful tool that Allah has given us to seek His guidance in all matters, and hence we should not hesitate to pray Istikhara before making any choice in our lives, whether big or small.

Some benefits of Istikhara

- **Guidance from Allah:** Istikhara is a means of seeking Allah's guidance in making a decision, as we believe that Allah knows what is best for us.
- **Peace of Mind:** The process of Istikhara brings a sense of tranquillity and peace of mind, knowing that the decision is in Allah's hands.
- **Inner Peace and Contentment:** The process of Istikhara allows individuals to surrender any worries and anxieties to Allah, knowing that He is in control. This surrender can bring a sense of inner peace and contentment, as we feel supported and guided by a higher power.
- **Clarity in Decision Making:** When faced with difficult choices, Istikhara can provide clarity and insight. By praying for guidance, we may receive signs and also inner feelings that help us understand which path to take. This can help us make informed decisions based on divine wisdom.
- **Strengthening Faith:** By seeking guidance through Istikhara, we deepen our faith and trust in Allah's plan. This fosters a stronger connection to spirituality and enhances our relationship with the Divine.
- **Overcoming Doubt:** When faced with multiple options or conflicting feelings, Istikhara can help overcome doubt and confusion. It aids in aligning our intentions with Allah's Will and opens up the heart and mind to a clearer understanding.
- **Protection us from Regret:** Making major life decisions without seeking divine guidance can sometimes lead to regret and feelings of uncertainty. Istikhara

provides a safeguard against potential regrets by allowing individuals to make choices with Allah's blessings and support.

- **Reliance on Allah:** By performing Istikhara, we express our dependence on Allah and acknowledge that only He has the ultimate knowledge and wisdom to guide us.
- **Istikhar is an act of worship:** Istikhara is an act of worship and an expression of one's reliance on Allah's wisdom and knowledge. By seeking His guidance, we are encouraged to place our trust in Allah's plan and decisions, recognising that He knows what is best for us.

The Prophet[P] *said, 'If any one of you is concerned about a decision he has to make, then let him pray two rakahs of non-obligatory prayer, then say: "O Allah, I ask for Your decision by Your knowledge and Your decree by Your ability, and I ask of You from Your great favour. For You are able and I am not able, and You know and I do not know, and You are the Knower of things concealed. O Allah, if You have known that this matter (naming it here) is good for me in my religion, my livelihood and the outcome of my affair, then decree it for me, make it easy for me and then bless it for me. And if You have known that this matter is bad for me in my religion, my livelihood and the outcome of my affair, then turn it away from me and turn me away from it, and decree for me what is good wherever it may be. And then make me content with it."* **Bukhari and Tirmidhi.**

How to perform Istikhara Prayer and Dua

- Make Intention for Istikhāra
- Perform ablution
- Pray two rakat of non-obligatory prayer
- Straight after the two rakat prayer recite the dua of Istikhara and mention your need

Istikhara dua with English translation and transliteration.

اللّٰهُمَّ إِنِّي أَسْتَخِيرُكَ بِعِلْمِكَ وَأَسْتَقْدِرُكَ بِقُدْرَتِكَ، وَأَسْأَلُكَ مِنْ فَضْلِكَ الْعَظِيمِ، فَإِنَّكَ تَقْدِرُ وَلَا أَقْدِرُ وَتَعْلَمُ وَلَا أَعْلَمُ وَأَنْتَ عَلَّامُ الْغُيُوبِ، اللّٰهُمَّ إِنْ كُنْتَ تَعْلَمُ أَنَّ هَذَا الْأَمْرَ خَيْرٌ لِي فِي دِينِي وَمَعَاشِي وَعَاقِبَةِ أَمْرِي فَاقْدُرْهُ لِي وَيَسِّرْهُ لِي ثُمَّ بَارِكْ لِي فِيهِ، وَإِنْ كُنْتَ تَعْلَمُ أَنَّ هَذَا الْأَمْرَ شَرٌّ لِي فِي دِينِي وَمَعَاشِي وَعَاقِبَةِ أَمْرِي فَاصْرِفْهُ عَنِّي وَاصْرِفْنِي عَنْهُ، وَاقْدُرْ لِي الْخَيْرَ حَيْثُ كَانَ ثُمَّ أَرْضِنِي بِهِ

Transliteration

Allahumma inni astakhiruka bi'ilmika, Wa astaqdiruka bi-qudratika, Wa asaluka min fadlika al-'azim Fainnaka taqdiru Wala aqdiru, Wa ta'lamu Wala a'lamu, Wa anta 'allamu l-ghuyub. Allahumma, in kunta ta'lam anna hadha-l-amra (mention the matter here for which you are seeking Allah's Guidance) Khairun li fi dini wa ma'ashi wa'aqibati amri Faqdirhu li wa yas-sirhu li thumma barik li Fihi, Wa in kunta ta'lamu anna hadhalamra shar-run li fi dini wa ma'ashi wa'aqibati amri Fasrifhu anni was-rifni anhu. Waqdir li al-khaira haithu kana Thumma ardini bihi.'

Translation of Istikhara Prayer in English

"O Allah, I consult You as You are All-Knowing and I appeal to You to give me power as You are Omnipotent, I ask You for Your great favour, for You have power and I do not, and You know all of the hidden matters. O, Allah!

If you know that this matter (then mention the matter for which you are seeking Allah's Guidance) is suitable for me in my religion, my livelihood, and for my life in the Hereafter, then make it (easy) for me. And if you know that this matter is not good for me in my religion, my livelihood, and my life in the Hereafter, then keep it away from me and take me away from it and choose what is good for me wherever it is and please me with it."

Some important rules of Istikhara

- It is essential to recite this prayer with sincerity, acknowledging in our hearts that only Allah can provide us with the guidance we seek, and to resolve to follow the guidance He gives us, even if it conflicts with our desires.

- We should also say the dua with firm conviction, not begging or pleading, but asking Allah clearly for guidance.

- We should not be impatient after our dua. We do not put Allah on a timetable. And we should not expect some sort of miracle, or a dream full of signs and symbols. These things are not necessary. We simply say our prayers and trust that Allah has heard us and will answer us in the best way.

The best time to pray Istikhara

Istikhara prayer can be performed at any permissible time of the day or night, which is convenient. However, our beloved Prophet[P] stressed to his companions that the third part of the night is the ideal time for supplication. Narrated Abu Huraira, Allah's Messenger[P] said, *"Our Lord, the Blessed, the Superior, comes every night down on the nearest Heaven to us when the last third of the night remains, saying: 'Is there anyone to invoke Me, so that I may respond to invocation? Is there anyone to ask Me, so that I may grant him his request? Is there anyone seeking My forgiveness, so that I may forgive him?"* **Bukhari.**

On another occasion, Abu Umamah[RA] reported that the Messenger of Allah[P] was asked: *"At what time does the supplication find the greatest response?"* He[P] replied, *"A supplication made during the middle of the last part of the night and after the conclusion of the obligatory prayers."* **Tirmidhi.**

It is not compulsory to sleep immediately after performing Istikhara.

The result of Istikharah is considered to be a sign of being inclined to do something and continuing to feel positive about it.

In addition, if the decision one is about to make is beneficial to them (in both worlds), the paths to it will open up; if it is not, then the paths will become obstructed, and Allah will direct them elsewhere. The beauty of Istikharah is that the person who seeks Allah's guidance will be content with Allah's decision, even if it diverts him from what he thought was good, as he will know that this is the result of his Istikharah. This is because Allah, the Creator, knows what is best and will guide His servants to what is best for them within His vast knowledge and infinite wisdom.

However, we must understand that Istikharah does not guarantee the absence of tests and trials in life.

Since Istikharah is a dua, Allah's response to it may come in any of the three ways as stated in the Hadith: *"There is no Muslim who offers a dua in which there is no sin or severing of family ties but Allah will give him one of three things in return: either He will answer his du'aa soon, or he will store it up for him in the Hereafter, or He will divert an equivalent evil away from him because of it."* **Ahmad.**

The Prophet[P] said, *"It is from the happiness of the son of Adam to practice Istikharah and be pleased with what Allah had ordained for him. And it is from the misery of the son of Adam to drop the Istikharah of Allah and be displeased at Allah's decrees."* **Tirmidhi and Ahmad.**

Unfortunately, many people ignore this beautiful *Sunnah* and resort to baseless or forbidden ways to make important decisions. Then, there are those who do Istikhara but have added bizarre myths and unreasonable expectations to it. They ask a stranger or a religious personality to do it for them and expect the results of Istikharah to be revealed to them in dreams, visions, or some special sign. All of this is nothing but acts of ignorance.

Istikharah is a dua that one needs to make for himself, at any time of the day and then execute the matter for which he prayed. If it is good, then Allah will make it easy for him and bless him in that, and if it is not good for him, then Allah will turn it away from him and will make easy for him that in which there is good by His permission.

For without a doubt, the person who makes Istikharah, seeking guidance from his Creator and advice from His creation, never regrets, as Allah says addressing the Prophet: *"Once you make a decision, put your trust in Allah. Surely Allah loves those who trust in Him."* Quran 3:159.

What to do after the Istikhara Prayer and Dua

After performing Istikhara, consult your heart by paying attention to your feelings and inclinations. While there may not be any immediate signs, Allah may guide you through your feelings and thoughts.

Repeat if Necessary. If you do not feel a clear answer after the first Istikhara, you can repeat the process and continue seeking Allah's guidance.

It is important to note that Istikhara is not a magic solution, and the answer may not always be immediate or apparent. It requires patience, trust in Allah, and the understanding that His wisdom surpasses human understanding. Additionally, seeking advice from knowledgeable individuals or scholars is encouraged when making important decisions.

Saad[RA] narrated that the Messenger of Allah[P] *said, "From (the signs of) the son of Adam's prosperity, is his satisfaction with what Allah decreed for him, and from the son of Adam's misery is his avoiding to seek guidance from Allah, and from the son of Adam's misery is his anger with what Allah decreed for him."* **Tirmidhi.**

Remember, Istikhara is not a guarantee of a specific outcome, but rather a means to seek Allah's guidance and acceptance of His will. We are encouraged to perform Istikhara with sincerity, patience, and faith, and to be open to signs or feelings that may guide us in our decisions.

May Allah[SWT] grant us the correct understanding of this important prayer and dua so that we are encouraged to perform it in our lives when crucial decisions need to be made.

Itiqaf – The retreat in a *Masjid* in the last 10 days of *Ramadan*

Itikaf is an Islamic practice that involves staying in a mosque for a specified number of days, devoting oneself to ibadah during this period, and abstaining from worldly affairs.

What is the meaning of *Itikaf*?

The literal meaning of the word suggests sticking to or adhering to something, or being regular in a particular activity. It is particularly practised during the last 10 days of

Ramadan when a person will seclude themselves in a part of the mosque and spend all their time worshipping Allah^{SWT}. *Itikaf* is a praiseworthy voluntary act.

Linguistically, it means devotion to a thing and sticking to it. In *Shariah*, it means that the Muslim clings to the mosque for dhikr, prayer, and recitation of the Quran while fasting.

The Purpose of *Itikaf*

The purpose of *Itikaf* is for an individual to devote their time to worshipping Allah^{SWT}. The Prophet^P used to observe *Itikaf* in a small tent inside the mosque, so that this place would be reserved only for the person observing *Itikaf* and he would not be distracted by other people in the Mosque, as he could not see them and they could not see him.   The intention of *Itikaf* is also to seek out *Laylat ul Qadr* and develop and strengthen one's bond with Allah^{SWT}.

Itikaf starts after sunset on the 20th day of *Ramadan* and ends when the moon for Eid is sighted. This means one must make all arrangements for donating to charities beforehand and before starting the *Itikaf*. This includes Zakat Ul Fitr, which must be paid before the Eid prayer.

Three types of *Itikaf*:

Sunnah Itikaf

This was the general practice of the Prophet^P, meaning to seclude oneself inside the *Masjid* for the last ten days of *Ramadan*.

Wajib *Itikaf*

This *Itikaf* becomes compulsory when a person makes a vow to Allah^{SWT} that if Allah fulfils a particular wish of theirs, then they will undertake to perform so many days of *Itikaf*. In this case, the moment their wish is fulfilled, it becomes compulsory for them to perform *Itikaf*. It becomes a *wajib* on them from that moment onward until performing *Itikaf*.

Nafil *Itikaf*

There is no specific time or number of days for Nafil *Itikaf*. A person may form the Niyyah for any number of days at any time of the year. Some would observe it in the last 10 days of *Ramadan* for a few days, joining those in *Sunnah Itikaf*.

Conditions of *Itikaf*

- *Itikaf* in the last 10 days of *Ramadan* can only be done by those who are fasting. It is not valid for someone who is not fasting, even if it is due to a valid excuse.

- *Itikaf* can only be done in a Mosque. Allah[SWT] says: *"... While you are doing Itikaf in mosques."* It is not valid in houses, shops, and other such places.
- *Itikaf* must be performed in the Jummah Mosque, where the Jummah prayer takes place, unless you are fulfilling a vow to observe a certain number of days in *Itikaf*, which does not include the day of Jummah.
- If someone in *Itikaf* deliberately breaks their fast, which is a sin in itself, they have to begin their *Itikaf* all over again. There is a difference between what is deliberate and what is forgetful. Illness and menstruation are in the same category as forgetfulness.
- If a person eats or drinks out of forgetfulness, or becomes ill, or a woman menstruates, they do not have to begin again, since it is not invalidated, and the person makes it up afterwards.
- If a person falls ill during *Itikaf*, they can return home, but they should complete their *Itikaf* once they are well again.
- It is not permitted to leave the mosque, except for essential necessities such as using the toilet or bathroom.
- It is not permitted to engage in conversation with anyone, but if he speaks briefly to some of the people, or someone comes to visit him and he talks to them, there is nothing wrong with that. His conversation should be in a low voice, so as not to distract any of those who are engaged in worship. His talk should be brief and should not distract him from the purpose of *Itikaf*.
- *Itikaf* begins before sunset on the 20th day of *Ramadan*, as the night that follows marks the start of the last ten nights.
- While in *Itikaf*, one is not permitted to visit the sick, follow funeral processions, or conduct any business transactions. When our beloved Prophet[P] was in *Itikaf*, he did not visit the sick or attend funerals. However, if one or both parents fall ill, it is an obligation in *Shariah* to go out and show familial devotion; otherwise, their *Itikaf* is invalidated.
- *Itikaf* finishes after Magrib on the last day.
- During *Itikaf*, one should devote one's time to worshipping Allah and should not be distracted by other people in the mosque. However, if you speak briefly to someone or someone who comes to visit you, there is nothing wrong with that.
- Simply being in the *Masjid* and among others who are also focused on worshipping Allah[SWT] results in positive energy, enabling one to exert even more effort during this time.

Virtues and Benefits of *Itikaf*

"Truly Allah loves those who turn [to Him] in repentance..."

Quran 2:222

"Whosoever for Allah's sake did even one day of Itikaf, Allah would keep him away from Jahannam by trenches."

Tabarani

Seeking Laylat ul Qadr

The evidence from the Prophet in seeking Laylat Ul Qadar in the last 10 days of *Ramadan* is in this Hadith.

Abu Saeed Al-Khudri[RA] said, *"The Messenger of Allah observed Itikaf in the first ten days of Ramadan; he then observed Itikaf in the middle of the ten days, staying inside a Turkish tent with a mat hanging at its door. He took hold of that mat and placed it in the nook of the tent. He then put his head out and talked with people, and they came near him, and he said, "I observed Itikaf in the first ten days in order to seek that night - i.e., Laylatul Qadr. I then observed Itikaf in the middle of ten days. Then (an angel) was sent to me and I was told that this night is among the last ten. Whoever amongst you desires to observe Itikaf should do so, and the people observed it along with him."* **Muslim.**

Another hadith Narrated Abu Said Al-Khudri: *"Allah's Apostle used to practice Itikaf in the middle ten days of Ramadan and once he stayed in Itikaf till the night of the twenty-first, and it was the night in the morning of which he used to come out of his Itikaf."* The Prophet *said, "Whoever was in Itikaf with me should stay in Itikaf for the last ten days, for I was informed (of the date) of the Night (of Qadr), but I have been caused to forget it. (In the dream) I saw myself prostrating in mud and water in the morning of that night. So, look for it in the last ten nights and the odd ones of them."* It rained that night, and the roof of the mosque dripped as it was made of leaf stalks of date palms. I saw with my own eyes the mark of mud and water on the forehead of the Prophet (i.e., in the morning of the twenty-first).

Performing *Itikaf* is the perfect opportunity to immerse oneself in worship and seek *Laylat al-Qadr*. *Itikaf* helps us separate ourselves from worldly desires and thoughts, allowing us to worship peacefully and unconditionally. This, in turn, will enable us to reap the fruits of the worship and therefore, make the most of the potential *Laylat ul Qadr* days.

2. The Reward of Sitting in *Itikaf*

Ibn Abbas[RA] reported that the Prophet[P] said about those who engage themselves in *Itikaf*: *"that he is safe from sin and he also gets that reward which everyone (outside Itikaf) gets for pious deeds."* **Ibn Majah.** This means that Allah[SWT] rewards the person for the deeds they would have done but could not do because they are in *Itikaf*. How merciful is our Lord!

Rewards in *Ramadan* are already multiplied by 70 or 100; therefore, taking time out to perform *Itikaf* can enable a person to reap the maximum benefits from this blessed month. Being a recommended act from the Prophet[P] means that there is already a reward for performing *Itikaf* in itself. Additionally, the time spent away from our busy lives allows us to immerse ourselves in Quran recitation and perform numerous *nawafil* prayers. *Itikaf*, therefore, encourages a person to develop and prosper in acts of worship, accumulating more and more rewards.

Also, Ali Ibn Hussain[RA] narrates from his father that the Prophet[P] *said, "He who observes the ten days of Itikaf during Ramadan will obtain the reward of two Hajj and two Umrah."* **Bayhaqi.** Subhan Allah, what a great reward for sitting in *Itikaf*.

3. A Time for Reflection

Itikaf is a great opportunity to reflect. Reflection allows us to look back on our lives, reviewing our strengths and weaknesses, and identifying areas for improvement going forward. Reflecting will also enable us to set goals and aspirations, looking at what we have already achieved and how we can further develop from this. As believers, we are encouraged to have a vision so we are constantly motivated and focused in life with lofty aims. Remember, the purpose of life is to worship Allah. Allah[SWT] says: *"And I did not create the jinn and mankind except to worship Me."* **Quran 51:56.**

Reflection also helps improve our mental health. It allows us to take a step back from our busy lives, calming our minds. This increases our concentration to worship Allah at this blessed time.

4. Protection from Hell

The Prophet[P] *said, "Whosoever for Allah's sake did even one day of Itikaf, Allah would keep him away from Jahannam by trenches."* **Tabarani.**

The month of *Ramadan* itself presents numerous opportunities for us to seek forgiveness from Allah[SWT]. Performing *Itikaf* is a bonus in this aspect. Not only did our

Prophet[P] mention being protected from Hell, but it also allowed us to reflect on and ponder our previous actions. Through this, we become alert to the necessity of seeking forgiveness. As humans, it is common to make mistakes even unintentionally. *Itikaf* enables us to reflect on our actions and continually seek protection from Hell.

What an amazing opportunity for us to gain such immense and abundant rewards, as well as to draw closer to Allah[SWT]. It is also an excellent opportunity to strengthen and boost our *Imaan* for the rest of the year.

The following are some ways to maximise *Itikaf*:

1. Purifying intentions
We must purify and correct our intentions before doing any act of worship. Our beloved Prophet[P] said, *"Verily actions are judged by intention."* **Bukhari and Muslim.**

We may have other underlying intentions in our hearts without even realising it. *Itikaf* is for those who intend to devote time to intense worship of Allah by praying, reciting dhikr, reading and understanding the Quran, making dua, and enhancing their knowledge of the deen, which will help them reflect on the purpose of life and ask for Allah's forgiveness.

Therefore, before doing any good deed, we need to correct our intentions so that we are more sincere in our worship. The better our intentions, the greater the rewards for the good we do.

Ibn Al-Mubaarak *said, "Maybe a small action is made great by its intention, and maybe a great action is made small by its intention."* Therefore, one must take every action to please Allah[SWT] solely.

2. Plan, Schedule, and Monitor Daily Worship
It is much better to plan and schedule our time in *Itikaf* so that we can spend it as effectively as possible. By setting daily targets, we can increase our chances of achieving them. Set a day and night routine working around the obligatory salah— that way we optimise and use our time effectively. Remember to vary our ibadah. Therefore, time is allocated for the Quran, Dhikr, learning the deen, reading the Seerah of the Prophet[P], and other similar activities. If we allocate and schedule our time effectively, we ensure that we are not only using our time efficiently but also maintaining varied concentration and focus, which will make us feel less tired.

3. Exerting oneself in worship during the last 10 nights
In a hadith recorded in Muslim: *"Allah's Messenger used to exert himself in devotion during the last ten nights to a greater extent than at any other time."* **Muslim.** Aisha[RA] reported: *"With the start of the last ten days of Ramadan, the Prophet[P] used to tighten his waist belt (i.e. work harder) and used to pray all night, and used to keep his family awake for the prayers."* **Bukhari.**

The last ten days and nights of *Ramadan* are the most blessed. Therefore, the person sitting *Itikaf* should exert themselves in worship on each night of the last ten nights, particularly the last ten odd-numbered nights, that is: 21, 23, 25, 27, and 29.

By worshipping in as many of the last ten nights as possible, there is a greater chance that we will catch *Laylatul Qadr,* the Night of Power, and gain the reward of over 83 years of worship! That is more than the average human life! Subhan Allah.

4.   Reciting the Quran abundantly

The Quran was revealed on the Night of Power, so we should increase our recitation even more during the last ten days and nights. The pious predecessors used to increase the amount of Quran they recited during this period. The reward for reciting each letter of the Quran during *Ramadan* is 700 Hashanah or more. Subhan Allah!

We should therefore set a target of completing at least one Quran during these last 10 days. There is plenty of time to do this; the most important thing is *Ibadha*. Also, try to understand and reflect on the meaning of what Allah[SWT] is saying to us. We should contemplate, ponder, and learn from the verses and implement them in our daily lives.

We should also recite Surah Yasin every day, particularly after Fajr time. We should also recite Surah Mulk and Surah Sajdah before going to sleep, and Surah Kahf every Jumma, just as we do outside *Ramadan*.

Other very rewarding Surahs we can recite in their entirety are Surah Zilzal, Al-Kaafirun, and Al-Ikhlas. Abdullah Ibn Abbas and Anas Ibn Malik[RA] reported that the Prophet[P] *said, "Whoever recited Surah Zilzl (Chapter 99) would get the reward of reciting half the Qur'an. Whoever recited Surah al-Kaafirun (Chapter 109) would get a reward as if reading a quarter of the Qur'an. Whoever recited Surah al-Ikhlas (Chapter 112) would get a reward as if reading one-third of the Qur'an.* **Tirmidhi.**

5.   Nawafil - Voluntary prayers

We should pray plenty of voluntary prayers as this will draw us closer to Allah[SWT]. Allah says in Hadith Qudsi: *"....And My slave keeps on coming closer to Me through performing Nawafil (voluntary deeds) until I love him."* **Bukhari.** Also, Rabiah Ibn Malik Al-Aslami[RA] reported that the Prophet[P] *said, "Ask (anything)." Rabiah[RA] said, "I ask of you to be your companion in paradise." The Prophet (pbuh) said, "Or anything else?" Rabiah[RA] said, "That is it." The Prophet[P] said to him: "Then help me by making many prostrations (i.e., Nawafil prayers)."* **Muslim.** This hadith encourages us to increase our *voluntary* prayers to gain the company of the Prophet[P] in *Jannah*.

The reward for praying the *fard* obligatory prayers outside of *Ramadan* is the greatest a Muslim can gain; however, in *Ramadan*, we receive the same reward for praying a *Nawafil* prayer. Subhaan Allah, how blessed we are. We should, therefore, strive to pray as many Nawafil as possible during *Itikaf* so we can get closer to Allah[SWT], gain the company of the Prophet[P] in *Jannah* as well, and gain the rewards of a *fard* prayer for each Nawafil prayer!

What *Sunnah* Nawafil prayers to pray during *Itikaf*?

- **Pray 12 Rakahs of *Sunnah* daily:** Two *Sunnah* of Fajr, four *Sunnah* and 2 *Sunnah* of Dhuhr and two *Sunnah* of Maghrib. Umm Habibah Ramilah bint Abu Sufyan[RA] narrated she heard the Prophet[P] saying: *"A house will be built in Paradise for every Muslim who offers twelve units of Prayers other than the obligatory ones in day and night, to seek the pleasure of Allah."* **Muslim.**

- **Salaatul Duha.** This prayer can be performed from 20 minutes after sunrise until 20 minutes before the beginning of Dhuhr time. We should remain seated after the Fajr prayer and recite the Quran or perform dhikr until 20 minutes after Sunrise, and pray Salaatul Duhaa, also known as Ishraq, at this time. If not, then we can still pray Salatul Duha any time before midday. Salatul-Dhuha consists of 2 – 12 Rakats, and it is preferable to perform 8 Rakats. The Prophet[P] *said, "Whoever prayed twelve rakats before midday, then Allah[SWT] will, as a reward, prepare a palace of gold for him in Paradise."* **Tirmidhi and Ibn Majah.** Subhan Allah!

- **Pray four *Sunnah*, two *Sunnah* and two Nawafil of Dhuhr.** Umm Habibah[RA] narrated that the Prophet[P] *said, "Whoever sticks to the habit of offering four rakats before Noon Prayer and four rakats after it, Allah will shield him against the Hell-Fire."* **Abu Dawud and Tirmidhi.**

- **Four Rakaahs of *Sunnah* of Asr.** The Prophet[P] said, *"May Allah have Mercy on the one who offers four Rakat before Asr prayer."* **Abu Dawud.** Here, our beloved Prophet[P] is praying for the mercy of Allah for those who pray the four Rakat of the Asr Prayer.

- **Two Rakaah *Sunnah* after entering *Masjid*.** Abu Qatadah[RA] narrated that the Prophet[P] *said, "If any one of you enters a mosque, he should pray two rakaah before sitting."* **Bukhari and Muslim.**

- **Tahiyyatul Wudu.** Two Rakat *Sunnah* after doing *Wudu*, i.e., Ablution. Abu Hurayrah[RA] reported that the Prophet[P] said to Bilal RA, *"Tell me about the best of your deeds (i.e. one which you deem the most rewarding) since your embracing Islam because I heard your footsteps in front of me in Paradise."* Bilal[RA] replied: *"I do not consider any act of mine more rewarding than that whenever I make ablution at any time of night or day, I perform Prayer for as much as was destined for me to do."* **Bukhari and Muslim.**

- **The most virtuous of all Nawafil Prayer is Tahajjud.** Allah[SWT] says: *"Establish worship at the going down of the sun until the dark of the night, and (the recital of) the Quran at dawn. Lo! (the recital of) the Quran at dawn is ever witnessed. And some part of the night awake for its recital, as voluntary worship for you. It may be that your Lord will raise you to a praised estate."* **Quran, 17:78-79.**

It is recommended to start the night vigil with two short Rakats, as per the Hadith of Abu Hurayrah RA, wherein the Prophet[P] said, "*If you get up for night prayer, start with two short Rakaats.*" **Muslim, Ahmad, and Abu Dawud.** We should aim to pray Tahajjud every night in the last 10 nights. If not, then we should pray it in as many nights as we possibly can, particularly on the nights of the 21,23,25,27 and 29th. This is the best time to reap the benefits of praying the Tahajjud prayers.

One should wake up a little earlier for Sehri, perform *Wudu*, and pray a minimum of two Rakats of Tahajjud. However, it is best to pray more. You may not have this opportunity outside *Ramadan* when the Shaytaan is released and we have less motivation to pray.

Regarding Tahajjud Abu Hurayrah RA, related that the Prophet[P] *said, "When the last one-third of the night remains, our Lord, the Glorious One descends towards the Heaven of the earth and proclaims: Who is that who supplicates for Me, and I grant his supplication? Who is that who begs Me for anything and I grant it to him? And who is that who seeks My forgiveness, and I forgive him?"* **Bukhari and Muslim.**

The last third portion of the night is the most blessed, and du'as are readily accepted at this time. Therefore, praying Tahajjud gives us the best opportunity to draw closer to Allah[SWT] and to make sincere dua, repent for our past and present sins, and to cry out and ask Allah for whatever is permissible.

6. Excessive Remembrance of Allah

Whilst in *Itikaf*, we should spend as much time as possible in the remembrance of Allah, keeping our lips moist in his glorification and praises. Surely, we will have utter regret in the Hereafter for each second wasted without remembering Allah[SWT], as this hadith indicates: Muadh Ibn Jabal[RA] said that the Prophet[P] *said, "The People of Paradise will not regret anything except one thing alone. That is the hour that passed them by in which they made no remembrance of Allah."* **Bayhaqi.**

The highest rank in *Jannah* is for those who remember Allah the most. Abu Said[RA] narrates that the Prophet[P] was asked: *"Which of the servants of Allah is best in rank before Allah on the Day of resurrection?"* He said, *"The ones who remember him* much." I said, "O Messenger of Allah, what about the fighter in the way of Allah?" He[P] responded: *"Even if he strikes the unbelievers and mushrikin with his sword until it breaks, and becomes red with their blood, truly those who do Dhikr are better than him in rank."* **Ahmad, Tirmidhi, and Bayhaqi.**

We should therefore remember Allah as much as we can and glorify him day and night. We should do this outside *Ramadan*, as well, in fact, until our very last breath. In *Itikaf*, we have the best opportunity to seclude ourselves and remember Allah.

The following are 11 Dhikr, supported by Hadith, that we can recite throughout the duration of *Itikaf*:

Note: We should try to recite each of these Dhikr 100 times each.

- Allahumma innaka 'afuwwun tuhibbul 'afwa fa'fu 'annee – Recite this abundantly during the last ten nights of *Ramadan*.
- Subhaanallah; Alhamdulillah; Allahu Akbar; Laa ilaaha illallah.
- La hawla wa la quwwata illa billah-hil aliyyil adheem.
- Asthaghfirullah-halladhee Laa ilaaha illa-huwal Hayyul Qayyuumu Wa athoobu Ilay. Or short version: Asthaghfirullah.
- Sub-haan'allaahi wa bi-ham'dihi sub-haan'allah-il adheem. Or short version: Sub-haan'allaahi wa bi-ham'dihi.
- Subhāna-llāhi, wa-l-hamdu li-llāhi, wa lā ilāha illā-llāhu, wa-llāhu akbar. Wa lā hawla wa lā quwwata illā bi-llāhi-l-aliyyi-l-azīm.
- Lā ilāha illā-llāhu waḥdahu lā sharīka lahu lahu-l-mulku wa lahu-l-ḥamdu yuhyi wa

  yumītu wa huwa ḥayyu-llā yamūtu abadan abada, ḏū-l-jalāli wa-l-ikrām, biyadihi-l-khayr, wa huwa alā kulli Shay-in qadīr.
- Or the shortened version: Laa ilaaha illal-laahu wahdahu laa shareeka lahu, lahul-mulku wa lahul-hamdu wa huwa 'alaa kulli shay-in qadeer.
- Radeetu billahi Rabban Wa bil Islami deenan Wabi Muhammadin Nabiyyan.

We should also recite much of durood e Ibrahim, which is the durood that is recited towards the end of Salaah. The shortest durood is Sallallahu Alayhi Wasallim.

7. Making Excessive Dua and Repentance
Itikaf is the best opportunity to repent and make long and sincere dua to Allah[SWT] whilst devoting ourselves to Allah in His house. Allah[SWT] says: *"When my servants ask you concerning me, (tell them) I am indeed close (to them). I listen to the prayer of every suppliant when he calls on me."* **Quran 2:186.**

Dua is a very honourable form of worship. The Prophet[P] said, "Nothing *is more honourable to Allah the Most High than Dua."* **Sahih Al-Jami.** Allah loves those who repent and love those who turn to him in sincere repentance, so repent unto him sincerely as much as possible: Allah[SWT] says, *"Truly Allah loves those who turn [to Him] in repentance..."* **Quran 2:222.**

Many of us rush our Dua, and quite often our hearts are not present whilst we are making Dua to Allah. That is why we lose out on many of the benefits and blessings of Dua. We need to be in a present state of mind and be mindful of what we are saying to Allah[SWT]. We should not let our minds wander and concentrate more, ensuring our hearts are present while asking Allah. We should imagine that Allah[SWT] is present before us and be humble in His presence, maintaining a state of complete humility.

It may also be helpful to create a list of what we want to ask Allah during our dua. We can then refer to this list as a reminder to ensure we cover everything we need to ask. This may help us prolong our dua and be more sincere in our intentions. We will not always remember everything we want to ask Allah unless we note it down and refer back to it when we need to.

The times when Dua is most accepted during *Itikaf* are:

- The third portion of the night, just before Sheri ends.
- Whilst fasting.
- Between Asr and Maghrib.
- Just before breaking the fast.
- In Jumma before and after the Khutba.
- Between Adhan and Iqamah.
- After Quran recitation.
- And of course, the Night of Qadr.

Let us make the most of *Ramadan*. Our beloved Prophet[P] *said, "The Angel Jibril appeared before me and said, Destruction to him who found the blessed month of Ramadan and let it pass by without gaining forgiveness..."* Upon that, I *said, "Ameen."* **Bukhari and Tabrani.**

We should ask Allah, whilst in *Itikaf*, to accept all our good deeds and efforts throughout *Ramadan* and be hopeful that Allah[SWT] will receive them from us. We should also have complete hope that Allah[SWT] will accept our Duas, if not in this world, then in the Hereafter. We should take his decree, for he knows best in all matters.

The Prophet[P] *said, "There is no Muslim who calls upon his Lord with a dua in which there is no sin or severing of family ties, but Allah[SWT] will give him one of three things: Either He will answer his prayer quickly, or He will store (the reward for) it in the Hereafter, or He will divert an equivalent evil away from him."* They said, *"We will say more dua."* Hepbuh said, *"Allah's bounty is greater."* **Ahmad and Tirmidhi.**

So, three ways Allah^{SWT} answers our *Dua*

4. **Yes.** You ask for something, and Allah^{SWT} gives it to you immediately. That is awesome. Just be grateful to Allah^{SWT} and thank Him.
5. **Yes, but not now.** You ask for something, and Allah^{SWT} delays giving it to you because He wants to draw you closer to Him through your desperate need for Him. Only Allah^{SWT} can help you. So, do not despair, be patient. Allah^{SWT} will avert any evil equivalent to the level of what you ask for.
6. **I have better plans for you.** Allah^{SWT} is withholding what you ask for. This is because what you ask for is not suitable for you, but you do not see it. Or He will give you something better on the Day of Judgement.

No doubt, there is wisdom behind Allah's decisions, which may take us years to understand and realise that Allah^{SWT} saved us from a terrible fate. We often make *dua* for what we want in this world, such as having a better job, a new house, or a car. There is no harm in asking for what is permissible, but more importantly, what we should be asking for, first and foremost, is strong *imaan,* and to be on the right path, because this is our precious asset and a great blessing. If *Imaan* is devoid in the heart, then we have lost everything and nothing is good. No matter how rich and famous we become, it will not benefit us in any way.

Also, remember to make dua at times of ease. We should not only beseech Allah when we are in difficulty but also at times of plenty. The Prophet^P said, *"Remember Allah during times of ease and He will remember you during times of hardship."* **Ahmad.**

The following dua should be recited as much as possible during the last 10 nights of *Ramadan*: Aisha^{RA} *said,* I asked the Prophet^P: *"O Messenger of Allah, if I know what night is the night of Qadar, what should I say during it?"* The Prophet^P *said, "Say: 'Allahumma innaka 'afuwwun tuhibbul 'afwa fa'fu 'annee.'* The translation of this dua is: "Say: O Allah, You are pardoning and You love to pardon, so pardon me." **Ahmad, Ibn Majah, and Tirmidhi.**

8. Practice the *Sunnah*

Following the *Sunnah* is a commandment of Allah^{SWT}. Allah^{SWT} says: *"Say (O Muhammad to mankind): 'If you (really) love Allah, then follow me (i.e. accept Islamic monotheism, follow the Quran and the Sunnah), Allah will love you and forgive you your sins. And Allah is Oft-Forgiving, Most Merciful."* **Quran: 3:31.** In another verse, Allah^{SWT} says: *"There certainly is an excellent example in Allah's Messenger for he who fears Allah and the last day and remembers Allah abundantly."* **Quran 33:21.** By following the *Sunnah* in every aspect of our daily lives, everything we do will become worship, even going to the toilet, having a bath, dressing, undressing, etc. In a hadith,

Anas[RA] reports: The Messenger of Allah[P] advised: *"Whoever cherishes my Sunnah, indeed he cherishes me and whoever loves me will be with me in Jannah."* **Tirmidhi.**

We should practice and implement the *Sunnah* throughout the duration of *Itikaf*, e.g., the *Sunnah* of awakening, using miswak, eating, drinking, going to the toilet, before sleeping, etc. When we do this, everything we do during our *Itikaf* will become worship and a source of reward. Remember, doing voluntary good deeds in *Ramadan* carries the reward of *fard!* SubhanAllah!

Our beloved Prophet[P] *said, "Whoever revives an aspect of my Sunnah that is forgotten after my death, he will have a reward equivalent to that of the people who follow him, without it detracting in the least from their reward."* **Tirmidhi.** Therefore, practice the *Sunnah* in *Ramadan* and outside *Ramadan*.

9. Refraining from sin and idle talk
Those who sit in *Itikaf* must take extra care and attention to ensure that they refrain from committing any sins. That includes guarding the ears, eyes, tongue, and heart, thereby deriving the maximum benefit from *Itikaf* and attaining a special closeness to Allah[SWT], as well as an increase and strengthening of *imaan*.

The mutakif (the person sitting in *Itikaf*) should remember that they are the guest of Allah[SWT] in his house and therefore they should be highly vigilant of their behaviour in the House of Allah. They must also avoid getting into idle discussions, debates, and arguments, which will be of no benefit but cause more harm than good.

Time will pass quickly, and if we waste our precious time during *Itikaf*, we will surely regret it forever. So, let us use this valuable time wisely, as this may be our last *Itikaf*; so let us treat it like our very last.

This does not mean that you do not talk at all. During Sheri and Iftar, you will certainly share food with other brothers who will be sitting in *Itikaf*. If there is an Alim amongst the group, then listen to his Nasiyah and the sound advice he will give, and feel free to ask questions about the deen. The purpose is to increase Islamic knowledge.

It is best not to bring your phone or any electronic device. If you wish to use the smartphone for an alarm, torch, or to check the time, etc., then put it on aeroplane mode and commit not to open it during the *Itikaf*.

10. Avoiding overeating and oversleeping
Excessive eating and sleeping during *Itikaf* is a major factor in stopping a person from maximising their *Itikaf*. Ibrahim al-Nakhai RA, one of the teachers of *Imam* Abu Hanifa RA, mentioned: *"The people ruined before you were done in by three characteristics: too much talking, too much eating, and too much sleeping."* Also, Ash-Shafi'i[RA] *said, "I have not filled myself in sixteen years because filling oneself makes the body heavy, removes clear understanding, induces sleep, and makes one weak for worship."*

Therefore, a person must ensure that they do not overeat or oversleep during *Itikaf*. Doing so will make a person feel heavy, tired, and lazy, resulting in that person not being as productive as they should be during *Itikaf*.

It would be better to set your limits and stick to them. Stay focused on your primary purpose for sitting in *Itikaf* and what you hope to achieve out of it.

11. Not leaving the *Masjid* unless necessary
It is not permitted for a person to leave the *Masjid* during *Itikaf* unless it is to answer the call of nature, make wudhu, take a bath, or to proclaim the adhan.

It is also not permitted to go out of *Masjid* to use a mobile phone. One should also try not to disturb others.

12. Giving to Charity
One of the most rewarding acts during *Ramadan*, particularly in the last ten days, is giving to charity. However, this cannot be done while on *Itikaf* if it means leaving the *Masjid*. Therefore, it is advisable to ensure that you have made all your donations before commencing your *Itikaf*. Nowadays, one can set up a standing order with their bank to automatically go out on each day of *Itikaf*.

We must continue to maintain *Ramadan* by performing good deeds after *Ramadan*.

May Allah enable us to make the best of the last ten days and nights of *Ramadan*. May Allah allow us to find the night of power, and may he accept our *Itikaf* and make it a salvation for us on the Day of Resurrection.

The Significance of Jummah (Friday) in Islam

"This day, I have perfected your religion for you, completed My favour upon you, and have chosen Islam as your religion."

Quran 5:3

"The best day during which the sun has risen is Friday. It is the day Adam pbuh was created. It is the day when Adam entered paradise and also when he was taken out from it. It is also the day on which the Day of Judgment will take place."

Muslim and Tirmidhi

We all know that Friday is an important day of the week for Muslims. There are many religious significances and virtues associated with this day. Abu Hurairah[RA] reported that the beloved Prophet[P] *said, "The best day during which the sun has risen is Friday. It is the day Adam[P] was created. It is the day when Adam entered paradise and also when he was taken out from it. It is also the day on which the Day of Judgment will take place."* **Muslim and Tirmidhi.**

As we know, we Muslims gather on Friday in mosques to pray *the Jummah* prayer collectively in the congregation. Before starting the prayer, the *Imam* delivers a speech, which is called the "Friday Sermon" or *"Khutbah"*. The *Imam* gives *naseeha* (advice/lessons) on religious matters and affairs during the sermon. Allah[SWT] says in the Quran: *"O you who believe! When the call is proclaimed for the Salah on Friday - jummah prayer, come to the remembrance of Allah, and leave off business (and every other thing). That is better for you if you did but know!"* **Quran 62:9. Here** we are commanded by Allah[SWT] to leave our businesses and work and anything else we are doing and come to the remembrance of Allah.

Friday is also the day when our *deen* was completed and perfected wherein Allah[SWT] says: *"This day, I have perfected your religion for you, completed My favour upon you, and have chosen Islam as your religion."* **Quran 5:3.**

The literal meaning of *Jummah* is congregation. Muslims offer *Jummah* prayer, and for this prayer, a special time is set aside. Due to the *khutba* (sermon) to be delivered by the *Imam* before the congregational prayer, the units of prayer during this time are reduced from four to two, so that appropriate time is apportioned for the *khutbah*.

It is stated in a hadith wherein our beloved Prophet[P] said, *"There is an hour on Friday and if a Muslim gets it while offering Salah and asks something from Allah, then Allah will definitely fulfil his demand." The Prophet[P] pointed out the shortness of that particular time with his hands".* **Bukhari** Scholars have said it is the last hour of the day, i.e., after the *asar* prayer until the *Maghrib* prayer.

The Prophet[P] said, *"If a man takes bath on Friday, cleans himself as much as he can, oils his hair, applies perfume available in his house, sets forth to the mosque, does not separate two people (to make a seat for himself), performs as many Prayers as written [by Allah] for him, remains silent when the Imam speaks, his sins between that Friday and the following Friday will be forgiven."* **Bukhari.**

The lesson we learn from this *hadith* is that we should take a bath on a Friday and clean ourselves thoroughly. When we enter the Mosque, we should not rush past people to reach the front row. If you wish to be in the front row, then go early to the Mosque. When we enter the Mosque, we should remain silent.

The importance of coming early for the *Jummah* prayers is highlighted in this *Hadith* wherein Abu Hurairah[RA] reported that the beloved Prophet[P] said, *"When it is jummah, the Angels stand at the gate of the Masjid and keep on writing the names of the persons coming to the Masjid in succession according to their arrivals. The example of the one who enters the Masjid in the earliest hour is that of one offering a camel (in sacrifice); the one coming next is like one offering a cow, and then a ram; and then a chicken; and then an egg respectively. When the Imam starts the Jummah Khutba, they (i.e., Angels) fold their papers and listen to the sermon."* **Bukhari.** Subhanallah! We see here the immense reward that comes from going early. We should make every effort to arrive at the *Masjid* early.

Abu Hurairah[RA] reported that the Prophet[P] said, *"The five [daily prescribed] prayers, and Friday [prayer] to the [next] Friday [prayer], and Ramadan to the next Ramadan, is the expiation of the sins committed in between them, so long as major sins are avoided."* **Muslim.** This is an excellent blessing for believers. One should never miss their five daily prayers and the *Jummah* prayers. Not only because it is an obligatory duty that we are fulfilling, but Allah[SWT] forgives our minor sins committed between them.

We are also required to recite Surah *Al-Kahf* every Friday. The Prophet[P] said, *"Whoever reads Surah Al-Kahf on the night of Friday, will have a light that will stretch between him and the Ancient House – i.e. the Kabah."* **Albani.** It does not take long to recite Surah *Al-Khaf*. If you have to work, try to read this Surah straight after *Fajr* before heading to work. Once you have this as a routine and a habit, it will become easier. Remember the purpose of life is to worship Allah[SWT] and fulfil His commandments. Therefore, adjust your timings to accommodate the tasks you need to perform. It is this that will take us to *Jannah*, which is our ultimate abode.

On this day, we are also required to send salutations to the beloved Prophet[P]. Regarding this, He[P] said, *"Among the best of your days is Friday. So, pray to Allah frequently on it to bless me, for such supplications of you will be presented to me."* **Abu Dawud.** There are many virtues in reciting the *durood* on Fridays, and we should do this abundantly.

It is highly recommended to offer two *rakah* (units) of prayer upon entering the *Masjid* on the day of *Jummah*, even if the *Imam* has begun to deliver the Sermon. For example, Sulaik Al-Ghatafani[RA] came on a Friday when the Prophet[P] was delivering the sermon. The companion sat down. So, the Prophet[P] said to him: *"O Sulaik! Stand and observe two rakah and make them short."* Then, he said, *"When any one of you comes on Friday, while the Imam delivers the sermon, he should observe two rakah and should make them short."* **Muslim.** The importance of offering the two *rakah* upon entering the *Masjid*, even if the *Khutbah* has started, is stressed here. This means it is very important to arrive early at the *Masjid*. If you are delayed for any reason, then offer the two *rakah* of supplementary prayer and make them short before sitting down, even if the *Imam* has started the *Khutba*.

When you enter the *Masjid* on a Friday and the sermon has started, then keep silent and listen to the *Khutbah*, because the Prophet[P] said, *"If you say to your companion: Listen attentively on a Friday when the Imam is delivering the khutbah, then you have engaged in idle talk."* **Muslim.** Therefore, absolute silence, and not even responding to anyone talking, is strongly recommended here.

Also, the Prophet[P] said, *"Do not choose the Friday night among all other nights for Qiyam (night vigil prayer), and do not choose Friday among all other days for fasting except that one of you have accustomed to."* **Muslim.** In another *Hadith,* the Prophet[P] said, *"None of you should observe fast on Friday unless he observes fast a day before or after it."* **Bukhari.** The lesson we learn from this is that we should not perform *tahjjud* on Friday, i.e., Thursday night, or fast during the day unless you are accustomed to it or fast the day before or after it.

We should walk to the *Masjid*. Abu Hurairah[RA] reported that the beloved Prophet[P] said, *"He who purifies (performs wudhu) himself in his house and then walks to one of the houses of Allah[SWT] (Masjid) for performing an obligatory Salah, one step of his will wipe out his sins and another step will elevate his rank (in Jannah)."* **Muslim.** We should make every effort to walk to the *Masjid*. Not only will this be rewarding, but it will also avoid you being frustrated and worried about finding a car park space when the *Masjid* car park is full. It is so sad that we see people coming in their cars late, and because they do not want to miss *Jummah*, they park in such a way that they block local residents' access to their driveways or garages, or park in a way that prevents others from driving out. By coming late and blocking someone's pathway, you are inadvertently sinning by breaching others' rights. You may be coming for prayers to fulfil your commandment of Allah^{SWT}, but you are also breaking *the rules of Huququl Ibad.*

One of the most worrying hadith related to Friday is this one, wherein our beloved Prophet^P *said, "There is no creature but that it is alert on Friday when it awakens until the sun sets, anxious of the Hour, except for humans and jinn."* **Abu Dawood.** The animals, the birds, and all the creatures on air, land, and sea anxiously await the *Qiyammah* (the HOUR) whilst we humans and jinn are heedless and oblivious to this. May Allah^{SWT} guide us to remember the final hour on Fridays, just as all the other creatures of Allah^{SWT} do.

Allah^{SWT} made it compulsory for all believers to ask Him to bestow upon the Prophet Muhammad^P His Blessings and Tranquillity. This act of asking Allah^{SWT} to show His Favour and Protection to our beloved Prophet^P is known as "*Durood.*" It is essentially a form of prayer, which Muslims are obligated to recite upon hearing, reading, or speaking the name of our beloved Prophet^P in order to pay him respect and praise in the most rightful manner.

The Prophet^P *said, "Whoever sends Salah upon me once, Allah will send Salah upon him ten-fold, and will erase ten sins from him, and will raise him ten degrees in status."* **Nasai and Haakim in Mustadrak.** The Prophet^P also *said, "The person closest to me on the Day of Judgement is the one who sent the most Salat upon me."* **Tirmidhi.**

Concerning *salat* and *durood* specifically on Fridays, the Prophet^P *said, "Of your best days is Friday. On its Adam was created, and on it, his (soul) was taken, and on it is the blowing (of the Trumpet), and on it is the Swoon. Therefore, increase in sending your Salat upon me, for your salat upon me are presented to me."* They *said, "O Messenger of Allah! And how will our Salat upon you be presented to you after you have perished?"* He replied: *"Indeed, Allah, the Mighty and Sublime, has prohibited the earth from (destroying) the bodies of the Prophets."* **Abu Dawud.**

Based on this, *Imam* Shafi (may Allah be pleased with him) used to say: *"I love to send plenty of salat upon the Messenger of Allah^P all the time, and I love it more so on the day of Jummah."*

So, there are plenty of rewards for reciting *salat* and *Salaam (durood)* every day, especially on Fridays. One may reap these rewards with whichever wording of *salat* and *Salaam (durood)* one uses.

Allah^{SWT} says: *"Indeed Allah and His angels bless the Prophet; O you who have faith! Invoke blessings on him and invoke Peace upon him in a worthy manner."* **Quran 33:56.**

There is a chapter of the Quran named Surah Jummah. This chapter, revealed in Madina, has eleven verses. One of the fundamental goals of the Chapter is to encourage the Muslims to congregate for the weekly establishment of the Friday prayer. The Muslims are advised to leave everything aside upon hearing the call to prayer and hasten toward the remembrance of Allah[SWT]. The Prophet[P] used to recite Surah Jummah in the first *rakah* (unit) and Surah Al-Munafiqoon in the second *rakah*. Surah Jummah opens with the glorification of Allah[SWT] and the Prophetic call, discussing the negligence of *Bani Isra'il* in listening to Allah[SWT] as they became too involved in hedonism (i.e., seeking pleasure). They were given the message and had the book of Allah[SWT], but failed to follow the guidance. Muslims are urged to keep the Friday prayer and not to get too involved in business that they forget Allah[SWT].

In summary, the following is what we are required to do on the day of *Jummah*:

- Take a bath on this day, apply perfume, use *a miswak*, trim your nails, and *arrive at the Masjid* early.
- Wear clean and presentable, or new, clothes to the Friday prayer.
- If possible, walk to the *Masjid* because one step will wipe out sins and another step will elevate the rank in *Jannah*.
- Attend the *Masjid* in good time for the *Jummah Khutbah* and prayer, and perform two *Rakah* prayers before sitting down.
- Do not push in between two people. If you arrive late, please sit in the available space you find.
- Do not separate two people to make a space for yourself. Sit in a space.
- Keep silent during the *Khutbah*. Do not even say to others to be quiet.
- Listen to the *Khutbah* of *Jummah* (Friday sermon) attentively. This includes not interrupting the speaker, not whispering or talking to the person next to you and not asking questions during the *Khutbah,* and staying silent even when you do not understand something.
- Make lots of *dua* to Allah[SWT] as the day of *Jummah* includes an hour during which all supplications are accepted.
- Give charity on the day of *Jummah* because it is more virtuous than any other day.
- Send lots of *Durood* on our beloved Prophet Muhammad[P].
- Recite Surah Al-Kahf on the day of *Jummah*. The beloved Prophet[P] said, *"Whoever reads Surah Al-Kahf on Friday, he will be illuminated with light between the two Fridays."* **Al-Haakim; Albani**
- Make many *duas* between the *Asr* and *Maghrib* prayers. Remember, it is on this day that the final hour will occur, so be mindful of this.
- Do not observe a fast on this day unless you fast the day before or after.

In some *Masajid*, the *Jummah Khutba* is not translated into the community language of the congregation being served, thereby denying the opportunity to receive *Nasiha* (advice) on the day when the majority of Muslims *attend the Masjid* once a week. Most people in the Muslim community will make every effort not to miss the *Jummah Khutbah*. The content of the Prophet's *Khutbah* was related to the current affairs of the time. He[P] spoke in a way that the people who heard him could understand. This meant that when the companions[RA] went back to their marketplaces and homes, they were able to heed the advice given and act upon it. Today, we see some, but not all, *imams* reading the Arabic text during the *Khutbah*. The congregation is unaware of its meaning and therefore derives no benefit from it. I urge the respected *Ulama* and *Imams* who have the responsibility of leading the *Jummah* prayer and the *Khutbah*, to at least provide some interpretation of what has been said in the speech so that our *Musallees*, particularly the youth, can benefit from this. Who knows, it could be that the *Khutbah* delivered on one such Friday could be a means for a person returning to Allah[SWT] and the turning point for a misguided young Muslim to return to practising his *deen*.

May Allah[SWT] grant us the *taufiq* to take heed of this important day of the week and guide us to fulfil the commandments of Allah[SWT] and the teachings of our beloved Prophet[P] as required on this virtuous and blessed day.

Time Management

"Know that the life of this world is but amusement and diversion and adornment and boasting to one another and competition in increase of wealth and children - like the example of a rain whose [resulting] plant growth pleases the tillers; then it dries and you see it turned yellow; then it becomes [scattered] debris. And in the Hereafter is severe punishment and forgiveness from Allah and approval. And what is the worldly life except the enjoyment of delusion?"

Quran 57:20

"What have I to do with this world? My example in the world is but like that of a traveller who rests in the shade of a tree, then is refreshed and moves on."

Tirmidhi

Managing the right balance between Deen and Dunya

If you are one of those people who is constantly rushing from one urgent matter to another; missing appointments; going late at meetings; forget doing tasks; not keep your word, and your workplace is a mess; and you spend all your time on last-minute; you pay penalties and late fees; the inside of your car is a mess; you cannot find that important document; your email inbox is overflowing; you work long hours, yet, there is always too much to do; then you need to sort out your life!

With all the technological advancements and time-saving devices, what has happened to the so-called time saved? Despite the tremendous development of time-saving gadgets, life has become busier than ever before. Where can we show anything for all the time that has been saved?

When people put Allah[SWT] first, just as the earlier Muslim civilisation did, vast development and advancement took place. Ibn Kathir, Ubaydullah ibn Hisn, RA, reports that whenever two companions met, they would not depart until they recited Sura Al-Asr to each other, reminding themselves of the eternal loss that everyone faces if they waste away their time in foolish pursuits.

We need to learn how to use our time effectively and wisely. Time management is the ability to use time productively and efficiently. It is about having the time to do everything that you need, without feeling stressed about it. As believers, it is finding the right balance between *deen* and *dunya*.

In the Islamic context, Time Management is more akin to life management. After all, our purpose in life is to worship Allah[SWT] throughout our lives. Remember, Allah[SWT] has created us for this *dunya* only to test us, but also not to shun the *dunya*. Our beloved Prophet[P] would recite this dua, which is in Sura Baqrah, frequently: "Allahumma Rabbana atina fid dunya hasanah wa fil aakhirati hasanah wa qina 'adhaban nar." **Quran 2:201,** *"O our Rabb! Grant us good in this world, good in the Hereafter and save us from the punishment of the fire."* **Bukhari.**

Those who have mastered good time management techniques and prioritised the obligatory acts in Islam seem to have *barakah* in their time, allowing them to accomplish everything they want to. In contrast, others are always rushing from task to task and become overwhelmed, never seeming to finish anything.

Ibn Masood[RA] reported that the Prophet[P] *said, "The son of Adam will not be dismissed from his Lord on the Day of Resurrection until he is questioned about five issues: his life and how he lived it, his youth and how he used it, his wealth and how he earned it and he spent it, and how he acted on his knowledge."* **Tirmidhi**. Therefore, we will all be asked on the Day of Judgement, how we used our time in this world.

We need to shift our focus to activities that are results-oriented, from being hurried to being effective, and dedicate uninterrupted time to the tasks that matter. You can then target your attention where it is most needed.

Ibn Abbas[RA] relates that our beloved Prophet[P] *said, "There are two bounties in which many people are deluded: 'Well-being and Free time."* **Bukhari.** According to this hadith, we learn that health, well-being and free time are two bounties that Allah[SWT] has bestowed upon every believer. We need to take advantage of it in accordance with our purpose in life.

Allah[SWT] says in the Quran: *"Know that the life of this world is but amusement and diversion and adornment and boasting to one another and competition in increase of wealth and children - like the example of a rain whose [resulting] plant growth pleases the tillers; then it dries and you see it turned yellow; then it becomes [scattered] debris. And in the Hereafter is severe punishment and forgiveness from Allah and approval. And what is the worldly life except the enjoyment of delusion."* **Quran 57:20.**

Our relationship with the *Dunya* is brief. The Prophet[P] *said, "What have I to do with this world? My example in the world is but like that of a traveller who rests in the shade of a tree, then is refreshed and moves on."* **Tirmidhi.** In another Hadith, the

Prophet[P]) advises a companion: *"Be in the world as though you were a traveller or wayfarer"*. **Bukhari.**

Therefore, make the most of your time in the *Dunya* preparing for the *Akhira*. Do not make the world the peak of your aspirations; otherwise, you will realise how awful a mistake you made. Allah[SWT] reminds us: *"Our Lord! We have now seen and heard, so send us back; we will do good – we do indeed (now) have firm faith."* **Quran 32:12.** Their pleas will be answered with: *"Did We not grant you a life long enough for him who would reflect (and take heed)? And there came to you a warner (too); therefore, taste now (the punishment), for the unjust have no helper."* **Quran 35:37.**

This comes back to our purpose in life, which is to worship Allah[SWT] by living a life that is pleasing to Him, so that we can reap the benefits in the Hereafter and not give too much priority to this world over the next. Allah[SWT] says: *"Nay, but you give preference to the life of this world, While the Hereafter is better and more enduring."* **Quran 87:16-17.** We are warned to utilise our precious time correctly.

Effective Time Management Tips:

Plan and Schedule your work

Planning and scheduling your work will reduce anxiety. You can do a to-do list and check off each task as you complete it. You cannot always remember what tasks you have to fulfil for the day, and writing them down is the best way to ensure you get everything done that needs to be done. Consider making it a habit to write out your "to-do" list for the next working day at the end of each workday. That way, you can hit the ground running the next morning. Most people keep a diary, digital or otherwise, for their work; that way, you can record every meeting and task that you have to fulfil. Those who do not work should also keep a diary and record, plan and schedule their tasks. That way, you do not forget and miss out on any promises you may have made to someone. Fulfilling promises is one of the attributes of the pious, and it is one of the most excellent means of attaining *Taqwa* (piety, consciousness of Allah). Allah says: "Absolutely, whoever fulfils his pledge and fears Allah much; verily, then Allah loves those who are *Al-Muttaqun* (the pious)." **Quran 3:76.**

Eliminate procrastination

Procrastination is an unhealthy habit. There are numerous reasons why people procrastinate. When a task needs to be done, it is essential to do it; otherwise, it is just going to linger in your unconscious mind, and this can make you feel more anxious or sometimes even depressed. When you eliminate delays, you will soon find yourself with more time than before. Try to do things you don't like to do first; that way, you will be able to enjoy the remaining tasks more. Shaytaan causes people to procrastinate, be lazy and delay performing good deeds. Abu Hurayrah[RA] *said,* The

Prophet[P] said, "Shaytaan puts three knots at the back of the head of any of you if he is asleep. On every knot, he reads and exhales the following words, 'The night is long, so stay asleep.' When one wakes up and remembers Allah, one knot is undone; and when one performs ablution, the second knot is undone, and when one prays, the third knot is undone and one gets up energetic with a good heart in the morning; otherwise, one gets up lazy and with a mischievous heart." **Bukhari.** The Shaytaan makes one procrastinate and lazy, he makes the sinner put off repenting, and he keeps him indulging in his own desires. Allah[SWT] says: *"Satan has taken hold of them, causing them to forget the remembrance of Allah. They are the party of Satan. Surely Satan's party is bound to lose."* **Quran 58:19.** So beware of this.

Prioritise your tasks based on importance and urgency

Look at your daily tasks and determine which are:

- Important and urgent: Do these tasks right away.
- Important but not urgent: Decide when to do these tasks.
- Urgent but not important: Delegate these tasks if possible.
- Not urgent and not important: Set these aside to do later.

Prioritising in this way helps you avoid feeling stressed out and worrying about whether you are getting things done or not. Prioritisation is a crucial survival skill for navigating stressful times. It brings order to chaos, creates calmness and space, and reduces stress.

Take a break between tasks

Rushing from task to task can be detrimental to our mood, effectiveness, and productivity. When completing numerous tasks without a break, it becomes harder to stay focused and motivated. Allow some downtime between tasks to clear your head and refresh yourself. Consider grabbing a brief nap or going for a short walk. If the prayer time falls between your tasks, then that is the best time to take a break and prioritise your Salah. By doing this, not only do you allow blood to circulate in your brain due to the *sujood* you will perform in prayer, but it also enables you to revitalise yourself and release radioactive toxins in your body. You will definitely become more energised and more efficient and effective in whatever task you undertake. In fact, never give up your salah even if you think your tasks are more important, because the Prophet[P] said, *"Between a man and shirk [associating others with Allah] and kufr there stands his giving up prayer."* **Muslim.**

Start Everything with "Bismillah" (in the name of Allah)

When you start anything with the name of Allah, it will bring blessings in whatever you are doing. The action you take after saying Bismillah will be considered an act of worship, and you will be rewarded for it. Therefore, when you start your car, read an article, or work on the computer, play with your grandchildren, attend a meeting, put your shoes on, change your clothes, etc., begin with *Bismillah* (in the name of Allah). This will also enable you to be conscious of Allah[SWT] at all times. Whatever you are doing, have the sincere intention of pleasing Allah[SWT]. For example, when you are going to work, have the intention that you are earning a halal means of living to sustain you and your family or when you exercise, have the intention that you wish to exercise so that you can be fitter to undertake the acts of worship, such as prayer, etc., better. Now, is this difficult to do? Certainly NOT! It is only *Shaytaan* who will prevent you from saying *Bismillah*, and yet by saying *Bismillah*, the *Shaytaan* will run away a mile!

Therefore, whatever you do in life, adapt your thought process to please Allah[SWT]. This is because whatever you do in life that pleases Allah[SWT] is considered an act of worship, and anything that displeases Allah is an act of sin. Allah[SWT] says: *"And I did not create the jinn and mankind except to worship Me."* **Quran 51:56.**

Schedule your day around your Salah, not the other way round

There is some wisdom in planning your daily schedule to incorporate the 5 daily prayers performed at their stipulated times. If you do this, then things will start to fall into place for your betterment. Whether you are working on a project for an extended period or about to embark on a journey, you must factor in your prayer time. Not only are you fulfilling the obligatory act of prayer, but Allah[SWT] will make your day full of *Barakah* (blessings).

The Prophet[P] said, *"Allah the exalted said, 'O son of Adam, free yourself from my worship (for some time), and I will fill your breast with contentment and put an end to your need. But if you do not do so, I will keep your hands ever busy and I will not put an end to your need."* **Tirmidhi.**

Wake up early

The first few hours of the morning after you awake are the most productive part of the day. Wake up early, and your hours will be blessed. The beloved Prophet[P] said, *"Allah has made the early hours blessed for my nation."* **Tirmidhi.** This means switching your lights off early to wake up early. You will find so many more blessings in your day. Never forget to start the day with *Fajr* prayers. Scientific studies show that those who get up early in the morning are the most successful ones, yet we Muslims get up to submit to Allah[SWT] at the beginning of the day. It is recommended to do your work in the early part of the day. There are many blessings in this, and you will achieve much more than you would by starting late. The Prophet[P] *said, "O Allah, bless my nation in their early mornings."* **Ibn Majah.**

Often, we neglect the *Fajr* prayer and *Isha* prayers because they are at the two extreme ends of the day and harder to do. Our beloved Prophet[P] *said, "No prayer is more burdensome to the hypocrites than the Fajr (dawn) prayer and the 'Isha' (night) prayer; and if they knew their merits, they would come to them even if they had to crawl to do so."* **Bukhari and Muslim.** So, perform these two prayers at their proper times.

Optimise Sleep

Getting the right amount of sleep can have a profound effect on your productivity, leaving you with more free time. Adequate sleep helps you with improved memory, improved mood, and clearer thinking. Additionally, there are numerous long-term benefits, including improved health, better weight control, and stronger immunity. However, avoid oversleeping, as this can have a detrimental impact on both your body and mind.

Try to make every effort to go to sleep after *Isha* as was the routine of our beloved Prophet Muhammad[P]. If you stay up late, you are sabotaging the next day.

Do not Multi-Task

The Prophet[P] had multiple roles in his life. He[P] was a father, husband, teacher, governor, friend, etc., but excelled at each one of those roles without exception. However, he[P] undertook one task at a time, giving complete focus, concentration, and attention on each task. For example, if he[P] were speaking or listening to someone, he would face them and give full attention. When he was with his family, he devoted his entire time to being in their presence.

One cannot focus and concentrate on doing two or more things at the same time. For example, you cannot speak to someone on the phone, but at the same time write an email. You cannot take an active part in a meeting and at the same time check your text messages on your smartphone. It is just not possible. Allah[SWT] did not make us this way. The Prophet[P] *said, "Allah loves whenever any of you does something, that he should perfect it."* **Tabarani.** If you consider multi-tasking as something where you go out to the shops to buy some items, but on the way, you visit your friend who lives near the shops, then that is okay – that is different.

Additionally, research indicates that multitasking can reduce productivity by up to 40%. Therefore, single-tasking is a *Sunnah*, doing each task with complete focus, attention, and dedication. If you do this, your tasks get the attention they deserve and get completed to their full potential.

In conclusion

Make time for Allah[SWT], and everything else will fall into place. Do it the other way round and you will never make time for Allah[SWT]. Make life management a priority, and time will work itself out. Do not rush to please everyone – you will become exhausted; instead, please Allah[SWT], and you will earn the respect, dignity, and honour of people through Allah's mercy.

Weigh up how much time we are spending pleasing Allah[SWT] and how much time we are spending displeasing Allah[SWT]. How much time do we spend doing things that neither benefit the *Akhirah* nor our *dunya*? How much of our time will we be glad to know, once we have died, and how much will we bitterly regret?

May Allah[SWT] give us all the *taufiq* to spend our time wisely and productively so that not only do we benefit in this *dunya* but also in the aak*hira.* Aameen.

The History and Background of the Four Schools of Thought in Islam

The four major schools of thought in Sunni Islam, known as the Madhabs, developed to provide guidance on interpreting Islamic law (Sharia). These schools are Hanafi, Maliki, Shafi'i, and Hanbali.

These schools provided the framework for Islamic legal thought and governance, shaping the religious and social practices of Muslim communities across the world.

The four major schools of thought in Sunni Islam, known as the **Madhabs**, developed to provide guidance on interpreting Islamic law (Sharia). These schools are the Hanafi, Maliki, Shafi'i, and Hanbali schools. They emerged from different regions and contexts within the Islamic world, each with distinct methodologies for interpreting the Quran, the Hadith (sayings and actions of the Prophet Muhammad), and other sources of Islamic jurisprudence.

The brief history and background of each of these schools

Imam **Abu Hanifa: History and Detailed Background**

Early Life and Education

Full Name: Nu'man ibn Thabit ibn Zuta ibn Marzuban

Birth: 699 CE in Kufa, Iraq

Death: 767 CE in Baghdad, Iraq

Imam Abu Hanifa was born into a prosperous merchant family in Kufa, a major centre of learning and commerce in the Islamic world at the time. His family was of Persian descent and had embraced Islam. Kufa, being a vibrant intellectual hub, exposed Abu Hanifa to various scholarly traditions and schools of thought from an early age.

Abu Hanifa initially followed his family's trade and was a successful silk merchant. However, his interest in religious studies grew, leading him to seek knowledge from various scholars in Kufa. He was particularly influenced by Hammad ibn Abi Sulayman, a leading jurist in Kufa, under whom he studied for 18 years.

Scholarly Contributions and Methodology

Imam Abu Hanifa's contributions to Islamic jurisprudence are profound and far-reaching. He is renowned for founding the **Hanafi school of thought**, the first of the four major Sunni schools of Islamic law.

Key Characteristics of His Methodology:

1. **Quran and *Sunnah***: Abu Hanifa prioritised the Quran and the Hadith (*Sunnah* of the Prophet Muhammad) as primary sources of law.

2. **Reason and Opinion (Ra'y)**: He made extensive use of reason and individual judgment (ra'y) when direct guidance from the Quran and Hadith was unavailable.

3. **Analogy (Qiyas)**: He employed analogy to extend principles from the Quran and Hadith to new situations.

4. **Consensus (Ijma)**: He respected the consensus of the early Muslim community and scholars.

5. **Istihsan (Juristic Preference)**: Abu Hanifa introduced the concept of istihsan, allowing jurists to opt for more equitable solutions in some instances where strict analogy might lead to unfair outcomes.

Challenges and Persecutions

Abu Hanifa's intellectual independence and prominence did not sit well with the political authorities of his time. He faced several challenges, particularly under the Umayyad and Abbasid Caliphates:

- **Refusal of Judicial Position**: Abu Hanifa was known for his integrity and independence. He famously refused the position of Qadi (judge) offered by the Umayyad Caliphate, fearing that it would compromise his impartiality. His refusal led to imprisonment and flogging.

- **Opposition to the Abbasid Caliphate**: Under the Abbasids, particularly Caliph al-Mansur, Abu Hanifa continued to face pressure. He was imprisoned again for refusing to support the Abbasid regime's policies and for his refusal to accept a judicial appointment, which he viewed as a potential conflict of interest.

Legacy

Imam Abu Hanifa's legacy is immense. He is credited with developing one of the most comprehensive and systematic schools of Islamic jurisprudence. The Hanafi school is characterised by its flexibility, rationality, and adaptability, making it widely adopted in various regions, including the Ottoman Empire, the Indian subcontinent, Central Asia, and parts of the Arab world.

Key Works:

- **Al-Fiqh al-Akbar**: A seminal work outlining the foundations of Islamic creed and theology.

- **Al-Musnad**: A collection of Hadiths narrated by Abu Hanifa, later compiled by his students.

- **Al-Fiqh al-Absat**: Another important theological work addressing various aspects of belief and doctrine.

Influence and Spread

The Hanafi school became the dominant legal school in the Abbasid Caliphate and later in the Ottoman Empire, due to its practical and inclusive approach. Abu Hanifa's emphasis on reason and adaptability contributed to the evolution of Islamic jurisprudence, enabling it to meet the needs of diverse societies.

Students and Followers

Imam Abu Hanifa trained many prominent scholars, including:

- **Abu Yusuf (Ya'qub ibn Ibrahim al-*Ansari*)**: His most famous student, who served as the Chief Judge (Qadi al-Qudat) under Caliph Harun al-Rashid.

- **Muhammad al-Shaybani**: Another key student who contributed significantly to the development and dissemination of Hanafi jurisprudence.

Through his students, Abu Hanifa's teachings were preserved and propagated, solidifying his school's influence in the Islamic world. His legacy endures as a testament to his intellectual rigour, ethical principles, and commitment to justice.

Imam Malik ibn Anas: History and Detailed Background

Early Life and Education

Full Name: Malik ibn Anas ibn Malik ibn Abi 'Amir al-Asbahi

Birth: 711 CE in Medina, Hejaz (modern-day Saudi Arabia)

Death: 795 CE in Medina, Hejaz

Imam Malik ibn Anas was born in Medina, the city which was the heart of Islamic learning and the residence of many companions of the Prophet Muhammad. His family had a long history of scholarship and devotion to the Islamic faith. His grandfather, Abu 'Amir, was a companion of the Prophet, and his family was deeply respected in Medina.

Education and Influences

From a young age, Malik showed a keen interest in learning. He studied under several renowned scholars of his time, particularly those who were direct students of the Prophet's companions. Some of his notable teachers included:

- **Rabi'ah ibn Abdurrahman (Rabi'ah al-Ra'y)**: Known for his rational approach to jurisprudence.

- **Nafi' Mawla Ibn 'Umar**: A freed slave of Abdullah ibn 'Umar, who narrated many hadiths from Ibn 'Umar, a prominent companion of the Prophet.

- **Zayd ibn Aslam**: A scholar who also narrated hadiths from several companions.

Malik's education in Medina, a city with a rich tradition of hadith transmission, deeply influenced his approach to Islamic jurisprudence.

Scholarly Contributions and Methodology

Imam Malik's contributions to Islamic jurisprudence are most notably encapsulated in the Maliki school of thought. His methodology and principles are distinct and highly respected.

Key Characteristics of His Methodology:

1. **Reliance on the Practices of Medina (Amal Ahl al-Madina)**: Malik gave significant importance to the practices of the people of Medina, considering them as living traditions that closely followed the actions of the Prophet Muhammad.

2. **Hadith and *Sunnah***: He extensively used hadiths (sayings and actions of the Prophet) as primary sources of law.

3. **Consensus (Ijma)**: The consensus of the scholars of Medina played a crucial role in Malik's jurisprudence.

4. **Public Interest (Maslahah Mursalah)**: Malik allowed for the consideration of public welfare in making legal decisions, which made his jurisprudence practical and flexible.

5. **Less Reliance on Analogy (Qiyas)**: Compared to the Hanafi school, Malik used analogy less frequently, preferring direct evidence from the Quran, *Sunnah*, and the practices of the people of Medina.

Major Works:

- **Al-Muwatta**: Malik's most famous work, which is one of the earliest and most authoritative collections of hadiths and legal principles. It is highly respected across all Sunni schools of thought and remains a crucial text for understanding early Islamic law and practice.

Challenges and Persecutions

Imam Malik's commitment to his principles occasionally brought him into conflict with the political authorities:

- **Persecution by the Abbasids**: Malik's stance on specific issues, such as his support for the legitimacy of the descendants of the Prophet's family over the Abbasids, led to tensions with the ruling authorities. He was reportedly flogged for his refusal to conform to specific political pressures.

Despite these challenges, Malik remained a highly respected figure, and his teachings continued to spread.

Legacy

Imam Malik's influence is vast and enduring. The Maliki school of thought, characterised by its reliance on the practices of Medina and its consideration of public interest, became widely adopted in various regions, including North and West Africa, parts of Egypt, and Andalusia (Spain).

Key Contributions:

- **Al-Muwatta**: As a pioneering compilation of hadith and jurisprudence, it laid the foundation for later Islamic legal works.

- **Promotion of Medina's Practices**: By emphasising the practices of the people of Medina, Malik provided a direct link to the Prophet's traditions, preserving the early Islamic ethos.

Influence and Spread

The Maliki school spread widely due to its practical approach to jurisprudence and the respect it commanded among scholars and rulers. In North Africa and Andalusia, the Maliki school became the dominant legal tradition, shaping the legal and cultural landscape of these regions.

Students and Followers

Imam Malik taught numerous students who later became prominent scholars themselves, ensuring the transmission of his methodologies and teachings. Some of his notable students included:

- **Al-Shafi'i (Muhammad ibn Idris al-Shafi'i)**: Founder of the Shafi'i school of thought, who studied under Malik and was greatly influenced by him.

- **Ibn al-Qasim**: A key transmitter of Malik's teachings in Egypt.

- **Sahnun ibn Sa'id**: His work "Al-Mudawwana" became a foundational text for Maliki jurisprudence.

Through his students and their writings, Malik's teachings continued to be studied and respected, solidifying his legacy as one of the great *Imam*s of Sunni Islam.

Imam Muhammad ibn Idris al-Shafi'i: History and Detailed Background

Early Life and Education

Full Name: Muhammad ibn Idris al-Shafi'i

Birth: 767 CE in Gaza, Palestine

Death: 820 CE in Fustat, Egypt

Imam al-Shafi'i was born in Gaza, but he moved to Mecca at a young age after the death of his father. His mother, who belonged to a noble Yemeni tribe, ensured he received a good education despite their modest means. Growing up in Mecca, a significant centre for Islamic learning, he memorised the Quran by the age of seven and was recognised for his prodigious intellect and memory.

Education and Influences

Al-Shafi'i's pursuit of knowledge took him to various centres of learning where he studied under some of the most prominent scholars of his time:

- **Malik ibn Anas:** Al-Shafi'i travelled to Medina to study under *Imam* Malik, where he memorised Malik's famous work, Al-Muwatta, and became deeply influenced by Malik's methodologies.

- **Muhammad ibn al-Hasan al-Shaybani:** In Iraq, al-Shafi'i studied under al-Shaybani, a leading disciple of Abu Hanifa, which exposed him to the Hanafi school of thought and its emphasis on reason and analogy.

- **Other Scholars:** He also interacted with and learned from other scholars in Yemen and Egypt, absorbing a diverse range of jurisprudential views.

Scholarly Contributions and Methodology

Imam al-Shafi'i is renowned for founding the Shafi'i school of thought, one of the four major Sunni schools of Islamic jurisprudence. His contributions significantly shaped Islamic legal theory and practice.

Key Characteristics of His Methodology:

1. Systematisation of Usul al-Fiqh: Al-Shafi'i is credited with developing the principles of Islamic jurisprudence *(usul al-fiqh)* into a coherent and systematic discipline. His work, Al-Risala, is the first to codify these principles, making a clear distinction between sources of law and their hierarchical order.

2. Sources of Law:

    - Quran: The primary and most authoritative source.

    - *Sunnah*: The practices and sayings of the Prophet Muhammad, which he emphasised, should be authentically verified.

    - Ijma (Consensus): The agreement of the Muslim community or scholars on a particular issue.

    - Qiyas (Analogy): The application of principles derived from the Quran and *Sunnah* to new situations through analogical reasoning.

3. Reconciliation of Differences: Al-Shafi'i sought to reconcile the differing methodologies of the Hanafi and Maliki schools by finding a balanced approach that respected both textual evidence and rational deduction.

Major Works

- Al-Risala: This foundational text on *usul al-fiqh* outlines the principles of Islamic jurisprudence and establishes the framework for deriving legal rulings.

- Kitab al-Umm: A comprehensive work covering various aspects of Islamic law, it reflects al-Shafi'i's mature legal opinions and methodologies.

Challenges and Persecutions

Throughout his life, *Imam* al-Shafi'i faced various challenges, including political opposition and imprisonment:

- Political Persecution: During his time in Yemen, al-Shafi'i was accused of supporting the Alawites and was imprisoned by the Abbasid authorities. He was later released due to the intercession of influential supporters.

- Scholarly Debates: Al-Shafi'i engaged in numerous debates with scholars from other schools, defending his methodologies and refining his legal theories. These debates helped to clarify and strengthen his positions.

Legacy

Imam al-Shafi'i's influence on Islamic jurisprudence is profound and enduring. The Shafi'i school of thought is characterised by its balanced approach, rigorous methodology, and systematic framework for interpreting Islamic law.

Key Contributions:

- Systematisation of Jurisprudence: By codifying the principles of Islamic jurisprudence, al-Shafi'i provided a clear and structured approach to legal reasoning, which became the foundation for subsequent legal theory.

- Integration of Hadith: His emphasis on authentic hadith as a primary source of law strengthened the role of prophetic traditions in Islamic jurisprudence.

Influence and Spread

The Shafi'i school spread widely due to its intellectual rigour and practical approach. It became the dominant legal school in various regions, including:

- Egypt: Al-Shafi'i spent his final years in Egypt, where his teachings gained a strong following and became deeply embedded in the local legal tradition.

- East Africa: The school spread to the coastal regions through trade and scholarly exchange.

- Southeast Asia: The Shafi'i school became the predominant legal tradition in countries such as Indonesia, Malaysia, and Brunei.

Students and Followers

Imam al-Shafi'i taught numerous students who carried forward his legacy and disseminated his teachings:

- Al-Muzani: A key disciple who authored important commentaries on al-Shafi'i's works.

- Al-Rabi' ibn Sulayman al-Muradi: One of his close companions who played a significant role in preserving and transmitting his teachings.

Through his students and their writings, al-Shafi'i's methodologies and principles continued to shape Islamic legal thought, ensuring his lasting impact on the Muslim world. His legacy is celebrated for bringing clarity, structure, and a balanced approach to the interpretation and application of Islamic law.

Imam Ahmad ibn Hanbal: History and Detailed Background

Early Life and Education

Full Name: Ahmad ibn Muhammad ibn Hanbal Abu 'Abd Allah al-Shaybani

Birth: 780 CE in Baghdad, Iraq

Death: 855 CE in Baghdad, Iraq

Imam Ahmad ibn Hanbal was born in Baghdad, the capital of the Abbasid Caliphate and a prominent centre of learning and culture. His family was of Arab origin, belonging to the Banu Shayban tribe. Ahmad's father died when he was young, and his mother raised him. His early education began in Baghdad, where he showed a keen interest in religious studies.

Education and Influences

Imam Ahmad's pursuit of knowledge led him to travel extensively in search of hadith and legal expertise. He studied under numerous scholars, accumulating a vast collection of hadith and deepening his understanding of Islamic jurisprudence.

Key Teachers:

- Hushaym ibn Bashir: One of the early scholars from whom Ahmad learned hadith.

- Sufyan ibn 'Uyaynah: A renowned hadith scholar in Mecca.

- Abdur-Razzaq as-San'ani: A prominent hadith collector in Yemen.

- *Imam* al-Shafi'i: Ahmad studied under al-Shafi'i in Baghdad and was significantly influenced by his teacher's methodologies in jurisprudence.

Imam Ahmad's commitment to seeking knowledge was evident in his travels to major Islamic centres like Mecca, Medina, Kufa, Basra, and Yemen.

Scholarly Contributions and Methodology

Imam Ahmad's contributions to Islamic jurisprudence are foundational, laying the groundwork for the establishment of the Hanbali school of thought, which is renowned for its strict adherence to textual sources.

Key Characteristics of His Methodology:

1. Primacy of the Quran and *Sunnah*: Ahmad placed paramount importance on the Quran and authentic hadiths as the primary sources of Islamic law.

2. Rejection of Analogy (Qiyas) and Opinion (Ra'y): He was cautious in using analogy and rejected the extensive use of personal opinion, preferring direct evidence from the texts.

3. Consensus (Ijma): He accepted the consensus of the early Muslim community (Sahaba) but was sceptical of claims of consensus in later generations.

4. Rejection of Innovations (Bid'ah): Ahmad was a staunch opponent of religious innovations, emphasising adherence to the practices of the Prophet and his companions.

Major Works:

- Musnad Ahmad ibn Hanbal: One of the most extensive collections of hadith, comprising over 30,000 narrations. This work is highly regarded for its comprehensive compilation of prophetic traditions.

Challenges and Persecutions

Imam Ahmad ibn Hanbal's life was marked by significant trials, especially during the Abbasid Caliphate's Mihna (Inquisition) under Caliph al-Ma'mun, al-Mu'tasim, and al-Wathiq.

- Mihna (Inquisition): The Abbasid Caliphs, influenced by the Mu'tazilite school of thought, enforced the doctrine that the Quran was created. Ahmad's refusal to accept this doctrine led to his imprisonment and torture.

- Staunch Defence of Orthodoxy: Despite severe persecution, Ahmad remained steadfast in his belief that the Quran was uncreated, viewing this as a matter of orthodoxy. His resilience earned him great respect and solidified his status as a defender of traditional Islamic beliefs.

Legacy

Imam Ahmad's legacy is profound and enduring. His strict adherence to the Quran and *Sunnah*, as well as his opposition to religious innovations, shaped the Hanbali school of thought, characterised by its conservative and text-based approach.

Key Contributions:

- Musnad Ahmad: His hadith collection remains a vital source for Islamic scholars.

- Development of Hanbali Jurisprudence: Ahmad's principles laid the foundation for the Hanbali school, emphasising textual evidence over speculative reasoning.

Influence and Spread

The Hanbali school, though initially less widespread compared to the Hanafi, Maliki, and Shafi'i schools, became influential in various regions, particularly:

- Arabian Peninsula: The Hanbali school gained prominence in Najd and later in the Hijaz.

- Modern Influence: The school experienced a resurgence with the rise of the Wahhabi movement in the 18th century, which adopted Hanbali principles and had a significant influence on contemporary Saudi Arabia.

Students and Followers

Imam Ahmad's teachings were preserved and disseminated by his numerous students, who played a crucial role in the spread of Hanbali jurisprudence:

- Ibn Hanbal's Sons: His sons, Salih and Abdullah, played a significant role in preserving his works and teachings.

- Al-Khallal: A key student who compiled and organised Hanbali jurisprudence.

- Ibn Qudamah: A later Hanbali scholar who wrote critical legal texts, such as "Al-Mughni," that became central to Hanbali *Fiqh*.

Final Years and Death

Imam Ahmad spent his final years in Baghdad, continuing to teach and compile hadith until he died in 855 CE. He was buried in Baghdad, and his funeral was attended by a large number of people, reflecting the deep respect and admiration he commanded within the Muslim community.

Imam Ahmad ibn Hanbal's commitment to Islamic orthodoxy, his vast knowledge of hadith, and his principled stance during the Mihna left an indelible mark on Islamic history. His legacy continues to influence Islamic thought and practice, particularly within the Hanbali school of thought.

The development of these schools was not an isolated process; scholars from different schools often interacted, debated, and influenced one another. Over time, the schools established distinct methodologies, but they also shared standard foundations in the Quran and the *Sunnah* (the traditions of the Prophet). These schools provided the framework for Islamic legal thought and governance, shaping the religious and social practices of Muslim communities across the world.

Translation, Tafsir, and Summary of the Last 15 Surahs in the Quran

The last 15 Surahs of the Quran are all short chapters that are rich in spiritual guidance, offering moral and ethical teachings, reminders of God's majesty, and instructions for righteous living. These Surahs, revealed mostly in Mecca, reflect the early period of the Islamic message and emphasise core themes like monotheism, divine justice, and the afterlife.

The last 15 Surahs of the Quran are all short chapters that are rich in spiritual guidance, offering moral and ethical teachings, reminders of God's majesty, and instructions for righteous living. These Surahs, mainly revealed in Mecca, reflect the early period of the Islamic message and emphasise core themes like monotheism, divine justice, and the afterlife.

Below is an English translation of these Surahs, along with brief Tafsir (interpretation) and summaries.

1. Surah Al-Fil (The Elephant) - Surah 105

Translation:

1. Have you not seen how your Lord dealt with the owners of the elephant?

2. Did He not make their plot go astray?

3. And He sent against them birds, in flocks,

4. Striking them with stones of baked clay.

5. And He made them like eaten straw.

Tafsir: This Surah refers to the event of the Year of the Elephant, when the Abyssinian King Abraha attempted to destroy the Kaaba in Mecca. Allah protected the Kaaba by sending flocks of birds that pelted Abraha's army with stones, causing their defeat. The Surah serves as a reminder of God's power and His protection over His sacred house.

Summary: Surah Al-Fil recounts a miraculous event where God's intervention saved the Kaaba from destruction, highlighting His protection over what is sacred and serving as a warning to those who plot against it.

2. Surah Quraysh (The Tribe of Quraysh) - Surah 106

Translation:

1. For the accustomed security of the Quraysh—

2. Their security during their journeys in the winter and the summer—

3. Let them worship the Lord of this House,

4. Who has fed them, [saving them] from hunger and made them safe from fear.

Tafsir: This Surah addresses the tribe of Quraysh, the custodians of the Kaaba. It reminds them of the blessings they enjoy, such as safety and prosperity, due to their association with the Kaaba. The Surah calls on them to worship Allah, who has provided for them and protected them.

Summary: Surah Quraysh emphasises the blessings that the tribe of Quraysh receives from Allah due to their role as guardians of the Kaaba and calls on them to worship the one true God who provides for their needs.

3. Surah Al-Ma'un (Small Kindnesses) - Surah 107

Translation:

1. Have you seen the one who denies the Recompense?

2. For that is the one who drives away the orphan

3. And does not encourage the feeding of people experiencing poverty.

4. So woe to those who pray,

5. But are heedless of their prayer—

6. Those who make a show [of their deeds]

7. And withhold [simple] assistance.

Tafsir: This Surah condemns those who neglect their social responsibilities and only perform religious duties for show. It criticises those who deny the Day of Judgment, mistreat orphans, and refuse to help people in need, emphasising the importance of sincerity in faith and actions.

Summary: Surah Al-Ma'un highlights the hypocrisy of those who perform religious rituals for show while neglecting their duties towards others, particularly orphans and people in need, emphasising that true faith involves sincere actions.

4. Surah Al-Kawthar (The Abundance) - Surah 108

Translation:

1. Indeed, We have granted you, [O Muhammad], al-Kawthar.

2. So pray to your Lord and sacrifice [to Him alone].

3. Indeed, your enemy is the one cut off.

Tafsir: Al-Kawthar is interpreted as a river in Paradise or a symbol of the abundant blessings bestowed upon the Prophet Muhammad. The Surah instructs the Prophet to remain devoted in worship and sacrifice, assuring him that his opponents will be cut off from all good.

Summary: Surah Al-Kawthar is a message of reassurance to the Prophet Muhammad, promising him abundant blessings and affirming that his detractors will be the ones who are truly deprived.

5. Surah Al-Kafirun (The Disbelievers) - Surah 109

Translation:

1. Say, "O disbelievers,

2. I do not worship what you worship.

3. Nor are you worshippers of what I worship.

4. Nor will I be a worshipper of what you worship.

5. Nor will you be worshippers of what I worship.

6.   For you is your religion, and for me is my religion."

Tafsir: This surah emphasises the clear distinction between the beliefs of Muslims and those of disbelievers. It asserts that there is no compromise in matters of faith and that each group will follow their own path without interference.

Summary: Surah Al-Kafirun serves as a declaration of the distinct religious identity of Muslims, rejecting any form of syncretism with disbelievers and affirming mutual non-interference in matters of faith.

6. Surah An-Nasr (The Divine Help) - Surah 110

Translation:

1.   When the victory of Allah has come and the conquest,

2.   And you see the people entering into the religion of Allah in multitudes,

3.   Then exalt [Him] with praise of your Lord and ask forgiveness of Him. Indeed, He is ever accepting of repentance.

Tafsir: This Surah was revealed near the end of the Prophet Muhammad's life, foretelling the victory of Islam and the conquest of Mecca. It instructs the Prophet to praise Allah and seek His forgiveness as his mission nears completion, emphasising humility and gratitude in the face of success.

Summary: Surah An-Nasr predicts the triumph of Islam and instructs the Prophet to continue in worship and repentance, emphasising that even in victory, humility before Allah is paramount.

7. Surah Al-Masad (The Palm Fibre) - Surah 111

Translation:

1.   May the hands of Abu Lahab be ruined, and ruined is he.

2.   His wealth will not avail him or that which he gained.

3.   He will [enter to] burn in a Fire of [blazing] flame,

4.   And his wife [as well]—the carrier of firewood.

5.   Around her neck is a rope of [twisted] fibre.

Tafsir: This Surah condemns Abu Lahab, an uncle of the Prophet who was a staunch opponent of Islam, along with his wife. Despite his wealth and status, Abu Lahab is doomed to punishment in the Hereafter, a sign that opposition to God's message leads to destruction.

Summary: Surah Al-Masad serves as a stern warning to those who oppose the message of Islam, using Abu Lahab and his wife as examples of the ultimate failure and punishment awaiting such individuals.

8. Surah Al-Ikhlas (The Purity) - Surah 112

Translation:

1. Say, "He is Allah, [Who is] One,

2. Allah, the Eternal Refuge.

3. He neither begets nor is born,

4. Nor is there to Him any equivalent."

Tafsir: This Surah is a profound declaration of the oneness and uniqueness of Allah. It refutes any notion of God having a son, parents, or equals. It encapsulates the core of Islamic monotheism and is often recited in prayers.

Summary: Surah Al-Ikhlas is a concise and powerful affirmation of Allah's absolute oneness, rejecting any form of polytheism and emphasising that God is unique and incomparable.

9. Surah Al-Falaq (The Daybreak) - Surah 113

Translation:

1. Say, "I seek refuge in the Lord of daybreak

2. From the evil of that which He created

3. And from the evil of darkness when it settles

4. And from the evil of the blowers in knots

5. And from the evil of an envier when he envies."

Tafsir: This Surah is a prayer for protection against various forms of evil, including those arising from creation, darkness, witchcraft, and envy. It emphasises the need for divine protection from harm and ill-intent in all its forms.

Summary: Surah Al-Falaq teaches believers to seek refuge in Allah from the dangers and evils that may affect them, whether they come from nature, darkness, magic, or the envy of others.

10. Surah An-Nas (The Mankind) - Surah 114

Translation:

1. Say, "I seek refuge in the Lord of mankind,

2. The Sovereign of mankind.

3. The God of mankind,

4. From the evil of the whisperer who withdraws—

5. Who whispers in the breasts of mankind—

6. Among jinn and men."

Tafsir: This Surah is another prayer for protection, specifically from the whispers of Satan and evil influences that can affect the hearts and minds of people. It underscores Allah's role as the protector of all humanity from spiritual harm.

Summary: Surah An-Nas is a plea for protection from the evil whispers of Satan and other harmful influences, reinforcing the need for seeking refuge in Allah, the ultimate protector of humanity.

11. Surah Al-Takathur (The Rivalry for Worldly Gain) - Surah 102

Translation:

1. The mutual rivalry for piling up [the good things of this world] diverts you [from the more serious things],

2. Until you visit the graves.

3. But no, you will soon know [the reality].

4. Again, you will soon know!

5. No, if you only knew with knowledge of certainty...

6. You will surely see the Hellfire!

7. Then you will surely see it with the eye of certainty.

8. Then, on that Day, you shall be asked about the delight [you indulged in, in this world].

Tafsir: This Surah warns against the distraction of accumulating worldly wealth and status. It reminds believers that life's true purpose is often forgotten in the pursuit of material gains, and that ultimately, everyone will be held accountable in the afterlife for how they used their blessings.

Summary: Surah Al-Takathur serves as a reminder that the pursuit of worldly gains can lead to negligence of the Hereafter, warning that everyone will be questioned about their indulgences on the Day of Judgment.

12. Surah Al-Asr (The Declining Day) - Surah 103

Translation:

1. By time,

2. Indeed, mankind is in loss,

3. Except for those who have believed and done righteous deeds and advised each other to the truth and advised each other to patience.

Tafsir: This short Surah highlights the importance of time and the fact that most people are wasting it. It outlines the four criteria for success: faith, righteous deeds, truthfulness, and patience. These qualities are essential for salvation and success in the Hereafter.

Summary: Surah Al-Asr emphasises the fleeting nature of time and urges believers to live a life of faith, good deeds, truthfulness, and patience to avoid being among those who are in loss.

13. Surah Al-Humazah (The Slanderer) - Surah 104

Translation:

1. Woe to every scorner and mocker,

2. Who collects wealth and [continuously] counts it.

3. He thinks that his wealth will make him immortal.

4. No! He will surely be thrown into the Crusher.

5. And what can make you know what is the Crusher?

6. It is the fire of Allah, [eternally] fueled,

7. Which mounts are directed at the heart.

8. Indeed, it [Hellfire] will be closed down upon them

9. In extended columns.

Tafsir: This Surah condemns those who indulge in slander and backbiting, and who amass wealth thinking it will protect them from death. It warns of a severe punishment in the Hereafter, where such people will be thrown into Hell, described here as the "Crusher," a fire that will crush their hearts.

Summary: Surah Al-Humazah warns against the evils of slander, mockery, and excessive love of wealth, emphasising that these behaviours lead to severe punishment in the afterlife.

14. Surah Al-Mutaffifin (The Defrauders) - Surah 83

Translation:

1. Woe to those who give less [than due],

2. Who, when they take a measure from people, take in full.

3. But if they give by measure or by weight, they cause loss.

4. Do they not think that they will be resurrected

5. For a tremendous Day—

6. The Day when mankind will stand before the Lord of the worlds?

7. No! Indeed, the record of the wicked is in sijjin.

8. And what can make you know what is sijjin?

9. It is their destination written.

10. Woe, that Day, to the deniers,

11. Who deny the Day of Recompense.

12. And none deny it except every sinful transgressor.

13. When Our verses are recited to him, he says, "Legends of the former peoples."

14. No! Rather, the stain has covered their hearts of that which they were earning.

15. No! Indeed, from their Lord, that Day, they will be partitioned.

16. Then indeed, they will [enter and] burn in Hellfire.

17. Then it will be said [to them], "This is what you used to deny."

18. No! Indeed, the record of the righteous is in 'illiyyun.

19. And what can make you know what is 'illiyyun?

20. It is their destination written.

21. The righteous will be in gardens [of Paradise],

22. On adorned couches, observing.

23. You will recognise in their faces the radiance of pleasure.

24. They will be given to drink [pure] wine [which was] sealed.

25. The last of it is musk. So, for this, let the competitors compete.

26. And its mixture is of Tasneem,

27. A spring from which those near to Allah drink.

28. Indeed, those who committed crimes used to laugh at those who believed in them.

29. And when they passed by them, they would exchange derisive glances.

30. And when they returned to their people, they would return jesting.

31. And when they saw them, they would say, "Indeed, those are truly lost."

32. But they had not been sent as guardians over them.

33. So Today those who believed are laughing at the disbelievers,

34. On adorned couches, observing.

35. Have the disbelievers not been rewarded [this Day] for what they used to do?

Tafsir: This Surah denounces those who cheat others in trade by giving less than due. It reminds them of the Day of Judgment, when all will be held accountable for their actions. It contrasts the fate of the wicked, who will be punished in Hell, with that of the righteous, who will enjoy the delights of Paradise.

Summary: Surah Al-Mutaffifin condemns dishonest trade practices and warns of the dire consequences in the Hereafter for those who defraud others, contrasting the punishments awaiting the wicked with the rewards for the righteous.

15. Surah Al-Inshiqaq (The Splitting) - Surah 84

Translation:

1. When the sky has split [open]

2. And has listened to its Lord and was obligated [to do so]

3. And when the earth has been extended

4. And has cast out that within it and relinquished it.

5. And has listened to its Lord and was obligated [to do so]—

6. O mankind, indeed you are labouring toward your Lord with [great] exertion and will meet it.

7. Then as for he who is given his record in his right hand,

8. He will be judged with an easy account

9. And return to his people in happiness.

10. But as for he who is given his record behind his back,

11. He will cry out for destruction

12. And [enter to] burn in a Blaze.

13. Indeed, he had [once] been among his people in happiness;

14. Indeed, he had thought he would never return [to Allah].

15. But yes! Indeed, his Lord was ever of him, Seeing.

16. So I swear by the twilight glow

17. And [by] the night and what it envelops

18. And [by] the moon when it becomes full

19. [That] you will surely embark upon [state] after [state].

20. So what is [the matter] with them [that] they do not believe,

21. And when the Qur'an is recited to them, they do not prostrate [to Allah]?

22. But those who have disbelieved deny,

23. And Allah is most knowing of what they keep within themselves.

24. So give them tidings of a painful punishment,

25. Except for those who believe and do righteous deeds. For them is a reward uninterrupted.

Tafsir: This Surah describes the events of the Day of Judgment, when the *Heavens* and the earth will obey God's command and reveal what has been hidden within them. It speaks of the different fates awaiting those who receive their records in their right hand (the righteous) versus those who receive them behind their backs (the wicked). It emphasises the inevitability of the Day of Judgment and the need for faith and righteous deeds.

Summary: Surah Al-Inshiqaq vividly describes the signs of the Day of Judgment and the consequences for the righteous and the wicked, urging humanity to believe in God and prepare for the inevitable meeting with Him.

Zakat – The Third Pillar of Islam

"My mercy encompasses all things, but I will specify it for the righteous who give Zakat."

Quran 7:156

"If somebody gives in charity something equal to a date from his honestly earned money – for nothing ascends to Allah except good – then Allah will take it in His right (hand) and bring it up for its owner as anyone of you brings up a baby horse, till it becomes as big as a mountain."

Bukhari

Islam is not just a religion but a complete way of life that acts as a guide for us Muslims and encourages us to walk on the path of peace, mercy, and forgiveness. Among the five pillars of Islam that frame the Muslim life, concern for the needy is extremely important.

Zakat is often translated as "almsgiving" or "charity," but it has a broader meaning and significance within Islam. According to Islamic principles, all things belong to Allah[SWT], and human beings are entrusted with wealth as a responsibility. The word Zakat means 'purification' and 'growth'. Our possessions are purified when we give a portion to those in need, and this act of giving balances and encourages new growth in our economy.

Zakat is one of the Five Pillars of Islam, a mandatory act of charity central to Islamic economics and social justice. It is a form of financial worship that requires Muslims to give a specific portion of their wealth to those in need, thereby purifying wealth, fostering social welfare, and reducing inequality within the community. Hence, by giving Zakat, a Muslim purifies their wealth and encourages personal and communal prosperity.

In essence, Zakat is a form of obligatory charity that Muslims are required to pay if they meet specific criteria. It is a means of purifying one's wealth and helping those in need. A generous person may also give as much as they please as 'Sadaqa' and is encouraged to give it away in secret, because when we give Zakat, it is only to please Allah[SWT] and not to show off or to gain status.

The intention–niyyah, to pay Zakat, must be made before giving it with a sincere heart, purely for the sake of Allah.

The purpose of Zakat is both spiritual and social

1. **Spiritual Purification:** By giving Zakat, a person purifies their heart from greed and selfishness, and their wealth from potential impurity. It promotes selflessness and humility.

2. **Economic Redistribution:** Zakat facilitates the redistribution of wealth in society, ensuring that the less fortunate have access to resources and that wealth is not concentrated in the hands of a few.

3. **Social Solidarity:** Zakat strengthens bonds between different segments of society, fostering a spirit of solidarity and cooperation, as the wealthy support the less fortunate.

Zakat helps maintain economic balance and purifies our wealth as it redistributes it from the rich to the poor, stabilises the financial condition of society, and ensures that each person benefits from the wealth. The rich people have to pay zakat so that differences and gaps between the rich and the poor are reduced, and this way we can guarantee human rights for all. The Zakat helps shape the character of the wealthy by saving them from greed and selfishness, and establishes the concepts of brotherhood and unity.

Wealth is usually earned individually by hard work and intense dedication. So, when we give or share even a small portion of this, it reflects our firm faith in Allah. It makes us realise what is provided by the Grace of Allah and what we spend. Allah is pleased with those who spend happily in His cause.

Beyond its material benefits, Zakat holds significant spiritual and social importance in Islam. By giving Zakat, Muslims fulfil a religious obligation and demonstrate their commitment to social justice and solidarity within the Muslim community. It serves as a reminder to Muslims of their responsibility to assist those less fortunate and contribute to the overall welfare of society.

The vital importance of Zakat is reflected in this verse of the Quran: *"My mercy encompasses all things, but I will specify it for the righteous who give Zakat."* **Quran 7:156.**

Important Aspects of Zakat

1. **Obligatory Charity**: Zakat is considered one of the five pillars of Islam, alongside Shahada (the profession of faith), Salat (prayer), Sawm (fasting), and *Hajj* (pilgrimage). It is obligatory for Muslims who meet the criteria to give a portion of their wealth to those in need.

2. **Calculation**: Zakat is typically calculated as 2.5% of a Muslim's total wealth, including savings, investments, gold, and silver, after deducting expenses such as debt and essential necessities. Certain assets, such as livestock and agricultural produce, will have different Zakat rates.

3. **Recipients**: Zakat is primarily meant for specific categories of recipients, as outlined in the Quran. Allah^SWT says: *"Zakat expenditures are only for the poor and for the needy and for those employed to collect [zakat] and for bringing hearts together [for Islam] and for freeing captives [or slaves] and for those in debt and the cause of Allah and for the [stranded] traveller - an obligation [imposed] by Allah. And Allah is Knowing and Wise."* **Quran 9:60.**

The categories outlined in the above verse consist of:

1. The Poor - *Al-Fuqara* - Individuals with low income or those experiencing poverty.
2. The Needy - *Al-Masakin* - Those facing financial difficulties and in need of assistance.
3. Those administering Zakat-*Al-Amilin* are designated individuals entrusted with the responsibility of collecting and disbursing Zakat.
4. Bringing Hearts Together - *Al-Muallaf* - Signifies friends of the Islamic community and/or newly converted Muslims.
5. To free those in bondage - Ar-*Riqab* - Encompasses individuals held involuntarily in captivity or slavery.
6. Those in debt, such as *Al-Gharmin*, represent those grappling with overwhelming debts and financial burdens.
7. In Allah's cause – F*isabillillah*- "In Allah's cause" refers to those who actively strive for the cause of Allah^SWT.
8. The stranded traveller – The traveller or wayfarer, facing adversity or being stranded.

In essence, these categories include the poor, the needy, those in debt, travellers, and those working to collect and distribute Zakat.

4. **Purpose**: Zakat serves several purposes within Islamic society. It aims to purify the wealth of the affluent, remind believers of their obligations to the less fortunate, foster a sense of social responsibility and solidarity, and ultimately contribute to the welfare and cohesion of the Muslim community.

5. **Collection and Distribution**: Historically, Zakat was collected and distributed by the state or Islamic authorities. In modern times, it is often managed by charitable organisations or individual Muslims who distribute it directly to those in need or through established channels.

6. **Paying Zakat**

   The obligation of paying Zakat, as mentioned in the Quran, does not apply to every Muslim. Zakat is binding on:

   - Muslim adults (who have reached the age of puberty)
   - Those sane of mind
   - Those in complete ownership of the *Nisab*

7. **Timing**

   Zakat is typically due annually, calculated based on a lunar calendar. Many Muslims choose to pay Zakat during the month of *Ramadan*, as the rewards for charitable acts are believed to be multiplied during this holiest month. It is important to calculate the assets and liabilities at the same time each lunar year.

8. **Spiritual Significance**

   Beyond its material impact, Zakat holds immense spiritual significance in Islam. It is seen as an act of worship and obedience to Allah[SWT], a means of spiritual purification, and a way to demonstrate gratitude for one's blessings.

9. **Rewards and Benefits**

   In addition to the tangible benefits of Zakat, there are profound spiritual rewards. The Quran and Hadith emphasise the blessings and merits of giving charity, elevating the status of the giver, and instilling a sense of contentment and gratitude.

   - Spiritual Purification: Purifies the soul and strengthens faith.
   - Social Solidarity: Fosters community bonds and empathy.
   - Alleviates Poverty: Effectively addresses economic disparities.
   - Empowers the Needy: Enables self-sufficiency.
   - Social Cohesion: Strengthens bonds within the Muslim community.
   - Barakah (Blessings): Brings prosperity and protection.
   - Forgiveness of Sins: Seeks forgiveness and spiritual growth.
   - Protection: Safeguards wealth from misfortunes.
   - Reward in the Hereafter: Earns blessings and Allah's pleasure.
   - Building a Just Society: Promotes social justice and fairness.

Overall, Zakat embodies the Islamic principles of compassion, justice, and social equity, playing a vital role in fostering a caring and supportive community where wealth is shared to ensure the well-being of all members.

10. **Calculating Zakat**

Below is a detailed guide on what assets and wealth to include and exclude:

Assets to Include:

1. **Cash and Bank Balances**: Include all cash in hand, as well as balances in checking, savings, and other bank accounts.
2. **Gold and Silver**: Include the market value of all gold and silver owned, whether in the form of jewellery, coins, or bullion.
3. **Stocks and Investments**: Include the market value of shares, stocks, bonds, and other investments. If you own a business, include the stock-in-trade and business inventory.
4. **Receivables**: Include any money owed to you that you are confident will be repaid. This includes personal loans and business receivables.
5. **Rental Income**: Include the income from rental properties. However, the property itself is not subject to Zakat; only the revenue generated from it is.
6. **Pension Funds**: Include accessible pension funds and retirement accounts. If the funds are not accessible without penalty, they may not need to be included until they become accessible.

Assets to Exclude:

1. **Primary Residence**: Exclude the home where you live, as it is considered a basic necessity.
2. **Personal Belongings**: Exclude personal items such as clothing, household furniture, utensils, and vehicles used for personal transportation.
3. **Non-Income Generating Property**: Exclude properties that do not generate income, such as a second home or land held for personal use.
4. **Debts**: Subtract any debts you owe from your total assets. This includes loans, credit card balances, and other personal debts.
5. **Non-Zakatable Investments**: Exclude investments that are not generating income and cannot be liquidated, such as non-dividend-paying stocks in a retirement account with penalties for early withdrawal.

By correctly identifying which assets to include and exclude, and accurately calculating your net wealth, you can fulfil your Zakat obligation per Islamic principles.

11. **Nisab Threshold:** Zakat is only obligatory if your total wealth and assets exceed the Nisab, which is the minimum amount of wealth one must have before one is liable to pay Zakat. The Nisab, which was set by our beloved Prophet[p] at the rate equivalent to the value of 87.48 grams of gold or 612.36 grams of silver. The exact amount can vary based on the current market value of gold and silver.

If one does not know any needy person, they may give the Zakat to a mosque or charitable organisation with the distinct purpose of helping the poor and sick.

When giving charity, we must be humble and never act as if we are doing a favour, because pride diminishes good deeds in Islam. We should be careful and make sure we give to the recipient with the utmost respect. We cannot boast that we gave to the charity. The Quran warns against this attitude.

Whatever we give to charity should be what we would accept if it were offered to us. Many people give away only those items which they feel are not good enough for themselves. The Quran clarifies this and has forbidden such acts. Allah[SWT] says: *"You who believe, you shall give to charity from the good things you earn, and from what we have produced for you from the earth. Do not pick out the bad therein to give away, when you yourselves do not accept it unless your eyes are closed. You should know that Almighty is Rich, Praiseworthy."* **Quran 2:267.**

In another verse, Allah[SWT] says: *"You cannot attain righteousness until you give to charity from the possessions you love. Whatever you give to charity, the Almighty is fully aware thereof."* **Quran 3:92.**

In a hadith narrated Ibn 'Abbas: The Prophet sent Muadh to Yemen and *said, "Invite the people to testify that none has the right to be worshipped but Allah and I am Allah's Apostle, and if they obey you to do so, then teach them that Allah has enjoined on them five prayers in every day and night, and if they obey you to do so, then teach them that Allah has made it obligatory for them to pay Zakat from their properties and it is to be taken from the wealthy among them and given to the poor."* **Bukhari.**

This Hadith demonstrates that Zakat was emphasised as an obligatory practice immediately after the establishment of prayer, with its primary purpose being the redistribution of wealth from the rich to the poor.

In another hadith narrated Abu Huraira, the Prophet[P] *said, "If somebody gives in charity something equal to a date from his honestly earned money – for nothing ascends to Allah except good – then Allah will take it in His right (hand) and bring it up for its owner as anyone of you brings up a baby horse, till it becomes as big as a mountain."* **Bukhari**

This hadith reinforces the notion of reward and spiritual purification from Zakat, emphasising that Allah blesses even small amounts of charity given sincerely.

Conclusion

Zakat is a profound institution in Islam with both individual and societal implications. It fosters personal spiritual growth through the purification of wealth and helps promote social welfare by addressing economic disparities. Rooted deeply in both the

Qur'an and Hadith, Zakat is an essential practice that ensures justice and compassion within the Muslim community, bridging the gap between the rich and the poor, and fostering an ethical and equitable society.

May Allah[SWT] make us fully understand the concept of Zakat and grant us the Taufiq to always be in the mood of giving and not miss a single year of Zakat.

3. Death & the Afterlife

"When their term is reached, neither can they delay it nor can they advance it an hour (or a moment)"

Quran 10: 49

"Every servant will be resurrected upon the way that they died."

Muslim

Preparing for Death and the Soul's Journey in the Afterlife

Imagine yourself at the moment of your death. What thoughts cross your mind? Will you panic? Will you have regrets? Or will you be looking forward to meeting Allah[SWT]? Now, this all depends on how you lived your life. Our beloved Prophet[P] said, *"Every servant will be resurrected upon the way that they died."* **Muslim**

The most important question we should ask ourselves in life is: Are we ready for death?

Sometimes we may not want to know about the processes that occur after we die because we are too afraid, or just do not want to think about it, because we believe we have a long life to live. However, this is not the attitude of a believer. We should be forthcoming in learning and understanding death so that we can live our lives accordingly. The Prophet[P] encouraged us to contemplate death and be prepared for it through good deeds. This is regarded as a sign of goodness.

Ibn Umar[RA] reports: *"I came to the Prophet[P] and I was the tenth of the first ten people (who embraced Islam). A man from among the Ansar got up and said, "O Prophet of Allah, who is the wisest and most prudent among the people?" The Prophet[P] replied: "Those who are most aware of death and prepare themselves for it. They are the wisest of people and will have honour in this world and a generous reward in the Hereafter."* Ibn Umar[RA] also said that Allah's Messenger[pbuh] *said, "You should remember the reality that brings an end to all worldly joys and pleasures, namely, death."* **Tabarani.**

We should continue striving to do good till death. The Prophet[P] said, *"If the Day of Judgment erupts while you are planting a new tree, carry on and plant it."* This means that even in our last moment on earth, if we have the opportunity to do one more deed, such as planting a tree, we should continue to do so. By doing this, we will reap the benefits as *sadaqah jariyah* in the Hereafter.

The soul's journey after death

Death is the termination of worldly life and the beginning of the afterlife. Death is merely seen as the separation of the soul from the human body, and its transfer from this world to the afterlife.

When a person is buried, the soul hears the receding footfall of the last of the people who followed the funeral, and the earth is levelled over them. The earth or even a rock hollowed out and sealed over with lead would not prevent the two angels, Munkar and Nakir, from reaching the soul.

The Soul's Journey after death is narrated in a detailed hadith. Upon the authority of Al-Bara ibn Aazib RA, who *said,* "We went out with the Prophet[P] to a burial of a man from the *Ansar* until we arrived at the grave, and he still had not been placed in the slot of the grave.

Then the Messenger of Allah[P] sat down, and we sat around him. You would have thought that birds were upon our heads from our silence, and in the hand of the Messenger of Allah[P] was a stick which he was poking the ground with. Then he began to look at the sky and the earth, and then up and down three times. Then he said to us: "Ask Allah for refuge from the torment of the grave." He repeated this command two or three times. Then he said, "O Allah, I seek refuge in you from the torment of the grave" three times. He then said:

"When the believer is about to depart from this world and go forward into the next world, angels with faces as bright as the sun descend from the *Heavens* and sit around him in throngs stretching as far as the eye can see. Then the Angel of Death comes and sits at his head and says, "Good soul, come out to forgiveness and pleasure from Allah!" Then his soul emerges like a drop of water flows from a water skin, and the angel takes hold of it. When he has grasped it, the other angels do not leave it in his hand even for the twinkling of an eye. They take it and place it in a perfumed shroud and fragrance issues from it like the sweetest scent of musk found on the face of the earth.'

"Then they bear it upwards and whenever they take it past a company of angels, they ask, 'Who is this good soul?' and the angels with the soul reply, 'So-and-so the son of so-and-so,' using the best names by which people used to call him in this world. They bring him to the lowest *Heaven* and ask for the gate to be opened for him. It is opened for him, and angels who are near Allah from each of the *Heavens* accompany him to the subsequent *Heaven* until he reaches the *Heaven* where Allah[SWT] is. Allah[SWT] says: 'Register the book of My slave in 'Illiyun and take him back to earth. I created them from it and I return them to it and I will bring them forth from it again.'

"His soul is then returned to his body, and two angels come to him. They make him sit up and say to him, 'Who is your Lord?' He replies, 'My Lord is Allah.' They ask him, 'What is your religion?' He replies, 'My religion is Islam.' They ask him, 'Who is this man who was sent among you?' He replies, 'The Messenger of Allah. Then a Voice from on high declares, 'My slave has spoken the truth, so spread out carpets from the Garden for him and open a gate of the Garden for him!'

"Then some of its fragrance and perfume comes to him, his grave is expanded for him as far as the eye can see, and a man with beautiful garments and a fragrant scent comes to him and says, 'Rejoice in what delights you for this is the day which you were promised.' He asks, 'Who are you? Yours is a face which presages good.' He replies, 'I am your good actions.' Then he says, 'O Lord, let the Last Hour come soon so that I may rejoin my family and my property!'

"When an unbeliever is about to depart from this world and go forward into the Next World, angels with black faces descend from the *Heavens* carrying rough haircloth and sit around him in throngs stretching as far as the eye can see. Then the Angel of Death comes and sits at his head and says, 'Foul soul, come out to the wrath and anger of Allah!' Then his soul divides within his body, and it is dragged out like a skewer is pulled out of wet wool. Then the angel takes hold of it. When he has grasped it, the other angels do not leave it in his hand even for the twinkling of an eye. They take it and wrap it in the rough haircloth, and a stench comes out of it like the worst stench of a corpse on the face of the earth.'

"Then they take it up and whenever they take it past a company of angels, they ask, 'Who is this foul soul?' and the angels with the soul reply, 'So-and-so the son of so-and-so,' using the worst names by which people used to call him in this world. They bring him to the lowest *Heaven* and ask for the gate to be opened for him. It does not get opened.'

"The Messenger of Allah, may Allah[pbuh] then recited the verse of the Quran, which translates: "Surely the gates of Heaven shall not be opened for those who reject Our signs as false and turn away from them in arrogance; nor shall they enter Paradise until a camel passes through the eye of a needle." **Quran 7:40.**

Then Allah[SWT] will say: "Register his book in Sijjin in the lowest earth." Then his soul is flung down. The Prophet then recited another verse, which translates: "Whoever associates anything with Allah, it is as though he has fallen from *Heaven* and the birds snatch him away or the wind sweeps him headlong into a place far away." **Quran 22:31.**

"Then his soul is returned to his body and two angels come and say to him, 'Who is your Lord?' He replies, 'Alas, alas, I do not know!' Then a voice calls from on high, 'My slave has lied, so spread out carpets from the Fire for him and open a gate of the Fire for him!' then a hot blast from it comes to him, and his grave is made so narrow for him that his ribs are pressed together, and a man with a hideous face and clothing and a foul odour comes to him and says, 'Grieve on account of what has brought you disgrace for this is the day which you were promised.' He asks, 'Who are you? Yours is a face which presages evil.' He replies, 'I am your bad actions.' Then he says, 'O Lord, do not let the Last Hour come!'" **Ahmed.**

Life in Barzakh – The "Interspace"

Life in the grave or Interspace is the next part of our journey after life on earth. An 'interspace' is something that separates two things: *Heaven* and earth, this world and the next world. This is the period between death and resurrection. The bliss or punishment of the Interspace is not the same as that of the Hereafter, but rather something that happens between the two worlds.

In death, the body remains in the ground while the soul is in the interspace or *Barzakh* between the two worlds. However, the two are still connected, and so the bliss or punishment happens to both of them. When Allah desires happiness or punishment for the soul, He connects it to the body. This is dependent on the Will of Allah and on a person's own actions. The soul is diffused in more than one place at the same time. The proof of this is that the Prophet[P] saw Musa[AS] on the Night Journey, standing in prayer in his grave, and he also saw him in the sixth and seventh *Heavens*.

How to prepare for death

Don't get too engrossed in the Dunya

We are required not to get too engrossed in this world. The Prophet[P] *said, "Live in this world as though you are a stranger or a traveller (passing through it)."* **Muslim.** This life is short and only one part of a long journey; therefore, we should be aware of the entire journey's itinerary, not just the part on earth, which includes life in the *Barzakh* and beyond. Once we understand what happens to our souls in the afterlife, we feel less afraid of dying, Insha'Allah.

Only Allah determines our timing of death

One of the mysteries of death is its timing. No one except Allah[SWT] has the knowledge of when a person dies. Allah[SWT] says, *"When their term is reached, neither can they delay it nor can they advance it an hour (or a moment)"* **(Quran 10:49).** No one knows where, how, or when we die. Allah[SWT] says: *"Surely Allah alone has the knowledge of the Hour. It is He Who sends down the rain and knows what is in the wombs, although no person knows what he will earn tomorrow, nor does he know in which land he will die. Indeed, Allah is All-Knowing and All-Aware."* **Quran 31:34.**

Allah[SWT] takes the souls of some of his slaves when they are asleep. Allah[SWT] says: *"Allah takes souls at the time of their death and [the souls] of those that do not die during their sleep. He retains those souls for which He has ordained death, whereas He releases the rest for an appointed term."* **Quran 39:42.**

When a companion once asked: *"When is the Day of Judgement?"* The Prophet[P] replied, *"What have you prepared for it?"* This implies the Day of Judgement is when a person dies.

How to overcome the fear of death

1. Knowing there are glad tidings for the Believer

Allah[SWT] says: *"Verily, those who say, 'Our Lord is Allah (alone) and then stand straight, on them the angel will descend (at the time of their death saying,) 'Fear not, nor grieve! But receive the glad tidings of Paradise which you have been promised."* **Quran 41: 30.** Therefore, the event of death is merely a transfer from one realm to another. Death is not extinction nor destruction, but the separation of the soul from the body.

Allah[SWT] says: *"Everyone shall taste death. And only on the Day of Resurrection, you shall be paid your wages in full. And whoever is removed from the fire and admitted to Paradise, he indeed is successful. The life of this world is only the enjoyment of deception (a deceiving thing)."* **Quran 3: 175.** In another verse, Allah[SWT] says: *"Wherever you may be, death will overtake you even if you are in a fortress built up strong and high."* **Quran 4:78.**

Therefore, death is inevitable and no one can escape it, whether rich or poor, healthy or sick, young or old, leader or follower, pious or not. Allah[SWT] says: *"Do they not think that they will be resurrected, on a Great Day? The Day when all mankind will stand before the Lord of the Worlds?"* **Quran 83:4-6.**

When we please Allah[SWT], Allah will love us. Our name is announced in the *Heavens* when this happens. In a hadith narrated by Abu Huraira RA, the Prophet[P] *said, "If Allah loves a person, He calls Jibrael saying, 'Allah loves so and so; O Jibrael love him.' And make an announcement amongst the inhabitants of the Heaven: "Allah loves so and so, therefore, you should love him also, and so all the inhabitants of the Heaven would love him, and then he is granted the pleasures of the people on the earth."* **Bukhari and Muslim.** Therefore, if you have lived your life pleasing Allah[SWT], there is nothing to worry about.

2. Consider Death as a Form of Rest

This world is full of trials and tribulations for a believer and is not a place of pleasure and enjoyment, but more of a test. The Prophet[P] said, *"The world is a prison for the believer and a paradise for the unbeliever."* **Muslim.**

Once, when the Prophet[P] passed by a funeral, he said, *"He is (now) in peace, secure from others, and others are in peace, secure from him."* The people asked: *"O Allah's Messenger! Who is in peace and from whom are others in peace?"* He[P] said, *"A believing servant (of Allah) is relieved from afflictions of this world upon his death, while upon the death of a wicked person, other people, land, trees, and animals are rid of his evil."* **Bukhari and Muslim.**

Allah[SWT] causes righteous people to do good deeds and makes it easy for them before their death so that Allah can take their souls while they are doing good. Anas[RA] reported that the Prophet[P] said, *"When Allah intends good for a servant of His, He uses him for good."* They asked: "How does Allah use him?" The Prophet[P] replied, *"He enables him to do good deeds and makes it easy for him before his death and then causes him to die while he is in that state of goodness."* **Ahmad and Tirmidhi.**

3. Death is better for a believer

The Prophet[P] said, *"There are two things that the son of Adam dislikes: death, although death is better for a believer than fitnah; and he dislikes having little wealth, but less wealth means less reckoning."* **Ahmad.** With regards to the Prophet's saying: less wealth means less reckoning, Abu Huraira[RA] reported: The Messenger of Allah[P]: *"The poor Muslims will enter Paradise before the rich by half of a day, the length of which is like five hundred years."* **Tirmidhi.**

The wealthy will have greater accountability for their wealth, including how they earned it and how they spent it. The Prophet[P] also said, *"The son of Adam will not be dismissed from his Lord on the Day of Resurrection until he is questioned about five matters: his life and how he lived it, his youth and how he expended it, his wealth and how he earned it and he spent it, and how he acted upon his knowledge."* **Tirmidhi,**

4. Life in this world is very short compared to the Hereafter.

The Prophet[P] said, *"This world in comparison with the Hereafter is like the amount of water one of you gets when he dips his finger in the sea. Let him see what his finger returns with."* **Muslim.**

This means this life is truly very short. As mentioned in the hadith, if we wish to know the reality of this world in comparison to the Hereafter, then put a finger in the sea and take it out, then look at what it comes back with. What it comes back with is nothing compared to the water in the sea. This is precisely what this world means in terms of its short duration and the perishing of its pleasures in comparison to the Hereafter, which is everlasting, and its pleasures are eternal. Allah^SWT says: *"But little is the enjoyment of the life of this world as compared with the Hereafter."* **Quran 9:38.**

Everything that one is given in this worldly life of riches and pleasures is short-term and mixed with pains and displeasures. A man will brag and boast about his worldly gains, but they are only temporary. They soon perish and are succeeded with sorrow and regret. Allah^SWT says: *"And whatever of things you have been given, are only for the enjoyment of worldly life and its adornment. And what is with Allah is better and more lasting; so, will you not then use reason?"* **Quran 28:60.**

5. If you are still breathing, you have time to repent before Death

The Prophet^P *said, "When any of you completes the last tashahhud of his prayer, let him seek refuge in Allah from four things, saying, 'O Allah, verily I seek refuge in you from the punishment of the Hellfire and the torment of the grave; from the fitnah of life and of death; and from the evil fitnah of the false messiah.'"* **Muslim and Nasai.**

The Prophet^P also *said, "Allah accepts the repentance of His slave so long as his spirit has not arrived at his throat."* **Tirmidhi.** Therefore, if we are still taking in oxygen, we still have time to repent to Allah and ask for forgiveness from the people whom we have wronged. It is better to keep our slate clean before we meet Allah^SWT, which can be at any moment!

Allah^SWT says: *"But of no avail is repentance of those who do evil until death approaches any one of them and then he says: 'Now I repent.' Nor is the repentance of those who die in the state of unbelief of any avail to them. For them, We have kept in readiness a painful chastisement."* **Quran 4:18.**

Umm Salamah^RA reported: The Messenger of Allah^P visited Abu Salamah^RA when his eyes were open, soon after he died. He^P closed his eyes for him and then said, *"When the soul is taken away, the sight follows it."* Some members of his family began to weep. He^P said, *"Do not supplicate for yourselves anything but good, for the angels say `amin' to what you say."* Then he^P said, *"O Allah! Forgive Abu Salamah, raise his rank among those who are rightly guided, and grant him a successor from his descendants who remain behind. Grant him pardon and us, too. O Rubb of the world.*

Make his grave spacious for him and give him light in it." **Muslim**. Subhana Allah! There are so many lessons we learn from this hadith.

6. It is not proper for a Person to wish for Death

It is *makruh* or disliked to wish for death or pray to Allah for it, due to poverty, distress, illness, or anything else. The Prophet[P] *said, "None of you should wish for death because of a calamity befalling him; but if he has to wish for death, he should say: 'O Allah! Keep me alive as long as life is better for me, and let me die if death is better for me. "* **Bukhari.** The wisdom in the prohibition against wishing for death is clear in the hadith narrated by Umm al-Fadl RA. He *said, "The Prophet[P] went to see Abbas RA. He found him wishing for death. Thereupon, the Prophet[P] said, 'O Abbas! O Uncle of Allah's Messenger! Do not wish for death. If you do good and live long, your good deeds will multiply. Then that is better for you. If you are not good and your death is delayed, you may seek Allah's forgiveness. That is better for you. So do not wish for death."* **Ahmad and Al-Hakim.**

This means that if you live long and are righteous, your good deeds will multiply; but if you are not good and your death is delayed, you have the opportunity to seek Allah[SWT]'s forgiveness. The believer is so blessed. We just need to understand it and appreciate it.

A long life in which a believer performs righteous deeds is better for them than death; on the other hand, the evil person who lives long is the worst. This is emphasised in the hadith where a man asked, *"O Messenger of Allah, which of the people is best?"* He[P] *said, "The one who lives long and does good."* The man asked further: *"Which of the people is worst?"* The Prophet[P] replied, *"The one who lives long and does evil."* **Ahmad and Tirmidhi.**

In another hadith, the Prophet[P] *said, "No one of you should wish for death. Either he is a doer of good and will do more, or he is a doer of evil but perhaps he may stop."* **Bukhari.**

It is permissible, however, when one fears persecution that puts one's faith at risk, as is indicated by the following supplication of the Messenger of Allah[P]: *"O Allah! I ask You for the means to do good, to avoid evil, and to love the poor, and I beseech You to forgive me and have mercy on me. When You subject my people to a trial, cause me to die without being affected by it. O Allah! I ask Your love, the love of those who love You, and the love of all such actions that bring one closer to Your Love."* **Tirmidhi.**

The Prophet[P] taught us that three things continue to benefit a believing person even after death. That is Charity which he had given, which continues to benefit others; Beneficial knowledge which he had left behind, for example, authored a book or taught people beneficial knowledge, and a righteous child who supplicates on his behalf. Allah's Messenger[P] said, *"When carried to his grave, a dead person is followed by three, two of which return (after his burial) and one remains with him: his relative, his property, and his deeds follow him; relatives and his property go back while his deeds remain with him."* **Bukhari**. Therefore, we should continue giving in charity, even if it is a little, until we die, and pass on good knowledge to those who seek it and focus on bringing up a righteous child.

7. If you love to meet Allah, Allah loves to meet you

The closer a person gets to death, the more likely they are to think about it. The fear of death or going through the pangs of death is quite a natural and normal thing to have; however, it is how that fear affects you and to what level you allow it to influence your life that determines whether or not the fear is an unhealthy one.

If you fear death, this hadith should bring you great comfort. The Prophet[P] said, *It was narrated from 'Aishah that the Messenger of Allah (ﷺ) said, 'Whoever loves to meet Allah, Allah loves to meet him, and whoever hates to meet Allah, Allah hates to meet him."* It was said to him: "O Messenger of Allah, does hating to meet Allah mean hating to meet death? For all of us hate death." He said, "No. Rather, that is only at the moment of death. But if he is given the glad tidings of the mercy and forgiveness of Allah, he loves to meet Allah and Allah loves to meet him; and if he is given the tidings of the punishment of Allah, he hates to meet Allah and Allah hates to meet him."* **Ibn Majah.**

Rather than focus our attention on the fear of death, it is better to shift that attention to the love of Allah[SWT]. Every time you have thought about what is going to happen at death or fearful thoughts of death, then simply train your mind to shift into thinking about the fact that Allah loves to meet us and we long to meet Him! Subhanallah! How great is that!

8. The Desirability of Having a Good Opinion about Allah

We should remember the boundless mercy of Allah[SWT] and have a good opinion of our Sustainer. Jabir[RA] reported: *"I heard the Messenger of Allah, peace be upon him, saying, three nights before his death, 'Let none of you die unless he has a good opinion of Allah'."* **Muslim.**

Umar ibn al-Khattab reported: Some prisoners of war were brought to the Prophet[P] and a nursing woman was among them. Whenever she found a child among the prisoners, she would take it to her chest and nurse it. *The Prophet said to us, "Do you think this woman would throw her child into the fire?" We said, "No, not if she was able to stop it."* The Prophet[P] said, *"Allah is more merciful to His servants than this mother is to her child."* **Bukhari and Muslim.**

This hadith teaches us that Allah[SWT] is the most merciful and forgiving, and encourages us to hold onto hope and expectation of forgiveness when we meet Allah[SWT]. We should be in the state most loved by Allah, since He is the most Gracious, the most Merciful, the most Beneficent, and the most Generous. He loves to forgive those with hope. It is reported by Anas[RA] that: *"the Prophet[P] went to see a young man who was on his deathbed. The Prophet[P] asked him: 'How are you?' The young man said, 'I hope for Allah's pardon, but I am fearful because of my sins.' The Prophet[P] said, 'These two things never gather in the heart of a person at such a time without Allah granting him what he hopes for and sheltering him from what he dreads'."* **Ibn Majah and Tirmidhi.**

In another hadith, the Prophet[P] *said, "Allah has one hundred parts of mercy, of which He sent down one between the jinn, mankind, the animals and the insects, by means of which they are compassionate and merciful to one another, and by means of which wild animals are kind to their offspring. And Allah has kept back ninety-nine parts of mercy with which to be merciful to His slaves of the Day of Resurrection."* **Muslim.**

It is through the Mercy of Allah that He will admit His believing slaves to Paradise on the Day of Resurrection. No one will ever enter Paradise because of his deeds alone, as the Prophet[P] *said, "No one's deeds will ever admit him to Paradise."* They said, *"Not even you, O Messenger of Allah?"* He[P] *said, "No, not even me unless Allah showers me with His Mercy. So, strive for near perfection. And no one should wish for death; he is either doing good so he will do more of that, or he is doing wrong so he may repent."* **Bukhari and Muslim.**

We must remain in a state between hoping for the Mercy of Allah and fearing His punishment, for Allah[SWT] says: *"Declare (O Muhammad) unto My slaves, that truly, I am the Oft-Forgiving, the Most-Merciful. And that My Torment is indeed the most painful torment."* **Quran 15:49-50.**

The Seven Types of Martyrs

There are seven kinds of martyrs apart from those killed in fighting for the cause of Allah. Abu Hurairah reported that Allah's Messenger[P] asked, *"Who do you consider to be a martyr?"* They said, *"O Allah's Prophet, he who is killed fighting for the cause of*

Allah." The Prophet[P] said, "(If this is so) then very few in my community will be martyrs! " They asked: "Who else are they, O Allah's Messenger?" The Prophet[P] replied: "There are seven kinds of martyrs other than those killed in the way of Allah. Someone who is killed by the plague is a martyr, someone who drowns is a martyr, someone who dies of pleurisy (inflammation around the lungs, which causes sharp chest pain) is a martyr, someone who dies of a disease of the belly is a martyr, someone who dies by fire is a martyr, someone who dies under a falling building is a martyr and a woman who dies in childbirth is a martyr." **Ahmad, Abu Dawud and Nasai.**

The bodies of such martyrs, during the Prophet's time, were washed. Later on, Muslims, during the days of Umar, Uthman, and Ali, may Allah be pleased with them, continued this practice of washing the bodies of such martyrs.

People who died during earthquakes, floods, etc., are all considered to have died as Martyrs.

The person who dies in debt

Abu Hurairah reported that the Messenger of Allah *said, "A believer's soul remains in suspense until all his debts are paid off."* **Ibn Majah and Tirmidhi.** This means that the judgment regarding a soul's salvation or perdition or its entry into Paradise is held in abeyance until its debts are fully paid off and settled. The Prophet[P] said, "If anyone takes other people's money intending to repay it and then he or she should die without settling the debt, Allah will pay the debt on his behalf. And if anyone takes money or property (of others) with the intention of destroying it, Allah will destroy him." **Bukhari.** This hadith serves as a grave warning to those who fail to settle their debts, with the intention of not repaying them, despite having the ability to do so. However, by the mercy of Allah, if one had the intention of paying back but died, then Allah[SWT] would forgive this burden.

May Allah[SWT] grant us the *taufiq* to be most aware of death and prepare for it; and may Allah[SWT] keep us steadfast in our *deen* till death in order to achieve our primary goal, which is to attain *Jannah*.

The Islamic Will

"Allah directs you concerning your children: for a male there is a share equal to that of two females. But, if they are (only) women, more than two, then they get two-thirds of what one leaves behind. If she is one, she gets one-half. As for his parents, for each of them, there is one-sixth of what he leaves in case he has a child. But, if he has no child and his parents have inherited him, then his mother gets one-third. If he has some brothers (or sisters), his mother gets one-sixth, all after (settling) the will he might have made, or a debt. You do not know who, out of your fathers and your sons, is closer to you in benefiting (you). All this is determined by Allah. Surely, Allah is All-Knowing, All-Wise."

Quran 4:11

"It is the duty of a Muslim who has anything to bequeath not to let two nights pass without writing a will about it."

Bukhari

Indeed, Allah is the One who gives life, and He is the One who takes it, and to Him shall we return. As Muslims, we are required to bear the anguish of losing a loved one with patience, to beseech our Creator to be merciful to the soul of the deceased, and most importantly, to remind ourselves of the temporary nature of this life, so that we may better prepare ourselves for the next.

Whilst many Muslims ensure funeral rites are properly observed whenever there is a death, there is much less emphasis given to ensuring the assets of the deceased are distributed amongst the rightful heirs in accordance with Quranic requirements. Yet this is an obligation on the inheritors that is best achieved through preparing a legally valid Islamic Will.

Islam has great emphasis on exiting this world in the best possible way. It was the practice of numerous prophets to gather their children before death and exhort them to remain steadfast in their faith and not to deviate from divine teachings, as mentioned in the Quranic verses.

The Prophet[P] visited several people on their deathbeds, including his own uncle Abu Talib, in order to encourage them to accept Islam. The Prophet[P] *said, "If a person's last words are Laa ilaaha ill-Allaah, Paradise will be guaranteed for him."* **Ahmad and Abu Dawud.**

People generally place great sentimental value on words uttered towards the end of life and on written instructions in the form of a will. It is good practice to include general moral guidance and advice for heirs, as well as specific instructions regarding the estate and the practicalities of washing, shrouding, and burial wishes, including the desire not to have a routine post-mortem examination carried out unless legally required.

How we handle our inheritance is the last impactful legacy we can leave in this world. We should therefore ensure that it is done in a manner pleasing to Allah^SWT. The Prophet *said, "It is not permissible for any Muslim who has something to Will to stay for two nights without having his last Will and Testament written and kept ready with him."* **Bukhari.**

A Will is a legally binding document that gives instructions on the way that our estate – that is, the assets we leave behind- should be distributed. In a conventional, non-Islamic Will, we simply leave what we want to whomever we want. For this reason, we often hear stories of people leaving all their money to charity or even their pets, rather than to relatives. Islam tells us something different. It pre-determines who inherits our assets.

Islam teaches us that the proportion each living heir is to receive has already been determined according to Quranic verses and prophetic statements. Each heir inherits based on what Allah^SWT has ordained, and this should be borne in mind when drafting a will.

Allah^SWT says: *Allah directs you concerning your children: for a male there is a share equal to that of two females. But, if they are (only) women, more than two, then they get two-thirds of what one leaves behind. If she is one, she gets one-half. As for his parents, each of them is entitled to one-sixth of what he leaves in the event that he has a child. However, if he has no children and his parents have inherited from him, then his mother gets one-third. If he has some brothers (or sisters), his mother gets one-sixth, all after (settling) the Will he might have made, or a debt. You do not know who, out of your fathers and your sons, is closer to you in benefiting you. Allah determines all this. Surely, Allah is All-Knowing, All-Wise.* **Quran 4:11.**

In the next verse, Allah^SWT says: *"You will inherit half of what your wives leave if they are childless. But if they have children, then 'your share is' one-fourth of the estate— after the fulfilment of bequests and debts. And your wives will inherit one-fourth of what you leave if you are childless. But if you have children, then your wives will receive* one-eighth of your estate—after the fulfilment of bequests and debts. And if a man or a woman leaves neither parents nor children but only a brother or a sister 'from their mother's side', they will each inherit one-sixth, but if they are more than one, they 'all' will share one-third of the estate—after the fulfilment of bequests and debts without harm 'to the heirs'. 'This is' a commandment from Allah. And Allah is All-Knowing, Most Forbearing." **Quran 4:12.**

We are obligated to distribute the wealth and assets of the deceased in accordance with these verses of the Quran. The pre-set inheritance is the key difference in an Islamic will.

We should also understand that any wealth we possess is not our wealth. The Quran states that Allah has dominion over everything in the *Heavens* and the earth. This comes up several times in the Quran, including in Ayatul Kursi. Allah says: *"Allah – there is no deity except Him, the Ever-Living, the Sustainer of [all] existence. Neither drowsiness overtakes Him nor sleep.* **To Him belongs whatever is in the Heavens and whatever is on the earth.** *Who is it that can intercede with Him except by His permission? He knows what is [presently] before them and what will be after them, and they encompass not a thing of His knowledge except for what He wills. His Kursi extends over the Heavens and the earth, and their preservation tires Him not. And He is the Most High, the Most Great."* **Quran 2:255.**

In a non-Muslim country, we definitely need to leave a Will that sets all of that out in detail, because domestic laws will otherwise revert to the laws of intestacy, i.e., the laws that apply when we die without a will, not the laws of Islam. As long as we detail how we want our assets to be distributed, English law, and most likely other domestic law in Western countries, will not interfere with that.

In many Muslim countries, the laws of intestacy are derived from *Shariah*, which is beneficial for residents of these countries because even if the deceased does not leave a Will, they will be adhering to their Islamic obligations. However, in the UK or any other non-Muslim country, having a Will is a must. This is because if we die without one, our assets will be distributed according to the law of the land, which may be contrary to Islamic law.

We need to have a Will that complies with both domestic laws and Islamic law, in order for it to be both valid in the country we live in and meet the Islamic criteria for asset distribution.

What is the law for Wills in Islam?

An Islamic will is a legally binding document that stipulates to whom a person will leave their assets, i.e., their property, possessions, and money, upon their return to Allah^{SWT}. The person must make it while they are alive. A Will is made to arrange one's property and assets, after one's death, for the benefit of others, and for charitable purposes.

Islam pre-determines who inherits the assets left behind by a Muslim, with the legacy being divided primarily between the spouse, children, and parents by using specific calculations. The Quran outlines in detail the fixed portion of an estate that particular relatives of the deceased are entitled to inherit. Some key inheritance rules according to *Shariah* law can be broken down as follows:

- **Husband:** Inherits 1/2 if the deceased has no children or 1/4 if the deceased has children.
- **Wife:** Inherits 1/4 if the deceased has no children or 1/8 if the deceased has children.
- **Daughters:** Inherit 1/2 if the deceased has only one daughter and no sons, or 2/3 if the deceased has multiple daughters and no sons (shared equally between all daughters).
- **Son and daughter:** Inherit a shared portion with a 2:1 ratio.
- Father: Inherits 1/6 if the deceased has children.
- **Mother:** Inherits 1/3 if the deceased has no children or siblings, or 1/6 if the deceased has children or siblings.

One should not leave everything to the surviving spouse after death. This is prohibited because the Quran mandates other beneficiaries. Unfortunately, many people do this a lot. While it is assumed that the surviving spouse will care for the children with what she receives, this is not necessarily the case. The survivor may get married. If the survivor also dies, the new spouse may be the beneficiary, accidentally disinheriting the children. Sadly, people unwittingly organise assets in a way that causes injustices upon death. Part of Islamic Inheritance is an awareness of how you own your wealth.

Since disputes with family members may arise, it is advisable to seek advice from a Scholar for Islamic guidelines and to obtain Sharia-compliant advice from those who specialise in this field, or to appoint a Muslim agency that provides a will-creating service. It is also recommended to consult a solicitor for legal advice and to help create a Will that meets the criteria of the law of the land. This is particularly the case for those who reside in non-Muslim countries.

How to create an Islamic will that is legal in the UK

In order to create an Islamic will that is legal in the UK, you must meet the following conditions according to UK law:

- Be 18 years old or over.
- Have the mental capacity to make a Will.
- Have a written Will because spoken declarations are not legally binding.
- Declare that you wrote the Will.
- Legally declare that this is your last Will; meaning that any other Wills that cover the same assets are now invalid.
- Sign the Will in the presence of two witnesses, neither of whom can be your spouse or a beneficiary of the Will.

There are several additional requirements that must be included in the UK Will for it to be Sharia-compliant, including:

- The executor must be a Muslim.
- The exact distribution of an estate can only be determined upon death.
- Any assets left must be specified, such as a particular car, piece of jewellery, or a certain amount of cash left to a charity.
- At least two-thirds of the estate must be distributed among living family members.
- One-third can be left to anyone who is not entitled to a fixed share, such as a son-in-law, daughter-in-law, or a UK-registered charity. Any money bequeathed to a non-registered charitable organisation cannot be taken into consideration to reduce inheritance tax liabilities.

Why do we need to create a Will?

Allah[SWT] has made it compulsory for His creation to make a Will. Allah[SWT] says: *"It has been ordained upon you, when death is near one of you, leaving wealth behind, to make a will in favour of parents and close relatives, impartially. This is incumbent upon the pious."* **Quran 2:180.**

The Prophet[P] *said, "It is the duty of a Muslim who has anything to bequeath not to let two nights pass without writing a will about it."* **Bukhari.** Also, the Prophet[P] said, *"When a person passes away, his ability to perform deeds stops except for three: Sadaqah Jariah (perpetual charity), Useful knowledge that people benefit from, and a good son who prays for the deceased."*

The importance of an Islamic Will and observing the Islamic laws of inheritance carries great blessings and mercy from our Creator. Unless one makes a valid Islamic Will, their estate will not be distributed in accordance with the Islamic laws of inheritance.

Suppose you die without leaving an Islamic Will under British jurisprudence. In that case, you risk your assets being distributed against your beliefs in accordance with the rules of intestacy, rather than the guidelines set out in the Quran. It can even end up going to a distant family member with whom you have rarely been in contact, or it can end up with the Treasury to be used by the Government as it sees fit. The only way to avoid the dreaded rules of intestacy is to write a legally valid will, which you can do with the help of a solicitor and a Scholar who specialises in Wills.

Abu Hurayrah[RA] narrated a hadith of the Prophet[P] that: *"A man may do good deeds for seventy years but if he acts unjustly when he leaves his last testament, the wickedness of his deed will be sealed upon him, and he will enter the fire. If (on the other hand), a man acts wickedly for seventy years but is just in his last will, the goodness of his deed will be sealed upon him, and he will enter the garden."* **Ibn Majah.**

What are the rules of Bequests?

Bequests are one of the main differences between Islamic Wills and other Wills. This allows the individual flexibility to do with their remaining assets and belongings as they see fit. However, it must be done within the maximum one-third spectrum and should not exceed that value for it to be a bequest.

One-third of the individual's assets are available to be accepted from individuals who are not entitled to receive two-thirds of the assets. This is an optional decision made at the individual's discretion. Bequests can be given to anyone; however, most Muslims who choose to include a bequest typically give it to charity.

In Islam, charity is highly praised, and as Muslims, we believe that good actions such as this will help benefit us on our journey to the afterlife. If a person decides to include a bequest in their will, they must ensure that they are specific about who or where their bequest will be going and how they wish for it to be distributed.

What are the benefits of creating a will?

- Prevent the state from deciding how to divide your estate.
- Save money for your heirs by distributing the inheritance.
- Prevent the inheritance from going to the wrong hands.

- Save hundreds or thousands of pounds in inheritance tax.
- Prevent family disputes
- If you are not legally married and have only performed a nikah, then a written Will ensures that your widow receives her share and a share of your family home. Otherwise, under the laws of intestacy, she will not.
- If you have step-children, foster children, or other dependents who are not blood relations, they will not automatically inherit anything without a Will.
- Allocate up to one-third of your estate towards *Sadaqah Jariyah* (perpetual charity) that will benefit you in the next life.

Allocation of the Assets

All the assets of the deceased must be distributed according to the Sharia stipulated in the Quran and Hadith, and order of priority:

Firstly, all funeral expenses should be paid. It is perfectly acceptable for these expenses to be met voluntarily by one or more family members.
Secondly, any outstanding debts should be repaid.
And thirdly, any bequests, i.e *wasiyyah,* should be honoured.

There are two stipulations to this:

- Their value does not exceed one-third of the value of the remaining net assets; that is, assets left after debts and funeral expenses are paid, and also on the condition that;
- The recipient of the bequest is not an individual who is entitled under *Shariah* to receive a share. For example: spouse, child, parent, etc., of the deceased.

We should consider establishing a bequest that is limited to a maximum of one-third of the deceased's net estate. A bequest is a special favour given to a Muslim by Allah[SWT] to compensate for a person's shortcomings through giving to charity as a *sadaqah jariyyah* or to provide for those who are not legal heirs. The bequest will form part of the will. Many Muslims choose to make a bequest to charity as a means of ensuring that some good deeds continue to benefit them even after they pass away, in the form of *sadaqah jariyah.*

How to Arrange an Islamic Will

There are two methods for writing an Islamic will and how it can be conducted, with the first being through an online process in which you create your Will by yourself with minimal assistance. The second method is through a trained specialist who will be able to answer every question and query, and can efficiently guide you through the process, including the Islamic requirements. It is highly recommended that you seek help from a Scholar and a Solicitor to ensure the Will is not only *Shariah*-compliant but also legally valid in the country of residence.

Once a Will is drafted, it should be kept safely. However, a Will should be revisited in case some important events occur in a person's life, such as the birth of a child, divorce, or marriage.

May Allah[SWT] grant us the *taufeeq* to fully understand the obligatory requirements of an Islamic Will and make us among those who implement it in the best possible way in order to not only benefit in this world but also the Hereafter.

How to shroud and wash the deceased according to the Quran and *Sunnah*

"Thereupon Allah sent forth a raven which scratched the earth, to show him how he might conceal the nakedness of his brother's body. [And Cain] cried out: "Oh, woe is me! Am I then too weak to do what this raven did, and to conceal the nakedness of my brother's body?" - and was thereupon smitten with remorse."

Quran 5:31

"If you perfume a dead body, do it three times."

Ahmad and Al-Hakim

When a Muslim dies, it is the responsibility of the family or other Muslims within the local community to wash and shroud according to the Islamic rites of washing the deceased. It is standard practice to have at least three members involved in the process of the ghusl and then shrouding.

At all times, the body of the deceased must be handled with great care and attention to ensure no harm or discomfort is caused. Any injury caused to the body is like causing injury whilst the person was alive, according to Islamic guidance. This is because, in Islam, human dignity is a right given by Allah[SWT] to all humans, who are referred to in the Quran as Allah's vicegerents on earth. Islam grants certain rights to humans before they are even born and others after their death. Whether dead or alive, the human body created by Allah[SWT] in the perfect shape must be given dignity and respect.

The importance of human respect and dignity given to a body is illustrated in this verse. Allah[SWT] says: *"Thereupon Allah sent forth a raven which scratched the earth, to show him how he might conceal the nakedness of his brother's body. [And Cain] cried out: "Oh, woe is me! Am I then too weak to do what this raven did, and to conceal the nakedness of my brother's body?" - and was thereupon smitten with remorse."* **Quran 5:31.**

When Adam[AS] son Cain was unsure of how to deal with the body of his brother Abel, whom he had murdered, Allah[SWT] sent a message in the form of a raven. Allah[SWT] used the crow to dig into the ground to bury another crow, thus indirectly showing Cain how to bury his brother's body with dignity.

Giving ghusl is a *Fard Kifayah* - a communal obligation that some members of the community must fulfil; otherwise, the whole community will be sinful. There are significant rewards for those who participate in the funeral process. The Prophet[P] *said, "Whoever follows a Muslim's funeral, out of faith and seeking to increase his account of good deeds, until he makes the funeral prayer for it will have a Qeeraat's worth of reward. And he whoever follows it until it is buried, will get two Qeeraats"* The Prophet[P] was then asked what two Qeeraats were, and he replied: *"They are equivalent to two huge mountains; [the smaller of the two is like Mount Uhud]."* **Bukhari and Muslim.**

Before washing the deceased

- The deceased's body should be washed in a clean, secluded, and private place where clean water and soap are available.
- For those involved in washing, it is best to be in the state of *wudhu.*
- It is *makruh,* i.e., detestable, for any person who is in the state *of janaabah, haidh or nifaas* to undertake the Ghusl, because they are classed as greater impurity.
- Gloves must always be worn when handling and washing the deceased.
- It is forbidden to mention to others any signs of disease, deformity or ailment that may be visible during the bathing of the deceased.
- The body of the deceased should be washed with water and, if available, lotus leaves or camphor, which is to be used in the final wash.
- The steps of the washing should be done at least three times. If washed more than three times, then an odd number of times as necessary can be done.
- Always be mindful of infection control and protecting the person performing the Ghusl.
- When washing the body of the deceased, a person should have *Ikhlaṣ* (sincerity), hoping for the reward from Allah[SWT].
- The washing of the body should be hastened, without any unnecessary delay, like the rest of the funeral process.
- It is preferable for the relatives of the deceased to perform the Ghusl with a knowledgeable person present, taking part in the process and guiding others.
- The *awrah* of the deceased should remain covered at all times.
- Before beginning the ghusl, make sure everything you require before and after the Ghusl are in place, including:
  - Gloves, towels, and aprons/scrubs.
  - Sidr and/or soap, camphor, and/or perfume.

- o Buckets, warm water, and pouring jugs, or a spray, to ensure it is operating correctly.
- o The shroud and coffin for after the ghusl should be ready in another room.
- o Sponges and cotton wool for cleaning the nose/ears.
- o Scissors for removing any bandages and clothing.
- A piece of cloth or a towel is wrapped around the hands of those who are washing the deceased, or gloves can be worn.

Be reminded that three things occur as you wash, shroud, and bury the dead:

- The body returns to the earth, from which it was made;
- The soul faces judgment;
- And the living are reminded that their time on Earth is limited and their opportunity to do good may end at any moment.

Who is entitled to wash the body?

The persons who may wash the deceased should be:

- Adult Muslims who are honest and trustworthy persons.
- Of the same gender as the deceased. Male members should wash the male deceased, and female members should wash the female deceased.
- For a young child, either males or females may do the ghusl.
- Knowledgeable individuals who are familiar with the Islamic method of washing the deceased should be present and participate in performing the ghusl, advising the deceased's relatives, who are encouraged to be involved in the process.
- Preferably in a state of wudhu.
- Should not be in ritual impurity where *Ghusl* is *fard* upon them.

Maintaining privacy and dignity at all times

- When washing a body, whatever you see during the washing and shrouding process must not be discussed with anyone outside of the immediate family.
- Privacy must be maintained at all times.
- Do not use water that is too cold or too hot; instead, it should be at a moderate, lukewarm temperature.

The whole process of Ghusl

The body of the deceased is washed just as a living person performs Ghusl, i.e., water must touch every part of the body, from head to toe.

Key stages:

- Istinjah
- Wudhu
- Ghusl

1. Gently untie the cloth covering the deceased from the head and feet.
2. Making sure the private parts of the deceased, particularly the *awrah,* remain covered, slowly remove clothing.
3. Remove any jewellery, watches, false teeth, etc. from the body.
4. Press the stomach of the deceased gently and massage it downwards to evacuate the bowels before the Ghusl is started. The process may be facilitated by one person raising the body from behind to a semi-upright or reclined position as the other compresses the abdomen. Working under the cover, use a gloved hand to discreetly and carefully wash away any refuse with warm water.
5. Use gloves and a fresh, new white cloth, or a sponge, to gently clean the private parts while they are covered. Gently lift the legs to gain access to the back and front. Use a white cloth to show how much more washing may be required. You may need to clean the deceased one, two, or as many times as necessary until the body is clean.
6. After cleaning the private areas of the body, dispose of the used cloth and gloves.
7. Ensure respect is shown to the deceased and the same cloth or gloves are not used for the remaining parts of the body. To do so would be disrespectful to the deceased and very unhygienic.
8. Use small wads of cotton to plug the ears and the nose to minimise the possibility of water entering these cavities during Ghusl. A thick pad of cotton may be placed over the mouth for the same purpose. Additionally, use your free hand to shield the openings during the Ghusl.
9. Perform the Wudhu.
   a. Gently clean the right hand by passing water between the fingers. Always start from the right side.
   b. Then repeat the same process for the left hand, up to the wrist.
   c. Wet some cotton wool and gently rub the mouth area
   d. Using some wet cotton, clean the inside of the nose as well.
   e. Now gently wash the face, just like we do in *Wudu.*
   f. Any braids should be untied and washed well, and the hair should be combed.
   g. Clean the right hand and arm. A person should lift the arm while another person gently washes it. Do the same for the left arm.
   h. Now clean the back of the head (*masah*), neck, ear, and top of the head.
   i. Wash both feet, including between the toes.

10. Using warm water and soap, wash the body thoroughly from head to toe. Usually, three washes are sufficient to cleanse the body adequately. If necessary, rewash

the body. It is the *Sunnah* of the Prophet[P] to wash the body an odd number of times, as mentioned in the following Hadith: *"Umm Atiyyah[RA] reported that the Prophet[P] came in while they were washing his daughter Zaynab RA. He instructed them: Wash her three, five, seven or more times if you find it necessary- using water and (ground leaves of) lotus"* **Bukhari and Muslim.**

11. Have one or more helpers turn the body on its left side. Using soap and warm water, wash the right half of the body thoroughly. Gently turn the body on its right side and repeat the process to clean the left side.

12. Wash the whole body with water only. Ensure that the body is thoroughly cleansed of all foreign matter, including soap scum and other debris.

13. Pat the body dry with a towel discreetly. Again, work under the covering in deference to the deceased's privacy.

14. Perfume or camphor may be applied to the body to add to its overall sanitary condition.

15. Transfer the covered body carefully to an adjacent table where the Kafan has already been spread out in the prescribed manner.

-

There are no sound narrations that mention the recitation of any specific supplications during the ghusl process.

If the body is decomposed or not intact due to being involved in an accident, assess if it is possible to wash the body with water. If not, then it is permissible to do Tayammum. For specific information or other scenarios, it is essential to consult with your local Islamic scholar or *Imam* for clarification.

Special Circumstances

Unforeseen circumstances may arise that require attention during the Ghusl. Common sense and decency should prevail, which dictate the line of possible action in such situations. For example, despite all precautions, body fluids may sometimes be discharged from the deceased after the Ghusl has been completed. It is then only necessary to clean the secretion and waste with water and rinse the whole body with water three times. It is not necessary to repeat the whole Ghusl. If the discharge continues, small wads of cotton may be used, which can be discreetly taped, if necessary, to stop the secretions.

Cases involving accident victims, autopsy, or contagious diseases are some other examples of situations requiring special handling and precautions. A knowledgeable professional would normally be able to suggest prudent lines of action in such circumstances that are compatible with the *Shariah*, local laws, and legitimate health concerns.

During the COVID-19 epidemic, special precautions and PPE protective clothing had to be worn. There were specific rules and guidelines produced, which were *Shariah*-compliant, that had to be applied during this period.

After the washing

- Those who wash the deceased are obligated to conceal anything that they see.
- For a woman, her hair should be braided into three braids and placed at the back of her head.
- It is recommended that those who washed the body of the deceased perform Ghusl afterwards or *Wudu*.

The Body is now ready for Shrouding

The Method of Shrouding

Shrouding the body of the deceased, even if it be with just one piece of cloth, is a collective obligation - *fard kifayah* of the Muslims.

Shrouding should begin immediately after washing the deceased's body. It is recommended to use white sheets made of inexpensive materials. Extravagance is not recommended in the *Kafan* - shroud. The material of the sheet should not have any stitching, nor silk, nor should any gold be used. The minimum shrouding consists of one cloth that covers the entire body. The perfect shroud for a male is three cloths, and for a female is five cloths.

1. The shroud should be nice, clean, and large enough to cover the entire body. This is based on a hadith wherein the Prophet[P] said, *"If one of you is a guardian to his deceased brother, he should give him the best shroud he can."* **Ibn Majah and Tirmidhi.**

2. A shroud should be white. Ibn Abbas reported that the Prophet[P] *said, "Wear white clothes, for these are your best clothes, and enshroud your dead in them."* **Tirmidhi, Abu Dawud and Ahmad.**

3. The shroud should be scented and perfumed. The Prophet[P] *said, "If you perfume a dead body, do it three times."* **Ahmad and Al-Hakim.**

4. The shroud should be three wraps for a man and five wraps for a woman, in light of what is narrated by the group from Aishah RA, who *said, "The Messenger of Allah[P] was wrapped in three pieces of new white sheets of cloth from Yemen, without a shirt or a turban."* **Tirmidhi.**

One wrap may suffice if nothing else is available. Two wraps will also suffice, but three wraps are preferable for those who can afford it, and the female deceased should be enshrouded in five sheets.

If a pilgrim dies, he is to be washed the same way as any non-pilgrim is washed. He should be shrouded in his *ihram*, which are the two pieces of seamless cloth that pilgrims wear during *Umrah* or *Hajj*. His head should not be covered, nor should any perfume be applied to his body, because the restrictions of ihram still apply to him. This is based on what the group reported from Ibn Abbas RA, who *said, "During the last hajj, a man, mounted on a horse, was close to Allah's Prophet[P] and was trying to learn more from him, when he suddenly fell off his mount. The horse kicked him and killed him."* When the Prophet[P] was told about him, he *said, "Wash him with water and lotus (leaves), then wrap him in his two sheets, and do not perfume his body nor cover his head, for Allah, the Exalted, will raise him on the Day of Resurrection with talbiyah (The prayer uttered during the hajj by the pilgrims) on his lips'."*

The Shroud Should Be Purchased with the Deceased's Money

A person who dies and leaves some money behind should have his shroud purchased with his money. If the deceased did not leave any money, then whoever is responsible for taking care of his living expenses should provide his shroud. In case the deceased leaves no money and there is no one to take care of him, then his shroud should be purchased by the Public Treasury of the Muslims. Otherwise, individual Muslims should take care of it. The same applies to both males and females.

The Process of Shrouding the Male Deceased

- The wrapping sheets should be opened and spread out one on top of the other.
- Roll up the front half of the top sheet towards the head – like a qamees (shirt).
- The deceased, covered with a sheet (satar), is lifted and laid on his back on the top sheet (Qamees).
- The Qamees is then unrolled over the front of the body, and once the body is covered, the satar (covering sheet) is removed.
- Some scent, perfume, or sandalwood paste may be put on those parts of the body upon which one rests during prostration, that is, the forehead, nose, hands, knees, and feet.
- If it is possible, the deceased's left hand should be placed on his chest, then put his right hand on the left hand as in the *Salah* (Prayer). If not, place the hands on the side of the body.
- The edge of the next sheet (Izaar) is then folded over the deceased's right side, then the other edge over his left side.
- Then the last sheet (Lifafah) should be folded the same way.
- These sheets should be fastened with a piece of cloth (tie ropes), one above the head, another under the feet, and two around the body.

- This completes the shrouding for the male.

The Process of Shrouding the Female Deceased

- All the sheets should be spread out in layers
- Roll up the front half of the top sheet towards the head – like a qamees (shirt).
- The deceased, covered with a sheet (satar), is lifted and laid on her back on the top sheet (Qamees).
- The Qamees is then unrolled over the front of the body, and once the body is covered, the satar (covering sheet) is removed.
- Some scent or perfume may be put on those parts of the body upon which one rests during prostration, that is, the forehead, nose, hands, knees, and feet.
- The Sinaband (loincloth) is bound around (acts like underwear).
- Put on the head veil.
- The deceased's left hand should be placed on her chest, then put her right hand on the left hand as in the Salat (Prayer).
- The edge of the Izaar sheet is folded over the deceased's right side, and then the other edge is folded over his left side.
- Then the last (Lifafah) sheet should be folded the same way.

These sheets should be fastened with a piece of cloth (tie ropes), one above the head, another under the feet, and two around the body.

The washed and shrouded body is now ready for burial.

May Allah[SWT] grant us the correct knowledge in washing and shrouding the deceased and help us to undertake this noble task, abiding by what is commanded by Allah[SWT] and our Prophet[P] and be ready to do this when a loved one passes away.

Overseas Burials – An Islamic Perspective

It is against the Sunnah to delay the burial of the deceased and to move the body of the deceased unnecessarily to another place. Our beloved Prophet pbuh stressed the importance of burying the dead as soon as possible. The process of Embalming, transporting, and getting the paperwork ready all delays the burial and at a huge cost to the bereaved relatives of the deceased.

"Breaking the bone of a dead person is equivalent to breaking it when the person is alive".

Ahmed

Introduction

People, even today, but not as many as before, transport the body of deceased relatives abroad for burial.

Before any transporting of bodies overseas, the bodies are legally required to undergo a process called embalming. We will discuss the process of embalming and the Islamic perspective of sending bodies overseas for burial. The intention of this brief description is to make people aware of the horrific process of embalming in the hope that it will prevent people from practising the tradition of overseas burial.

Those who have observed this Embalming process would have been horrified by what they saw, which is the normal standard practice of the Embalmer.

It is against the *Sunnah* to delay the burial of the deceased and to move the body of the deceased unnecessarily to another place. Our beloved Prophet[p] stressed the importance of burying the dead as soon as possible. The process of Embalming, transporting, and getting the paperwork ready all delays the burial and at a huge cost to the bereaved relatives of the deceased.

Human dignity and the sanctity of the deceased

In Islam, human dignity is a right given by Allah[SWT] to all people, who are referred to as Allah's representatives on earth. Islam grants certain rights to humans even before they are born, and other rights after their death. Whether they are dead or alive, the dignity and respect required include that of the human body, created by Allah[SWT] in perfect shape.

As an indication of the respect given to the human body even during armed conflict, the Prophet[P] instructed Muslim soldiers to avoid targeting the faces of enemy combatants during a military engagement on the battlefield. In a Hadith narrated by his wife Aishah RA, the Prophet[P] *said, "Breaking the bone of a dead person is equivalent to breaking it when the person is alive".* **Ahmed.** This Hadith underlies the fundamental principle of respecting dead bodies in Islam, and in one sense, any crime committed against a dead body remains punishable in the same way as it was when the person was alive.   Burying dead bodies as soon as possible is therefore one of the ways of ensuring the dignity and respect of the dead and respecting the feelings of their living loved ones.

With regards to the burial of the dead as soon as possible, Abu Hurayrah[RA] narrated that the Prophet[P] *said, "Make haste in burying the deceased: because if it is the janazah of a pious servant, then enjoin this goodness with its station quickly; and if it is the janazah of an evil person then quickly dispose of such a load from your shoulders."* **Bukhari.** This hadith makes it clear that delaying the burial for any reason, including repatriation for overseas burial, goes against the teachings of Islam.

The Process of Embalming

Embalming is a process to preserve bodies from the time of death until they can be buried or, in the cases of other beliefs, cremated. Embalming is legally required when a body is taken out of the country. The embalmer usually provides a certificate. There are three main reasons why a body is embalmed. They are: Preservation; Presentation; and Sanitation

Preservation

Preservation of the body is vital to ensure that, during transportation or in the event of keeping the body for later burial, it does not begin to decompose and smell, and remains intact. Once the body is embalmed, it remains intact for about 14 days. If the body is not embalmed, it would begin to disintegrate in two days, depending on the climate, the environment, and the deceased person.

Presentation

The appropriate use of chemicals ensures that the body appears in its natural state, as if the person is asleep. The use of these chemicals maintains the natural colour of the face. Embalmers also use plastic eye cases to prevent the eyelids from sinking into the eye sockets, giving the appearance that the person is in a deep sleep. Some families, though not Muslims, also require embalmers to stitch the jaws together to prevent the mouth from remaining open.

Sanitation

To ensure the body is free of disease and impurities, the embalmer must remove or effectively treat the impurities. To do this, the embalmer must treat all the organs of the body with a different chemical compound.

It is the standard practice among many non-Muslims to embalm because there is no urgency in burial, so that the bereaved and family members can view the deceased in good form.

However, for the Muslims who choose to bury their loved ones abroad, before the repatriation of a deceased to another country can happen, the body will need to be prepared for transport. There is a legal requirement for the deceased to be embalmed before they can be taken overseas. During this process, the natural fluids of the body, including the blood, are replaced with a chemical solution of preservatives to slow down the effects of natural deterioration and decomposition.

The Embalming Process

The invasive nature of the embalming process involves the following steps:

1. The body is placed on a stainless steel or porcelain table, then washed with a germicide, insecticide, and olfaction. The insides of the nose and mouth are swabbed with the solution.
2. Rigour mortis, i.e., stiffness, is relieved by massage. Rarely, but sometimes, tendons and muscles are cut to place the body in a more natural pose if limbs are distorted by disease, for example, through arthritis.
3. Facial features are set by putting cotton in the nose, eye caps below the eyelids, and a mouth former is formed in the mouth, and cotton or gauze is placed in the throat to absorb purging fluids. The mouth is then tied shut with wire or sutures.
4. Arterial embalming begins by injecting embalming fluid into an artery while the blood is drained from a nearby vein or the heart. The two gallons or so needed is usually a mixture of formaldehyde or other chemicals and water. In cases of certain cancers, certain diabetic conditions, or due to the drugs used before death, where body deterioration has already begun, a stronger or waterless solution is likely to be used for better body preservation. Chemicals are also injected into other areas of the body using a syringe.

5. The second part of the embalming process is called cavity embalming. A trocar bar - a long, pointed, metal tube attached to a suction hose is inserted close to the navel. The embalmer uses it to puncture the stomach, bladder, large intestines, and lungs. Gas and fluids are withdrawn before cavity fluid, a more potent mixture of formaldehyde, is injected into the torso. The Embalming fluid is a mixture of formaldehyde, a strong tissue preservative and disinfectant, and alcohol in the form of methanol, propanediol, a compound similar to antifreeze and water.

6. The anus and vagina may be packed with cotton or gauze to prevent seepage if necessary. A close-fitting plastic garment may also be used.

7. Incisions and holes made in the body are sewn closed or filled with trocar buttons. The body is rewashed and dried.

8. Finally, the body is shrouded and placed in the casket.

It can be argued that this process is a form of mutilation of the body. The embalmer is not a physician or a surgeon, and the deceased undergoes an undignified process of being naked, being handled by an embalmer, vigorously massaged, and turned over to push the blood out and distribute the preserving fluid. Men embalm women; also naked and handled in the same way by a non-mahram.

Islam teaches utmost respect for the dead and to treat the body with dignity and care. The Prophet[P] forbade us from mutilating dead bodies. In fact, Muslims cannot cut the nails or hair of the deceased, yet during the Embalming process, the cutting of the flesh, draining out all the blood, replacing it with toxins, and sewing it up again takes place.

Honouring the dead body and its dignified burial is a fundamental Islamic obligation, and in no way or form is any harm, disrespect, or damage permitted to the natural composition and construction of the body before burial. Our beloved Prophet[P] ordered a *ghusl* for the body, and only males would handle the male deceased, and female members would handle the female deceased. Hepbuh never mentioned anything about Embalming.

Transportation overseas

A dead body is transferred within the cargo hold of a plane with the rest of the luggage, within a specially sealed coffin, and is subjected to too much movement during the journey. Arrangements would also need to be made in the country of burial for the body to be released by border guard authorities and transferred to the burial site. Booking the necessary travel tickets cannot be completed until certificates from the coroner are received and all the required documents are in place, which will cause a delay in the burial process.

Financial Cost

Repatriation of a body from the UK to a foreign country is very costly, which may cause a financial burden on the family. Instead, this money could be spent on things that will benefit the deceased and others, such as digging a well or feeding the poor, as *sadaqah jariyah* for the deceased.

The involvement of the coroner

In all cases where the deceased is sent abroad, a coroner must sign a certificate before this can be done. It does not matter whether the body requires a post-mortem or not; all bodies need to be certified before they are allowed to go abroad.

Burial in the land or city in which the deceased has died

The practice at the time of the Prophet[P] and the time of the *Sahabah* was to bury the deceased in the graveyard of the land or city in which they died. It is not proven in any hadith or report that the Prophet[P] either allowed or approved the transportation of a dead body from one location to another for any reason or purpose, even though Mecca and Madinah may only have been a few miles away for a deceased to be buried. Therefore, transporting the body for repatriation to another country, let alone a few miles away, goes against the teachings of Islam.

The Companions of the Prophet were buried in the place where they died.

We all know that there is a virtue attached to passing away and being buried in the blessed city of Madinah, as affirmed in various narrations, including in Bukhari and Tirmidhi. However, during the time of the Prophet[P] and the companions, the general practice was to bury the deceased in the location where they passed away. This includes the *martyrs* who were buried in *Uhud* and not in the graveyard of *Jannatul Baqi* in Madinah.

Many companions passed away in the surrounding regions of Makkah and Madīnah, but their bodies were not brought to Makkah or Madīnah for burial. For example, the mother of believers, Maymunah, passed away in a place known as Sarif, approximately ten miles from Makkah. She was buried in Sarif and not in the blessed city of Makkah. Similarly, we find that there are many graves of companions all over the world. Their bodies were not transported back to Makkah, Madinah, or the capitals of the Muslim world. From this, we deduce that it is preferable for the deceased to be buried in the city or town of their death.

The Prophet[P] *said, "Do not delay three things: First: Ṣalah when its time begins. Second: Janazah Salah when the deceased is present, and Third: The marriage of a woman when you find her a suitable match."* **Tirmidhi**. This hadith makes it clear that the *Janazah Salah* of the deceased should not be delayed, as this will inevitably happen were it to be transported overseas.

Conclusion

It must be noted that there is no precedent set for the repatriation of a body in Islam. There are no verses of the Quran, hadith, or *Sunnah* that promote this act, and the process of sending bodies abroad has no Islamic value for the deceased or living and goes against Islamic teachings.

Some people believe that there is a virtue or significance attached to burying a deceased person in their birthplace or place of origin, or with their ancestors. There is no basis for this belief in Islamic jurisprudence. It is therefore necessary to challenge this belief by refraining from this practice and encouraging others to do the same.

The embalming process is nothing but the mutilation of the deceased's body, is undignified, and has no place in Islam. This process is prohibited because it violates the sanctity of a deceased person. In addition to this, much of the deceased's body is kept uncovered during this process, and where *non-marham* men handle the deceased women.

How can we make ghusl for our dead brother or sister, taking great care to wash away impurities, but meanwhile pump the body full of toxic substances and stab them with a sharp instrument?

Some may argue that repatriation of the deceased allows relatives to participate in the funeral process and is what the deceased would have wanted. However, this is nothing but ignorance and misunderstanding of Islamic teachings.

A body should be buried as soon as possible after death, and burial should not be delayed unnecessarily, such as by transporting the body from one country to another. The *Sunnah* is to be buried where you die, so if there is a Muslim graveyard in the country the person dies in or graveyards with a Muslim section, as is the case in the UK, then the person should be buried there.

Proper burial of Muslims is *fard kifayah* – a community obligation. If it is not done correctly by individuals, we are all liable for punishment.

May Allah[SWT] grant us the *taufiq* to apply the principles ordained in the *Shariah* with regard to burials, and may He[SWT] forgive us for what has been done out of ignorance in the past and help us on the correct path.

The Concept of Jannah (Paradise) in Islam

"They will not taste death therein except the first death, and He will have protected them from the punishment of Hell."

Quran 44:56

"When you ask from Allah, ask Him for Al-Firdaus, for it is the best and highest part of Paradise. Above it is the Throne of the Most Merciful, and from it flow the rivers of Paradise."

Bukhari

Jannah is the eternal home of peace, pleasure, and nearness to Allah, promised to those who believe and act righteously. The term "Jannah" in Arabic means "garden", which conveys this abode's lush, beautiful, and tranquil nature. Unlike any worldly garden, Jannah is not subject to time, decay, or imperfection. It is mentioned in the Quran more than 140 times, reinforcing its centrality in Islamic theology and spirituality. Allah[SWT] describes Jannah as: *"Gardens of perpetual bliss: they shall enter there, as well as the righteous among their fathers, their spouses, and their offspring..."* **Quran 13:23**.

In Jannah, believers will enjoy:

Eternal life without death

In Jannah, life is everlasting. Once admitted, believers will never die again. The trials and fears associated with death, such as separation from loved ones or the unknown, are completely eliminated. This eternal life is a divine reward from Allah, where there is no end, and the soul is at perfect peace.

Allah[SWT] says: *"They will not taste death therein except the first death, and He will have protected them from the punishment of Hell."* **Quran 44:56.**

Youth without ageing

All inhabitants of Jannah will be in the prime of youth, typically described as being around 33 years old. This youth is not temporary but perpetual, with no signs of ageing. Beauty, strength, and vitality are permanently preserved. There is no decline in faculties or appearance—everyone remains at their best forever.

Health without illness

In Jannah, there is no pain, disease, or disability. The body and soul are in perfect harmony and function. Believers are free from the anxieties of health issues, both mental and physical. There are no hospitals, medications, or suffering. This total well-being enhances the enjoyment of Paradise's blessings.

Joy without sorrow

Jannah is a place of absolute happiness and contentment. There is no grief, stress, or heartache. The pain of this world, loss, betrayal, failure, and fear, has no place in Paradise. Every moment is filled with peace, love, and a deep sense of belonging and joy. Allah says: *"No fear will there be concerning them, nor will they grieve."* **Quran 2:62.**

Fulfilment without boredom

In Paradise, every desire is fulfilled, yet there is no monotony or boredom. The experiences, pleasures, and blessings are ever-renewing. Whether it's food, companionship, scenery, or worship of Allah, everything is profoundly satisfying and continuously refreshing. The human need for novelty and purpose is met entirely.

Jannah, in essence, is the ultimate manifestation of divine mercy; a place where every human longing is met in its purest and most enduring form. It is the final goal of every believer and the destination for which this worldly life is a test and preparation.

The Levels of Jannah

The levels of Jannah are graded based on each individual's faith, obedience, and struggle. Allah is just and rewards proportionally. Allah^SWT says: *"For all are degrees (or ranks) according to what they have done."* **Quran 6:132**

Jannatul Firdaus – The Highest Level

Jannatul Firdaus is described as the supreme level of Paradise, located directly under the Arsh (Throne) of Allah. It is reserved for the most elite of believers, such as the Prophets, truthful, martyrs, and those of highest *Taqwa*. Prophet Muhammad^P said:

"When you ask from Allah, ask Him for Al-Firdaus, for it is the best and highest part of Paradise. Above it is the Throne of the Most Merciful, and from it flow the rivers of Paradise." **Bukhari.**

The 100 Levels of Jannah

The Prophet[P] explained that there are 100 levels of Paradise, each distinct in beauty and reward, with a vast distance between them. He[P], said: *"Paradise has one hundred levels. The distance between each two levels is like the distance between Heaven and the Earth."*

Tirmidhi. The higher the level, the greater the reward, light, closeness to Allah, and comfort.

Who Will Be Granted Jannah?

The Believers (Al-Muminoon)

True believers who affirm the Oneness of Allah (Tawheed), follow His commands, and avoid His prohibitions will be admitted to Paradise. Allah[SWT] says: *"Indeed, those who believe and do righteous deeds – they will have the Gardens of Paradise as a lodging."* **Quran 18:107.**   Faith without action is incomplete. True belief (Iman) must be supported by righteous deeds.

The Righteous and God-Conscious (Al-Muttaqoon)

Those who live with Taqwa – a constant awareness of Allah and fear of displeasing Him- are specifically mentioned as the people of Jannah. Allah[SWT] says: *"Indeed, the righteous will be amid gardens and springs. Enter it in peace, safe and secure!"* **Quran 15:45-46.** *Taqwa* encompasses sincerity, humility, obedience, patience, and the avoidance of both major and minor sins. It is the defining trait of those closest to Allah.

The Repentant (At-Tawwaboon)

Jannah is not only for the sinless, but for those who sincerely repent after making mistakes. Allah[SWT] says: *"Except those who repent, believe and do righteous deeds, for them Allah will replace their evil deeds with good."* **Quran 25:70**. This verse highlights the hope and mercy of Allah. Even those who committed major sins can earn Jannah through genuine repentance *(Tawbah)* and reform.

The Patient (As-Sabiroon)

Those who exercise patience in the face of trials, poverty, injustice, and loss will receive a special reward in Paradise. Allah^{SWT} says: *"Indeed, the patient will be given their reward without measure."***Quran 39:10**.

Patience is not passive. It is an act of strength, resilience, and trust in Allah. The people of patience are honoured with elevated ranks.

The Martyrs (Ash-Shuhadaa)

Martyrs who die in the path of Allah, defending truth, justice, or faith, are granted immediate entry into Jannah and receive unique rewards. Allah^{SWT} says: *"Do not think of those who are killed in the Way of Allah as dead. Nay, they are alive, receiving provision from their Lord."* **Quran 3:169**.

Martyrdom is not limited to the battlefield. Even those who die protecting their family or faith, or due to disease like plague, can be considered martyrs.

What Awaits in Jannah?

Jannah contains pleasures that no eye has seen, no ear has heard, and no mind has imagined. Allah^{SWT} says: *"No soul knows what delights of the eye are kept hidden for them as a reward for what they used to do."* **Quran 32:17.**

This verse emphasises the limitless and unimaginable nature of Paradise. It's a realm where pleasures go beyond human perception. The delights of Jannah are not just superior in degree—they are entirely unlike anything experienced in this world, designed by the Creator for ultimate joy.

Flowing rivers of water, milk, honey, and wine (pure and non-intoxicating)

Allah^{SWT} says: *"...rivers of water unaltered, rivers of milk the taste of which never changes, rivers of wine delicious to those who drink, and rivers of purified honey..."* **Quran 47:15.**

Jannah is described as a paradise of rivers, each symbolising purity and pleasure. Water that is crystal clear; Milk with a taste that never changes; Honey that is pure and filtered; Wine, unlike worldly wine, which gives joy without intoxication or harm.

Fruits of every kind in abundance

Allah^{SWT} says: *"...and for them therein are fruits and for them is whatever they request."* ***Quran 36:57.*** Believers will have access to every type of fruit, in unimaginable abundance, freshness, and flavour. These fruits will be readily available, delivered effortlessly by servants or even brought forth by one's mere desire.

Trees whose shade stretches eternally

The trees of Paradise are unlike any on Earth. Their shade stretches for miles, offering a cool, comforting space. Some Hadith mention a rider could travel for a hundred years under the shade of one tree without reaching its end, symbolising vastness and serenity.

Palaces and Tents

Palaces made of gold, pearls, and transparent jewels. The architecture of Jannah is beyond luxury. Believers will have palaces built from bricks of gold and silver, foundations of pearls, and walls made from transparent gems, allowing light and beauty to radiate from every direction.

Each believer is promised a personal home, far grander than any worldly mansion. These dwellings reflect one's deeds and rank in Paradise, and no one will be without a place to call their own. Allah^{SWT} says: *"...for them will be palaces (in Paradise), and above them palaces built high..."***Quran 25:10.**

Rooms with high ceilings and rivers beneath. The elevated rooms of Jannah are lofty and spacious, built on hills or above flowing rivers—the natural beauty and divine construction merge to provide constant peace, stunning scenic views, and a refreshing coolness.

Eternal Youth and Companions

Believers will be 33 years old, in perfect health. Everyone in Jannah will remain forever youthful, at the peak of physical and mental perfection. There will be no ageing, fatigue, or weakness—only vitality and joy.

Married couples will be reunited

Spouses who believe will be reunited in eternal companionship, enjoying a loving and perfect relationship. There will be no disputes or heartbreak, only mutual love and closeness, forever.

In addition to earthly spouses, believers will also have pure companions—the Hoor al-Ayn—created especially for Paradise, possessing unmatched beauty, purity, and affection. These companions embody love and loyalty, contributing to emotional and spiritual fulfilment.

Peace and Joy

There will be no anger, envy, hatred, or regret. All negative emotions will be removed entirely from the hearts of Paradise's inhabitants. There is no jealousy, grudges, or sorrow. Everyone lives in harmony, content with their place and blessings. Allah^{SWT} says: *"And We will remove whatever is in their breasts of resentment..."* **Quran 7:43.**

Greetings of "Peace" from angels and Allah Himself

One of the most honoured rewards is the greeting of peace. The Angels will continuously greet the believers with "Peace" as they enter and dwell in Jannah. Most significantly, Allah Himself will say "Peace" to the righteous, a moment of eternal honour and closeness to the Creator. Allah^{SWT} says: *"Peace—a word from a Merciful Lord."* **Quran 36:58.**

Jannah is the perfect and eternal home for the soul, rich with physical comforts, emotional peace, spiritual joy, and the ultimate reward: the pleasure and nearness of Allah^{SWT}.

Seeing Allah – The Greatest Reward

Allah^{SWT} says: *"Some faces that Day shall be radiant, looking at their Lord."* **Quran 75:22-23.** This is the ultimate honour, the Sublime Vision. For the people of Jannah, seeing Allah^{SWT} will surpass every other pleasure.

Motivations for Taqwa, Righteousness, and Repentance

Jannah Requires Effort

Paradise is the prize for the struggle of the soul against desires, laziness, and sin. Allah^{SWT} says: *"Race one with another in hastening toward forgiveness from your Lord and toward Paradise..."* **Quran 57:21.**

Every Good Deed Counts

Even small acts of kindness, like smiling, feeding someone, or removing harm from the road, can lead to Paradise. Allah^{SWT} says: *"Save yourselves from Hell-fire even by giving half a date in charity."* **Bukhari and Muslim.**

Taqwa is the Key to Every Good

Allah[SWT] says: *"Whoever fears Allah – He will make for him a way out and provide for him from where he does not expect..."* **Quran 65:2-3.** Taqwa leads to peace in this life, forgiveness, and eternal joy.

Repentance is Always Open

No matter how sinful a person is, Allah loves those who return to Him. Sincere repentance erases the past. Our beloved Prophet[P] said, *"Allah is more joyful at the repentance of His servant than one who finds his lost camel in the desert."* **Muslim.**

In Conclusion

The description of Jannah in Islam is not only a narrative of reward but also a motivational map for living a better life. It inspires self-discipline, hope, repentance, and love for Allah.

Every believer, regardless of their background, is invited to strive for Jannah. Allah[SWT] says: *"And Paradise will be brought near to the righteous, not far – [It will be said], 'This is what you were promised – for every returner [to Allah] and keeper [of His covenant].'"* **Quran 50:31-32**.

May Allah[SWT] bless us with the strength and guidance to remain steadfast in our faith and strive sincerely, so that we may be granted entry into Jannah.

The Concept of Jahannam (Hellfire) in Islam

"And indeed, Hell is the promised place for them all. It has seven gates; for every gate is of them a portion designated."

Quran 15:43–44

"Some people will come out of the Fire through His Mercy. They will enter Paradise."

Bukhari

In Islam, Jahannam, often translated as Hellfire, is the place of punishment and torment in the Hereafter for those who have disbelieved in Allah, committed grave sins without repentance, or turned away from divine guidance. The Quran and Hadith describe Jahannam in vivid and powerful language to emphasise the severity of its torment and the consequences of rejecting faith or indulging persistently in sin.

Learning about Hell can be unsettling

Learning about Hell, especially the graphic descriptions in Islam, can be unsettling. However, it is essential to discuss how and why Islam addresses this topic in a manner that is honest and compassionate.

First, it is essential to understand that Islam teaches that God is not only All-Powerful but also the Most Merciful. The two most frequently mentioned names of God in the Quran are *Ar-Rahman* (The Entirely Merciful) and *Ar-Raheem* (The Especially Merciful).

So why mention Hell at all? Because Islam believes in both mercy and justice. If people commit great injustices, knowingly deny the truth, or cause harm with arrogance and never repent, then the concept of Hell becomes part of justice. It's not about scaring people for no reason, but about being real with what's at stake.

The descriptions of Hell in Islam are indeed intense: fire, regret, thirst, and darkness. But they are there to wake us up, not to break us. Like warning signs on a dangerous road, they are meant to steer people away from destruction, not to paralyse them with fear. At the same time, Islam constantly pairs these warnings with hope, offering the promise of forgiveness, repentance, and Paradise. In fact, the Quran states that God forgives all sins for those who repent sincerely.

Imagine someone rejected every sign of truth, misled others, and lived a life of cruelty with no remorse; would a just God ignore that? Hell is not for those who struggle or make mistakes; it is for those who knowingly rebel against truth with arrogance until the end. But even then, Muslims believe it is God alone who decides, with full knowledge, who goes where. Our role isn't to judge; our role is to call with love and concern, and to pray for guidance and mercy for everyone.

So yes, Hell is part of Islamic belief, but so is a deep commitment to mercy, justice, and compassion. The goal is not to terrify, but to awaken and to invite people to a path of light, peace, and ultimate salvation.

Nature and Description of Jahannam in Islam

Levels and Gates

Jahannam is not a uniform place; the Quran describes it as having seven distinct gates or levels, each prepared for different types of sinners based on the gravity of their actions and the nature of their disbelief or rebellion against God. Scholars often interpret these levels to range in severity, from lighter punishments to the most extreme torments reserved for the most arrogant and stubborn rejecters of faith. Allah^{SWT} says: *"And indeed, Hell is the promised place for them all. It has seven gates; for every gate is of them a portion designated."* **Quran 15:43–44.**

Each gate may correspond to a specific category of sin or disbelief, such as hypocrisy, polytheism, arrogance, or injustice.

Intense Suffering and Punishment

Jahannam is depicted as a place of unimaginable torment—blazing fire, scorching winds, boiling water, molten brass, and iron chains. The environment is not only physically unbearable but also emotionally and spiritually crushing.

This suffering is not metaphorical; it is real, multilayered, and eternal for some. Allah^{SWT} says: *"Then fear the Fire, whose fuel is men and stones, prepared for the disbelievers."* **Quran 2:24.**

The fuel of this fire, human beings and stones, indicates the horrifying nature of this fire. The mention of skin burning and being replaced to continue the experience of pain signifies that the punishment is continuous and recurring, and not dulled over time. Allah[SWT] says: *"Their skins will be roasted in it, and whenever their skins are burned out, We will replace them with new ones so they may taste the punishment."* **Quran 4:56**.

This verse reflects both the power of divine retribution and a deterrent for sin and disbelief.

Eternal vs. Temporary Punishment

Disbelievers – Eternal Residents

For those who die in a state of disbelief, having consciously rejected Allah and His messengers, Jahannam is an eternal abode. The Quran explicitly states that they will never exit from it, and all mercy will be withdrawn from them.

Allah[SWT] says: *"Indeed, those who disbelieve and die while they are disbelievers— upon them will be the curse of Allah... they will abide therein [Hell] forever."* **Quran 2:161-162**.

Sinful Believers – Temporary Punishment

Muslims who believed in Allah but committed major sins without repentance may be punished in Hell for a time. However, the intercession of the Prophet (pbuh) and Allah's mercy will ultimately rescue many of them, allowing them to enter Paradise in the end. The Prophet[P] said: *"Some people will come out of the Fire through His Mercy. They will enter Paradise."* **Bukhari.** This shows that belief in Allah is the foundation of salvation, even if it is accompanied by sin, though such a fate still carries a serious risk.

Consequences for Those Destined for Jahannam

Loss of All Reward and Mercy from Allah

In the Hereafter, those who are destined for Jahannam will face the complete withdrawal of Allah's mercy, the very essence of spiritual salvation. Their good deeds, even if numerous in the worldly sense, will be rendered null and void if not accompanied by genuine faith (Iman) and sincerity. This spiritual disconnection is the most devastating of all punishments.

Allah^SWT says: *"And We will regard what they have done of deeds and make them as dust dispersed."***Quran 25:23.**

This means their actions will have no eternal value. They will not be rewarded for charity, prayer, or even justice if it was not done for the sake of Allah and based upon proper belief. The loss of Divine Mercy (Rahmah) is a state of absolute spiritual exile, where the soul is no longer a recipient of divine compassion, guidance, or light.

In other verses, Allah^SWT says: *"Indeed, those who disbelieve and die while they are disbelievers—upon them will be the curse of Allah, the angels, and the people all together. They will abide therein forever; the punishment will not be lightened for them, nor will they be reprieved."* **Quran 2:161-162.**

Endless Regret and Remorse

The Quran repeatedly describes the people of Jahannam as being in a state of constant, agonising regret. Once they realise the truth, when it's too late, they will beg for another chance to return to earthly life and rectify their deeds. But these pleas will be firmly denied.

Allah^SWT says: "[They will say,] 'Our Lord, remove us; we will do righteousness—other than what we were doing!' But did We not grant you life enough for whoever would remember therein to remember, and the warner had come to you? So taste [the punishment], for there is no helper for the wrongdoers." **Quran 35:37.**

This is not just ordinary regret; it is a torment of the soul, where every memory of missed opportunities, neglected prayers, rejected truth, and sins becomes a source of torture. Their realisation comes only after the gates of mercy have been closed forever.

Allah^SWT says: *"They will cry out therein, 'Our Lord, bring us out; we will do righteousness, not what we used to do..'... But indeed, My verses had come to you, but you denied them and were arrogant, and you were among the disbelievers."* **Quran 39:58-59**

Isolation from the Righteous

One of the psychological punishments of Hell is the complete separation from loved ones, righteous people, and the community of believers. Hell is a place of loneliness, hatred, and blame, where even the bonds of family and friendship disintegrate. The righteous will be gathered in the light of Paradise, but the inhabitants of Hell will be surrounded only by fellow wrongdoers and the fierce, unmerciful angels of punishment. Allah^SWT says: *"And they will approach one another, blaming each other. They will say, 'Indeed, you used to come at us from the right.'"* **Quran 37:27-28.**

Instead of companionship, there will be mutual blame and abandonment. Even Shaytan (Satan) will disown his followers on the Day of Judgment: Allah^SWT says, *"And Satan will say when the matter has been decided, 'Indeed, Allah promised you the promise of truth. And I promised you, but I betrayed you... So do not blame me; blame yourselves.'"* **Quran 14:22.** The loss of community and love adds to the despair and dehumanisation experienced in Jahannam.

Spiritual and Physical Torment

Hell is not just spiritual, it is also a place of vivid, agonising physical punishment described with terrifying imagery in the Quran. The torments include:

- **Boiling Water and Pus to Drink -** The people of Hell will be forced to drink scalding fluids that destroy them from within: Allah^SWT says, *"And they will be given to drink scalding water that will sever their intestines."*
- **Quran 47:15.** They will cry out for relief, but be given boiling pus and filth: Allah^SWT says: *"And if they call for relief, they will be relieved with water like molten brass, which scalds their faces. Wretched is the drink, and evil is the resting place."* **Quran 18:29.**

- **Shackles and Garments of Molten Pitch –** Allah^SWT says: *"You will see the criminals bound together in shackles. Their garments of liquid pitch and their faces covered by the Fire."* **Quran 14:49-50.** These are symbols of utter humiliation and dehumanisation, showing how the residents of Hell are stripped of dignity and subjected to excruciating punishment in full view. Allah^SWT says: *"Indeed, We have prepared for the disbelievers chains and shackles and a blazing fire."***Quran 76:4.** These punishments are not temporary—they are relentlessly ongoing.

Eternal Despair and Hopelessness

In the Quran, despair is one of the worst torments of Hell. The people of Jahannam are shown as stripped of all hope; there will be no light, no release, no end to the pain. The Quran describes them as: Grimacing with disfigured faces; Living in constant fire; Emotionally broken and spiritually destroyed.

Allah^SWT says: *"But as for those whose scales are light—their souls will be in Hell, abiding eternally. The Fire will burn their faces, and they will grin with displaced lips."*

Quran 23:103-104. Their very facial expression becomes an image of horror, a manifestation of eternal grief and rejection. In another verse, Allah[SWT] says: *"They will not be killed so that they die, nor will its punishment be lightened for them. Thus do We recompense every ungrateful one."* **Quran 35:36.**

They will wish for death, but death itself will flee. This state of eternal despair is the final, unrelenting punishment: the realisation that there is no escape, no hope, and no second chance.

How to Avoid Jahannam

Tawheed (Monotheism) – Believing in Allah Alone

The cornerstone of Islamic belief is Tawheed, the oneness of Allah. Associating partners with Him (shirk) is an unforgivable sin if not repented before death. Tawheed brings protection from eternal punishment. Allah[SWT] says: *"Indeed, he who associates others with Allah—Allah has forbidden him Paradise, and his refuge is the Fire."* **Quran 5:72**.

Repentance (Tawbah)

Allah is described in the Quran as Oft-Forgiving, Most Merciful, and He invites sinners to return to Him. Sincere repentance, with regret, intention not to return to sin, and stopping the sin, wipes out even major sins.

Allah[SWT] says: *"Say, 'O My servants who have transgressed against themselves [by sinning], do not despair of the mercy of Allah. Indeed, Allah forgives all sins."* **Quran 39:53.**

This verse is a source of hope for all sinners, showing that no sin is too great for Allah to forgive.

Righteous Deeds and Obedience to Allah

Acts like prayer, fasting, giving charity, truthfulness, and justice are means to cleanse one's soul and earn Allah's pleasure. These deeds weigh heavily on the scales on the Day of Judgment. Allah[SWT] says: *"But as for he who feared the standing before his Lord and restrained himself from [evil] desires, then indeed, Paradise will be [his] refuge."* **Quran 79:40-41.**

Avoiding Major Sins and Persisting in Minor Ones

Major sins include murder, adultery, theft, backbiting, and arrogance. Regular repentance and seeking forgiveness protect one from both major and minor sins that accumulate over time. Allah^{SWT} says: *"If you avoid the major sins which you are forbidden, We will remove from you your lesser sins and admit you to a noble entrance [i.e., Paradise]."* **Quran 4:31**.

Following the Prophet Muhammad^P

The Prophet^P is the best example of how to live a life that pleases Allah. Following his Sunnah in actions, speech, and beliefs ensures staying on the straight path. Allah^{SWT} says: *"Say, [O Muhammad], 'If you should love Allah, then follow me, so Allah will love you and forgive you your sins.'"* **Quran 3:31.**

Having Hope and Mercy

Even with the severe warnings about Jahannam, Islam offers a message of infinite hope and divine mercy. The gates of repentance are open until death. The Prophet^P described Allah as being more merciful to His servants than a mother is to her child.

The Prophet^P Encouraged Believers to:

Seek Forgiveness (Istighfar) Constantly, Even for Sins They May Not Be Aware Of

The Prophet^P was the most spiritually aware and sinless of all humans, yet he would seek Allah's forgiveness more than 70 times a day. This practice emphasises that, regardless of one's level of piety, Istighfar (asking Allah for forgiveness) should be a constant in a Muslim's life. It cleanses the heart, removes minor sins, and draws the believer closer to Allah.   The Prophet^P said, *"By Allah, I seek forgiveness from Allah and I repent to Him more than seventy times in a day."* **Bukhari.**

Sins that are forgotten, hidden, or committed unknowingly can accumulate, so regular Istighfar serves as a shield against spiritual decay. Allah^{SWT} says: *"And ask forgiveness of your Lord and then repent to Him. Indeed, my Lord is Merciful and Loving."* **Quran 11:90.**

Make Tawbah (Repentance) Immediately After Committing a Sin

Tawbah (repentance) is a major act of worship that wipes the slate clean, if it is done sincerely. The Prophet^P taught that delaying repentance opens the door to sin further and hardens the heart. True *Tawbah* includes: Sincere regret for the sin; Immediate cessation of the act; Firm intention not to return to it; Returning rights or seeking forgiveness if others were harmed.

Allah^SWT says: *"O you who have believed, repent to Allah with sincere repentance. Perhaps your Lord will remove from you your misdeeds and admit you into gardens beneath which rivers flow."* **Quran 66:8.** The Prophet^P said: *"The one who repents from sin is like one who did not sin at all."* **Ibn Majah.**

Immediate *Tawbah* prevents the sin from becoming a pattern, which over time can lead to spiritual blindness and eventual punishment.

Increase in Good Deeds, Which Erase Bad Deeds

The Prophet (pbuh) encouraged believers to actively perform righteous deeds actively, especially after committing a sin, because good deeds can erase bad ones through Allah's mercy. These include: Daily prayers; Charity; Fasting; Kindness to others; Helping the needy; Remembrance of Allah (dhikr).   Allah^SWT says: *"Indeed, good deeds erase bad deeds. That is a reminder for those who remember."* **Quran 11:114.**

The Prophet^P said: *"Be conscious of Allah wherever you are. Follow the bad deed with a good one—it will erase it. And behave with good character toward people."* **Tirmidhi.** By increasing good actions, the scales of judgment tilt in favour of the believer, and it becomes a sign of sincerity and love for Allah.

Having Husn az-Zann (Good Opinion of Allah), Trusting His Mercy, Justice, and Forgiveness

The Prophet^P consistently taught that no matter how grave one's sins may be, a believer must never despair of Allah's mercy. Having Husn az-Zann, a good assumption of Allah, means trusting that: Allah^SWT is Al-Ghaffar (The Most Forgiving); His mercy outweighs His wrath; and He judges with perfect justice and knowledge.

Allah^SWT says: *"Say, 'O My servants who have transgressed against themselves [by sinning], do not despair of the mercy of Allah. Indeed, Allah forgives all sins.'"* **Quran 39:53.** In a Hadith Qudsi, the Prophet^P said, from Allah^SWT: *"I am as My servant thinks I am. So let him think of Me as he wills."* **Bukhari**

Having this mindset does not excuse sin but empowers the believer to return to Allah again and again, knowing that He is never tired of accepting sincere repentance, even if it happens a thousand times.

In another Hadith Qudsi, the Prophet^P said: *"If you come to Me with sins nearly as great as the Earth, and then meet Me not associating anything with Me, I will bring you forgiveness nearly as great as it."* **Tirmidhi.** The overall message is one of balance:

the fear of Jahannam should motivate action, but hope in Allah should encourage perseverance and prevent despair.

May Allah^{SWT} bless us with guidance and the ability to truly understand this topic, so that we may stay away from sins that lead to Jahannam and sincerely turn to Him in repentance whenever we fall short.

4. The Unseen & the Supernatural

The World of the Noble Angels

"And indeed he (Muhammad) saw him (Jibreel) in the clear horizon (towards east)."

Quran 81:23.

"The Messenger of Allah[P] said, "The angels are created from light, just as the jinn are created from smokeless fire and mankind is created from what you have been told about."

Muslim

The World of the Noble Angels

The Angels form a world distinct from that of mankind and the jinn. It is a noble world, completely pure. They are noble and pious, worshipping Allah^SWT as He should be worshipped, fulfilling whatever Allah^SWT commands them to do and never disobeying Him.

Angels are described in great detail in the Quran and Hadith. They are involved with man throughout life. From the moment a person is conceived in his mother's womb until his death and beyond, Angels play a significant role in human life. They accompany the human being, protecting him and keeping a record of all his good and bad deeds. They bring forth the soul of the deceased and bring comfort or inflict torment in the grave.

Belief in the Angels is one of the articles of faith, and a person's *Imaan* is not complete unless they believe in them. With regards to this, Allah^SWT says: *"The Messenger (Muhammad) believes in what has been sent down to him from his Lord, and (so do) the believers. Each one believes in Allah, His Angels, and His Messengers. (They say) "We make no distinction between one another of His Messengers."* **Quran 2:285.**

This means our firm belief in their existence; that they are the slaves of Allah^SWT, like mankind and *jinn*. They fulfil the commandments of Allah^SWT and are not able to do anything except what Allah^SWT has enabled them to do. Death is possible for them, but Allah^SWT has given them a long life, and they do not die until their appointed time comes.

The Angels have various duties. Among them are messengers, some are bearers of the *Arsh* - the Throne of Almighty Allah^SWT, some are the keepers of Paradise, some are the keepers of Hell, and then some record man's deeds and those who manage the clouds and the rain, etc.

Physical Characteristics of Angels

Allah^SWT has created the Angels with light. Ayesha^RA reported: *"The Messenger of Allah^P said, 'The angels are created from light, just as the jinn are created from smokeless fire and mankind is created from what you have been told about.'"* **Muslim.**

There is no mention of which light they were created from, so we cannot indulge in saying more on this matter. Since the Angels have bodies of light that are of low density, mankind cannot see them. Allah^SWT has not given our eyes the ability to see them.

Apart from our beloved Prophet^P no one has seen the Angels in their proper form. He^P saw *Jibreel* twice in the nature in which Allah^SWT created him, but human beings can see them only if they appear in human form. This aspect is mentioned in the Quran:

"And indeed he (Muhammad) saw him (Jibreel) in the clear horizon (towards east)." **Quran 81:23.**

They are great in size. Our beloved Prophet[P] said, describing *Jibreel*: *"I saw Jibreel descending from Heaven, and his great size filled the space between Heaven and earth."* **Muslim.** Also, Abd Allah ibn Masood[RA] *said, "Muhammad[P] saw Jibreel with six hundred wings."* **Bukhari.**

Among the greatest angels are those who carry the Throne of Allah, who were described in the Hadith where the beloved Prophet[P] *said, "I have been permitted to speak about one of the angels of Allah who carry the Throne. The distance between his ear-lobes and his shoulders is equivalent to a seven-hundred-year journey'"* **Abu Dawood.**

The angels are not all of one size or status; there are differences between them just as there are differences in virtue.

Angels do not eat or drink - This is indicated by the conversation between Prophet Ibrahim[AS] and the angels who visited him. Allah[SWT] says: *"Then he turned quickly to his household, brought out a calf, and placed it before them. He said, 'Will you not eat?' (When they did not eat), he conceived a fear of them. They said, 'Fear not,' and they gave him glad tidings of a son endowed with knowledge."* **Quran 51:26-28.**

The Angels remember and worship Allah tirelessly. **Allah**[SWT] says, *"They celebrate His praises night and day, nor do they ever slacken."* **Quran 21:20**. In another verse, Allah[SWT] says: *". . . For in the presence of your Lord are those who celebrate His praises by night and by day. And they never become tired."* **Quran 41.38.**

The Angels are great in number. Only Allah[SWT] knows the number of angels. However, we can say that they are far more than we can count. The Prophet[P] did say that an angel comes to the earth with a drop of rain, and its turn does not come again.

The Prophet[P] *said, "Indeed I see what you do not see, and I hear what you do not hear. The Heavens squeak, and they have the right to squeak because there is no space within it wider than 4 fingers' width except that an angel is prostrating to Allah[SWT]."* **Thirmidi.**

The Prophet[P] when he ascended to the heavens with Jibril, showed him the sheer quantity of angels that exist. The Prophet[P] *said*, Jibril said to me: *"This is Bayt al-Mamur, 70,000 Angels worship here every day, and when they leave, they never return."* **Bukhari.** Therefore, just imagine the vast number of Angels Allah[SWT] has created.

Their great powers - The angels possess great powers bestowed upon them by Allah[SWT], including the ability to take on various forms. Allah[SWT] has given the angels the ability to take on forms other than their own. Allah[SWT] sent *Jibreel* to Maryam[AS] in the form of a man, as Allah[SWT] says: *". . . Then We sent to her Our angel, and he appeared before her as a man in all respects."* **Quran 19:17.**

Their fast speed - The greatest speed known to man today is the speed of light; the angels can travel much faster than this. Hardly had an enquirer completed a question to our beloved Prophet (pbuh*) when Jibreel* would bring the answer from Allah[SWT].

The Angels do not enter a home where there is a dog present or pictures of dogs. The Prophet[P] gave us advice on how to avoid a home that repels angels. He[P] *said, "Angels do not enter a house wherein there is a soorah (image) or a dog."* **Bukhari.** Therefore, we must not display photographs and keep dogs as pets, but scholars say there is no harm in having a guard dog outside the home and caring for them.

The psychological function of the Angels

The Angels have been given the responsibility of providing positive mental energy by inspiring good thoughts in our minds. This lends support against demonic whispering into our minds. The Prophet[P] *said, "Satan has a portion over the son of Adam and the angel has a share over him. The devil directs man to commit evil actions and deny the truth and the angel encourages man to do good actions and believe in the truth."* **Tirmidhi.**

The Prophet[P] also *said, "When a man enters his house or goes to bed, an angel and a devil hasten to him. The angel says, 'End it off good!' and the devil says, 'End it off with bad!'"* **Ibn Hibban.**

There is a profound benefit to be gained from these narrations in terms of our mental health. While many factors contribute to our overall mental well-being, cognitions— i.e., thoughts—are among the most relevant to mental health professionals. Cognitive therapy involves challenging and replacing negative thoughts about ourselves and the world. Mindfulness aims to nurture a non-judgmental approach to negative thought patterns, enabling us to de-identify with them, thereby allowing the passive removal of those thoughts from our minds.

From these narrations, we learn about the psychological support available to us through the angels to counteract negative thinking. Therefore, from an Islamic perspective, adopting a lifestyle that invites the presence of Angels is a crucial aspect of good mental hygiene. Increasing the Angelic support around us is about restraining from what repels angels and committing to what attracts them.

The Angels Pray for the Believers

One of the most profound and empowering ways angels affect us on a spiritual level is through the prayers they offer on our behalf. Understanding that these noble and majestic creatures are a source of support for believers helps those going through difficulties in isolation and calamity. Knowing that there are heavenly beings that are praying for one's success helps one deal with loneliness.

Allah^{SWT} says: *"The Heavens almost break from above them, and the angels exalt their Lord with praise and ask forgiveness for those on earth. Unquestionably, it is Allah who is the Forgiving, the Merciful."* **Quran 42:5.**

In another verse, Allah^{SWT} says: *"Those [angels] who carry the Throne and those around it exalt their Lord with praise and believe in Him and ask forgiveness for those who have believed, "Our Lord, You have encompassed all things in mercy and knowledge, so forgive those who have repented and followed Your way and protect them from the punishment of Hellfire. Our Lord, and admit them to gardens of perpetual residence which You have promised them and whoever was righteous among their fathers, their spouses, and their offspring. Indeed, it is You who is the Exalted in Might, the Wise. And protect them from evil. And he whom You protect from evil on that day has received mercy from You, and that is the great attainment."* **Quran 40:7-9.**

Particular actions have been associated with the prayers of angels. The Prophet *said, "The angels send prayers on a person so long as he stays in his place of prayer. They say, 'O Allah, honour him, O Allah, have mercy on him,' And you are in a state of salah as long as you are waiting for salah."* **Bukhari.** Other examples include being among those in the first row for salah and filling in a gap to ensure the line is complete for prayer.

One of the most powerful deeds is visiting the sick, which results in 70,000 angels praying for your forgiveness.

There is also a narration that describes angels whose daily task is to make a special prayer for or against a person depending on their actions that day. The Prophet *said, "Every day two angels come down from the sky and one of them says, 'O Allah! Give to the one who spends in Your Cause, and the other angel says, 'O Allah! Destroy the one who withholds.'"* **Bukhari.**

The Angels Protect and Love the Believers

There are guardian Angels that protect us from physical and spiritual danger. Allah^{SWT} says: *"For each one are successive (angels) before and behind him who protect him by the decree of Allah."* **Quran 13:11.** In another verse, Allah^{SWT} says: *"Yes, if you hold on* to patience and piety, and the enemy comes rushing at you, your Lord will help you with five thousand angels having marks [of distinction]." **Quran 3:125.**

As for spiritual danger, we are told that reciting the Verse of the *Ayatul Kursi* before going to bed results in an Angel coming to protect us from demonic forces until morning.

This is emphasised in this hadith wherein Abu Hurayrah[RA] *said, "Allah's Messenger[P] put me in charge of the Zakah of Ramadan (i.e., Zakat l-Fiṭr). Someone came to me and started scooping up some of the foodstuff [of Zakah] with both hands. I caught him and told him that I would take him to Allah's Messenger[P]." Then Abu Hurayrah told the whole narration and added, "He (i.e., the thief) said, 'Whenever you go to your bed, recite the Verse of Al-Kursi (2:255) for then a guardian from Allah will be guarding you, and Satan will not approach you till dawn.'" On that, the Prophet[P] said, "He told you the truth, though he is a liar, and he (the thief) himself was Satan."* **Bukhari.**

Believing in the angels allows us to have courage in the face of danger and hardship. There is great comfort and security in knowing that Allah sends Angels to protect us from hardships that have not been written for us.

The Angels not only pray for us, protect us, and support us, but they also can feel genuine love for us. This forges a connection between the Angels and the individual, resulting in further support and protection. Such a person lives in this world with the Angels on their side throughout life.

The Prophet *said, When Allah loves a person, He calls Jibril and tells him, "Allah loves so-and-so, so love him." Then Jibril loves him and calls out to the inhabitants of the Heavens, "Allah loves so-and-so, so love him." So, the inhabitants of the Heavens love him, and he will find acceptance on earth.* **Bukhari.**

The Angels also seek out people doing *dhikr.* The Prophet[P] *said, "Allah has Angels who go around the highways and byways, seeking out the people of dhikr. If they find some people who are remembering Allah, they call out, "Come to what you are looking for!" And they encompass them with their wings up to the first Heaven."* **Bukhari.** Subhan Allah, how blessed are the believers!

The various duties of the Angels:

The Archangel: *Jibreel* (Gabriel) - Jibreel is one of the four greatest of angels. He is appointed to convey revelations to the Prophets by Allah[SWT].

The Angel of The Trumpet: *Israfeel* - This is the angel who will blow the trumpet. His name is mentioned among the four great Angels in the *hadiths. Israfeel* will blow twice. In the first instance, Doomsday will occur, and in the second, the resurrection will occur.

The Angel of Death: *Izraeel* - The duty of this angel is to take the souls of people whose time of death has come. He is called *"Malak-ul Mawt"* - the angel of death. Allah says: Say: *"The Angel of Death, put in charge of you, will (duly) take your souls: then shall you be brought back to your Lord".* **Quran 32:11.**

The Prophet[P] said, *"When a Muslim is about to go into the afterlife and leave this world, the angel of death comes and sits at his head. Then angels descend from the sky with faces like the sun, bringing a shroud from the shrouds of paradise, and perfume from the perfumes of paradise. They all sit with the angel of death as far as the eye can see. So, the angel of death says 'O tranquil soul, come out to forgiveness from Allah[SWT] and His pleasure.' So he removes the soul, which seeps out like water seeps out from a waterskin."* **Ahmad.**

The Prophet[P] also described how death occurs for evil criminals. *"The Angel of death says, 'O filthy soul, come out to anger from Allah[SWT]. 'The soul sinks deep into the body, so when it is pulled out it breaks vessels and nerves just like a stick with branches being pulled from a heap of wool."* **Ahmad.**

The description of the soul breaking through vessels and nerves does not refer to physical damage to vessels and nerves, but to a spiritual reality that we are unaware of.

The angel that controls the events in this realm: Mikail (Michael) - He is one of the four great angels, and He is responsible for the pouring of rain, the blowing of the wind, natural events such as the ordering of seasons, and the management of supplications of the created beings.

The Angels Kiraaman Kaatibin – The two Angels on our Shoulders - They are the two Angels who are attendants on the right and left of humans. The angel on the right is responsible for recording the good deeds and manners; the angel on the left is responsible for recording the evil deeds and manners.

The Angels Munkar and Nakir - They are the Angels that question man after he dies in the grave. These two Angels question the dead by way of the following questions and treat them according to the answers that they receive: "Who is your Lord, What is your religion, and Who is your Prophet?" This is stated by the Prophet[P] who *said, "It is in the grave when it is said to him: Who is your Lord? What is your religion? Who is your prophet?"* **Tirmidhi.**

The descriptions of the angels in the Quran and *Sunnah* are not just interesting facts to store in our brains; instead, they can serve to inspire the heart with awe and wonder when contemplating the majestic nature of these entities. Imagine that the cosmos is filled with these sublime creatures that play an active role in our lives in many different capacities. Such a thought can turn the most mundane of activities into a spectacle when viewed through the prism of faith.

For example, when we are on our way to seek knowledge, we should know that the Angels lower their wings for the seeker of knowledge. As the Prophet[P] said, *"He who follows a path in quest of knowledge, Allah will make the path of Jannah easy to him. The Angels lower their wings over the seeker of knowledge, being pleased with what he does."* **Abu Dawud.**

Allah[SWT], in his grandeur and might, has created beings whom we are not able to see and that are beyond our comprehension, but only mankind and *jinn* will be questioned on the Day of Judgement for what they did on Earth.

May Allah[SWT] grant us the correct understanding of our *deen* and the role that the Noble Angels play in our midst. Aameen.

The World of the Jinn

"Indeed We created man from dried clay of black smooth mud. And We created the jinn before that from the smokeless flame of fire"

Quran 15:26-27

"The Jinn are of three types: a type that has wings and they fly through the air; a type that looks like snakes and dogs; and a type that stops for a rest then resumes its journey."

Tahawi and Tabarani

The World of the Jinn

The existence of a parallel world has always fascinated people. Some people believe spirits are the souls of dead people or ghosts. Some say spirits are forces of good and evil, battling against one another to gain influence over humanity. Both of these explanations are more folklore and fantasy. The true explanation of such a world comes from our scriptures; the Quran and Hadith.

The *jinn* are in a world of their own, different from that of the humans or the angels. They do, however, possess some characteristics in common with humans, such as the ability to think and reflect. Similarly, they also have the ability to choose between the path of good and the path of evil in the same manner as humans. They, however, differ from humans in all other characteristics, including their origin. As Allah[SWT] says: *"....Indeed, he sees you, he and his tribe, from where you do not see them...."* **Quran 7:27.** This verse confirms that Allah[SWT] has not given us humans the ability to see the jinn.

All Shaytaans are *Jinns*, but not all *Jinns* are *Shaytaans*. The bad Jinns are called *Shaytaan*. The leader of all the *Shaytaans*, i.e. bad *Jinns*, is called *Iblees*. He is the source of all evil, and his followers, or soldiers, are also *Shaytaans*.

Iblees lured Adam and Eve to eat the forbidden fruit of *Heaven*, and thus, they were kicked out of *Heaven*, which is why we humans live on Earth instead of in Heaven.

Iblees continues to try to harm, lie, manipulate, and lure humans into doing all kinds of nasty things and lead them to hell with the help of his followers. They scare, manipulate, lie, sometimes possess humans, and do all manner of evil things. The other *Jinns*, i.e. the good ones, are usually *Jinns* who have embraced Islam. They pray, obey Allah[SWT], and do good things.

Since *Shaytaan* is a type of *jinn*, this topic is crucial for us, and we should be knowledgeable about it so that we can protect ourselves. It is no coincidence that Allah[SWT] has mentioned *Shaytaan*, his goals, his plots, and his allies throughout the entire Quran. This is because *Shaytaan* is man's greatest enemy. The believer must know the key to defending oneself from *Shaytaan*.

Who or what are the Jinn?

The origins of the *jinn* are mentioned in the Quran and the *Sunnah*. Allah[SWT] says: *"Indeed We created man from dried clay of black smooth mud. And We created the jinn before that from the smokeless flame of fire"* **Quran 15:26-27.** Thus, the *jinn* were created before man. As for their physical origin, our beloved Prophet[P] has confirmed the above verse when he said, *"The Angels were created from light and the Jinn from smokeless fire."* **Muslim.**

Like humans, they too are required to worship Allah[SWT] and follow Islam. Their purpose in life is the same as ours, as Allah[SWT] says: *"I did not create the Jinn and mankind except to worship Me."* **Quran 51:56.**

Jinns can thus be Muslims or non-Muslims. The disbelieving *Jinns* are also called devils/*Shaytaan*. *Jinns* can also become Muslims, as they did during the time of the Prophet[P], when a group of them were amazed by the recitation of the Quran. Allah[SWT] orders the Prophet to tell the people of this event: *"Say (O' Muhammed): It has been revealed to me that a group of jinn listened and said, 'Indeed we have heard a marvellous Quran. It guides unto righteousness so we have believed in it, and we will never make partners with our Lord."* **Quran 72:1-2.**

Jinns eat and drink, they marry, have children, and they die. The life span, however, is far greater than ours. They will also be subject to a Final Reckoning by Allah[SWT] and be accountable for all their actions during their lifetime. They will be present with mankind on the Day of Judgment and will either go to Paradise or Hell.

The Different Types of *Jinn*

Allah[SWT] has created different types of *jinn*. Surah Al-Jinn reveals that there are various categories of *jinn*: believers, disbelievers, misguided, and the guided. The Prophet[P] said, *"The Jinn are of three types: a type that has wings and they fly through the air; a* type that looks like snakes and dogs; and a type that stops for a rest then resumes its journey." **Tahawi and Tabarani.**

Every Human has a Jinn (devil) attached

The Prophet[P] *said, "There is none amongst you with whom is not an attached from amongst the Jinn (Devil)".* They (the Companions) *said, O Allah's Messenger, with you too? Thereupon, He[P] said, "Yes, but Allah helps me against him and so I am safe from his hand and he does not command me but for good*." *Muslim*

We humans also have angels protecting us, as the beloved Prophet[P] says: *"There is none amongst you but to whom there is assigned a constant companion from among the jinn and a constant companion from among the angels."* **Muslim.**

Their Abilities

What distinguishes the *jinn* from mankind is their powers and abilities. *Jinn* are given many powers; as a test from Allah[SWT]. If they oppress others with these powers, then they will be held accountable. One of the powers of the *jinn* is that they can take on any physical form they like. Thus, they can appear as humans, animals, trees, and anything else.

Jinn can see us, but we cannot see them. Allah[SWT] says: *"Verily, he and qabeeluhu (his soldiers from the jinn or his tribe) see you from where you cannot see them."* **Quran 7:27.**

The Shaytaan is our Open Enemy

Allah[SWT] says: *"Indeed, Shaytaan is an enemy to you; so, take him as an enemy. He only invites his party to be among the companions of the Blaze."* **Quran 35:6.**

How to Protect Ourselves from Shaytaan

We must make a strict routine to think about the Greatness of Allah[SWT]. Allah[SWT] repeatedly reminds us in the Quran of the fact that Shaytaan is our chief foe, whose main objective is to spread mischief and make us unable to distinguish between right and wrong. Allah[SWT] says: *"Shaytaan only wants to cause between your animosity and hatred through intoxicants and gambling and to avert you from the remembrance of Allah and from prayer. So, will you not desist?"* **Quran, 5: 91.**

In other verses, Allah[SWT] says: *"O you, who have believed, enter into Islam completely [and perfectly] and do not follow the footsteps of Shaytaan. Indeed, he is to you a clear enemy. But if you deviate after clear proofs have come to you, and then know that Allah is the Exalted in Might and Wise."* **Quran, 2: 208-209.**

This means Allah^SWT has clearly warned us to stay safe from the Shaytaanic evil by sticking to our Islamic devotion and beliefs. After being aware that *Shaytaan* is always ready to stray us from the right path, we have to safeguard our *imaan*. Just as we protect our homes and properties, we must also take defensive measures against this devil, as we cannot fight it, but we can only guard ourselves against it.

Abdullah bin Khubaib^RA reported: The Prophet^P said to me, *"Recite Surat Al-Ikhlas and Al-Mu'awwidhatain (Surat Al-Falaq and Surat An-Nas) three times at dawn and dusk. It will suffice you in all respects."* **Abu Dawud and Tirmidhi.** These three chapters of the Quran are just a few of the verses that we can recite every morning and evening to ward off the presence of the devil from our lives.

What else could we do to guard ourselves from the Shaytaan?

Staying in the state of *Wudu* (ablution)

It is the *Sunnah* of the beloved Prophet^P to remain in the condition of complete cleanliness and *Wudu* (ablution). This act has been emphasised for us to follow, as it prevents us from acting immorally. When we perform this action, whether for regular prayers or Quran recitation, we try to remain positive and calm, as we know that if we speak or do anything ill, we will not remain clean spiritually. So, staying away from evil feelings and being morally active means we have to shun any possible attempt by *Shaytaan* to mislead us.

Recite or Listen to the Quran

Read the Quran daily. It is one of the best ways to ward off Shaytaan. In a hadith narrated by Abu Huraira RA, the Prophet^P *said, "Do not make your houses as graveyards. Shaytaan runs away from the house in which Surah Baqarah is recited.".* **Muslim.**

If you are not able to recite the whole of Surah Baqarah every day, then at least make sure that you recite *Ayat-al Kursi* every day, along with other chapters of the Quran.

Observe Supplications during various actions

Start everything with the name of Allah^SWT so that we can seek refuge from the evils of Shaytaan. For example, when leaving your house, seek shelter from being accompanied by Shaytaan, because the Prophet^P *said, "Whoever says (upon leaving his house): "Bismillah, tawakkaltu 'alallah, wa la hawla wa la quwwata illa billah [I begin with the Name of Allah; I trust in Allah; there is no altering of conditions but by the Power of Allah]" it will be said to him: "You are guided, defended and protected." The devil will go far away from him".* **Abu Dawud and Tirmidhi.**

Whenever you enter your house or start a meal, begin with the name of Allah[SWT] and seek refuge from Shaytaan, because the Prophet[P] *said, "When a man enters his house and mention Allah's name on entering and on his food, the devil says: You have no place to spend the night and no evening meal; but when he enters without mentioning Allah's name on entering, the devil says: You have found a place to spend the night, and when he does not mention Allah's name at his food, he says: You have found a place to spend the night and an evening meal."* **Muslim.**

Also, recite the *dua* when entering your home: "*Bismil-lahi walajna, wabismil-lahi kharajna, waAAala rabbina tawakkalna*", which means "In the name of Allah we enter and in the name of Allah we leave, and upon our Lord we place our trust."

The Quran and Dhikr serve as antidotes to the many evils we face daily; they are effective ways to utilise our time, and they bring immense rewards. Every time Allah's name is mentioned, *Shaytaan* stays far away from there. So, keep your tongue moist with the remembrance of Allah[SWT].

Wake Up for Fajr

Many people struggle to wake up for the early morning prayers at the right time. Many people complain about *Fajr* being the most difficult *salah* for them. However, if you do not like to wake up for *Fajr*, then remember this: *"It was mentioned before the Prophet[P] that there was a man who slept the night till morning (after sunrise). The beloved Prophet[P] said, "He is a man in whose ears (or ear) Shaytaan had urinated."* **Bukhari.**

It is the *Shaytaan* that allows us not to wake up at *Fajr* at the right time, and we need to make deliberate efforts every day to fight him.

In another hadith, Abu Hurayrah[RA] reported that the Prophet[P] *said, "During your sleep, Shaytaan ties three knots at the back of the head of each one of you, and he seals each knot with the following words: 'The night is long, so keep on sleeping.' When that person wakes up and remembers Allah, one knot is undone; when he makes ablution the second knot is undone; and when he prays, all his knots are undone, and he gets up in the morning active and in good spirits, otherwise he gets up in bad spirits and sluggish."* **Bukhari and Muslim**

Do not believe in superstitions

The Quran strongly opposes various superstitious beliefs. Believing Fortune Tellers and Astrologers is considered to be among the major sins. Allah[SWT] says in the Quran: *"And do not pursue that of which you have no knowledge. Indeed, the hearing, the sight and the heart - about all those [one] will be questioned."* **Quran 17:36.**

In another verse, Allah^{SWT} says: *"[He is] Knower of the unseen, and He does not disclose His [knowledge of the] unseen to anyone."* **Quran 72:26.**

Further, Allah^{SWT} says: *"Indeed, Allah [alone] has knowledge of the Hour and sends down the rain and knows what is in the wombs. And no soul perceives what it will earn tomorrow, and no soul perceives in what land it will die. Indeed, Allah is Knowing and Acquainted."* **Quran 31:34.**

Allah^{SWT} also says: *"O you who have believed, indeed, intoxicants, gambling, [sacrificing on] stone alters [to other than Allah], and divining arrows are but defilement from the work of Shaytaan, so avoid it that you may be successful."* **Quran 5:90.**

No matter how righteous you may think you are, *Shaytaan* can be very influential, but he has no power or authority over us. Mankind can overcome *Shaytaan* by following the teachings of the Quran and *Sunnah.*

Allah^{SWT} says: *"And Shaytaan will say when the matter has been concluded, 'Indeed, Allah had promised you the promise of truth. And I promised you, but I betrayed you. But I had no authority over you except that I invited you, and you responded to me. So, do not blame me; but blame yourselves. I cannot be called to your aid, nor can you be called to my aid. Indeed, I deny your association of me [with Allah] before. Indeed, for the wrongdoers is a painful punishment."* **Quran 14:22.** So have total trust in Allah. He is our protector.

May Allah^{SWT} protect us from *Shaytan* and remind us to supplicate as prescribed in the Quran and *Sunnah.* Aameen.

The Evil Eye and how to protect yourself against it

"Do they envy others for the bounty that Allah has bestowed upon them? (Let them bear in mind that) We bestowed upon the house of Abraham the Book and Wisdom, and We bestowed upon them a mighty dominion."

Quran 4:54

"The Prophet once saw a young girl who had a certain expression on her face, so he said, 'Seek an Islamic formula for her because the evil eye touches her."

Bukhari

The Evil Eye and how to protect yourself against it

What is the Evil Eye?

The term "evil eye" typically refers to harm that befalls a person due to someone else's jealousy or envy towards them. The misfortune of the victim may manifest itself as sickness; loss of wealth or family; or a streak of general hardship or setback. The person inflicting the evil eye may do so with or without intention.

The Evil Eye, or *Ayn*, as it is known in Arabic, is an illness that some people are said to carry, unfortunately. It entails looking at a blessing someone has with amazement or appreciation. This then leads to dwelling on the matter, continually looking at the person who has the thing that he feels jealous of, and subsequently leading to an attack described as rays emitting from a person's eyes and soul, affecting them physically or mentally and causing the person to become ill.

One does not need to physically look at someone to give them an "evil eye". Even a blind person can give the evil eye. A person can give the evil eye merely by listening to a description of someone's blessings. The evil eye is like an arrow that comes from the soul of the one who envies the one who is envied and on whom the evil eye is put. Sometimes it hits him and sometimes it misses. If the target is exposed and unprotected, it will affect him, but if the target is cautious and armed, the arrow will have no effect and may even come back on the one who launched it.

To prevent casting an evil eye onto others, Allah[SWT] is telling us not to envy others and to be satisfied with the bounties that have been bestowed upon us, and not look at others' bounties. Allah[SWT] says: *"Do they envy others for the bounty that Allah has bestowed upon them? (Let them bear in mind that) We bestowed upon the house of Abraham the Book and Wisdom, and We bestowed upon them a mighty dominion."* **Quran 4:54**.

Our beloved Prophet[P] said, *"The evil eye is real and if anything were to overtake the divine decree, it would be the evil eye..."* **Muslim, Tirmidhi, and Ahmad.** The Prophet[P] spoke about the reality of the evil eye and advised his followers to recite specific verses of the Quran to protect themselves.

In another *Hadith*, Umme Salamah[RA] *said, "The Prophet once saw a young girl who had a certain expression on her face, so he said, 'Seek an Islamic formula for her because the evil eye touches her."* **Bukhari.**

Allah[SWT] revealed Surah *al Falaq* for protection. He says in the Quran: *"Say: 'I seek refuge with the Lord of the Dawn, from the mischief of created things; from the mischief of darkness as it overspreads; from the mischief of those who practice secret arts; and from the mischief of the envious one as he practices envy.'"* **Quran 113:1-5**.

The Prophet[P] also rebuked followers who admired someone or something without praising Allah[SWT]. He[P] *said, "Whenever one of you sees something with his brother that amazes him, ask Allah to bless him."* **Ibn Majah.** Thus, we need to say Masha Allah - "Allah has willed it."

It may not be Evil Eye

Unfortunately, some Muslims blame every little thing that goes "wrong" in their lives on the evil eye. People are accused of "giving an eye" to someone without any basis. This is wrong. There are instances when someone suffers from a psychological condition such as mental illness, but it gets attributed to the evil eye. Sadly, when this happens, medical treatment is not sought. We must be careful to recognise that there are biological disorders that may cause specific symptoms, and it is incumbent upon us to seek medical attention for such illnesses.

We must also recognise that when things go wrong in our lives, we may be facing a test from Allah[SWT], and need to respond with reflection and repentance, not assert it to the evil eye.

Envy is of varying degrees

The first and worst are those who simply wish to destroy the bounty, regardless of whether they receive it or not. They only want to destroy that blessing because it was not given to them in the first place. The second level is where a person wants a blessing to be taken away from someone else because they hope it will come to them. This person not only seeks to remove the bounty but also works to claim it for himself. The third is where he wishes for himself a blessing like that which someone else has without wanting it to be taken away from the other person. This is permissible and is not called *hasad* (destructive jealousy/envy); instead, it is called *"Ghibtah"* (envy that is free from malice).

Hasad – the destructive form of jealousy - causes a great deal of harm. The Prophet[P] said, *"There has come to you the disease of the nations before you, jealousy and hatred. This is the 'shaver' (destroyer); I do not say that it shaves hair, but that it shaves (destroys) faith. By the One in Whose Hand is my soul, you will not enter Paradise until you believe and you will not believe until you love one another. Shall I not tell you of that which will strengthen love between you? Spread the greetings of peace amongst yourselves."* **Tirmidhi.**

Hasad not only spoils the peace of mind, but it also weakens faith in Allah[SWT], because when a person becomes jealous of another, they think that Allah[SWT] has not been fair enough with them, although they do not know what blessings Allah[SWT] has given to each of His servants. Indeed, Allah does justice better than anybody can think of. Allah[SWT] has bestowed mercy and blessings to everyone, and He tests people in different ways. As Allah[SWT] says: *"And We will surely test you with something of fear and hunger and a loss of wealth and lives and fruits, but give good tidings to the patient."* **Quran 2:155.**

Some people may have less in terms of wealth, beauty, health, or children, while others may have more. This is the *Qadr* of Allah, and we need to overcome these tests by being patient. A person with a tremendous amount of wealth is also tested on how they earned it and how they spend it.

With regards to this, Allah[SWT] says: *"And Allah has favoured some of you over others in provision. But those who were favoured would not hand over their provision to those whom their right hands possess so that they would be equal to them therein. Then is it the favour of Allah they reject?"* **Quran 16:71.**

One important incident in which an evil eye was cast was narrated by Sahl ibn Haneef RA. The beloved Prophet[P] came out and travelled with him towards Makkah until they were in the mountain pass of Al-Kharar in Al-Jahfah. There, Sahl ibn Haneef[RA] did *ghusl* (i.e., bathed), and he was a handsome white-skinned man with beautiful skin. A companion, Amir ibn Rabeeah RA, looked at him while he was performing *ghusl* and said, *"I have never seen such skin as beautiful as this, not even the skin of a virgin."* Upon those words, Sahl fell to the ground. They went to the Prophet and *said, "O Messenger of Allah, can you do anything for Sahl because by Allah he cannot raise his head."* He[P] said, *"Do you accuse anyone with regard to him?"* They said, *"'Amir ibn*

236

Rabeeah looked at him." So, they called Amir and rebuked him strongly. Hepbuh *said,* *"Why would one of you kill his brother? If you see something that you like, then pray* *for blessings for him."* Then he said to him: *"Wash yourself for him."* So, he washed his face, hands, forearms, knees, and the sides of his feet, and inside his *izaar* (lower garment) in the vessel. Then that water was poured over him (i.e., Sahl), and a man poured it over his head and back from behind. He did that to him. Then, Sahl got up and joined the people, and there was nothing wrong with him. "Ahmad **and Albani**.

The lesson we learn from this incident is that the evil eye is real and the remedy shown by our beloved Prophet[P].

Protection from the Evil Eye

Only Allah[SWT] can protect us from harm, and believing otherwise is a form of *shirk*. Some misguided Muslims try to defend themselves from the evil eye with talismans, *taveez*, beads, a small Quran hanging around their necks, and such things. Many unscrupulous traders in this field will charge an enormous amount of money. The so-called lucky charms do not offer any protection. For guidance on this matter, it is advisable to consult a learned expert in the field of *Ruqyah*.

The best protection against the evil eye is that which brings one closer to Allah[SWT] through *dhikr*, i.e., the remembrance of Allah[SWT], *Salah*, and reading the Quran. These remedies can be found in the authentic sources of the Quran and *Hadith*, not from hearsay, old wives' tales, or un-Islamic traditions.

As believers, when we see good in others, we should say "Masha Allah", meaning "Allah has willed it". We recite this when praising or admiring someone or something, as a reminder to ourselves and others that all good things come from Allah[SWT]. Jealousy and envy should not enter the heart of a person who believes that it is Allah[SWT] who has bestowed blessings on people according to His Will.

Ruqyah

Ruqyah is the use of words from the Quran which are recited as a way of curing an afflicted person. Reciting *ruqyah*, as advised by the Prophet[P] has the effect of strengthening the faith of a believer, and reminding them of Allah's power. This strength of mind and renewed faith may help one to resist or fight against any evil or illness directed their way.

Allah says in the Quran: *"We send down stage by stage in the Quran, that which is a* *healing and a mercy to those who believe..."* **Quran 17:82.**

The most recommended verses to read include:

Surah *Al-Fatiha*; The last two surahs of the Quran (*Al-Falaq and An-Nas*) and *Ayat Al-Kursi*.

There are other recommended *duas* that one can recite, and these can be obtained from scholars and those who are knowledgeable in the field of *Ruqya*.

Conditions for *Ruqyah* to be successful

- **Intention** - *Ruqyah is* a dua. The intention should always be to ask Allah[SWT] to remove evil from the words of the Quran.
- **Conviction** - One should recite loudly and clearly, with firm conviction and belief in Allah[SWT], who Alone gives cure.
- **Patience and Consistency** - Like all treatments, consistency is key. Daily recitation, *dua,* and other treatments must be maintained for positive results.

Seeking Protection for Children

Since young children are unable to recite *Ruqyah*, parents should always recite *Ayat al-Kursi* and the last 3 Surahs of the Quran and blow on them. Children are more vulnerable to the evil eye. It is essential, therefore, to teach them these *ayats* as soon as possible and instruct them to recite them and blow on themselves.

Dangers of social media

The internet and social media are now a big part of our lives today. Sadly, this has made us much more vulnerable to the evil eye. We should be cautious of posting pictures of ourselves, our children, and our possessions on social media. At the same time, we should not envy the blessings of others. We should reflect on how using social media affects our health, family relations, spirituality, and ultimately our relationship with Allah[SWT].

How to Stop Envying Others

- If something pleases you, then say *MashaAllah Barak Allahu Feek* (What Allah has willed; May Allah bless you).
- Give gifts and do good to those whom you envy.
- Praise them when you wish to criticise them.
- Make *dua* for them, even if you are reluctant to do so.
- Be aware of how deadly envy is and how it will only return to harm you.
- Be content with Allah's decree.

- Say *Bismillah* (in the name of Allah) before undressing and entering the toilet. This puts a screen between us and the jinn. **Tabarani**
- Recite the specific *dua* before entering the toilet: (Bismillah) Allahumma innee A'uzu bika minal-khubuthi wal-khaba-ith - Translation: "In the name of Allah. O Allah, I seek protection in you from the male and female shayateen."
- Mention Allah's name when entering your home and before eating. This way, the Shaytaan cannot spend the night in your home, nor can he partake in your meal.
- Jabir[RA] reported: I heard Messenger of Allah[P] saying, "If a person mentions the Name of Allah upon entering his house or eating, Shaytan says, addressing his followers: 'You will find nowhere to spend the night and no dinner.' But if he enters without mentioning the Name of Allah, Shaytan says (to his followers); 'You have found (a place) to spend the night in, and if he does not mention the Name of Allah at the time of eating, Shaytan says: 'You have found (a place) to spend the night in as well as food.'" **Muslim.**
- When entering your home, make a habit of saying Asalaamo Allaikum even if no one is at home and recite the *dua* of entering the house "Bismillaahi walajnaa, wa bismillaahi kharajnaa, wa alaaRabblnaa tawakkalnaa." – Translation: "In the Name of Allah we enter, in the Name of Allah we leave, and upon our Lord we depend." Then recite Surah Ikhlas and Darood sharif.
- When leaving your home to recite: *"Bismillaahi, tawakkaltu alallaahi, wa laa hawla wa laa quwwata ' illaa billaah."* Translation: "In the Name of Allah, I have placed my trust in Allah; there is no might and no power except by Allah." **Abu Dawood.** This is a source of guidance and protection, and the devils cannot get to you. Also, make a habit of reciting A*ayatul Kursi.*
- Recite A*ayatul Kursi* in the morning, evening, and before sleeping. This protects you from the *jinn.* **Bukhari and Tabarani.**
- Reciting A*'udhu bikalima tillahit tammati min sharri ma khalaq.* Translation: "I seek refuge in the perfect words of Allah from the evil of that which He has created." This *dua* will protect you from vermin and other harmful creatures. **Nasai**
- Recite the last two verses of Surah Baqarah before sleeping. This will suffice. **Bukhari**
- Do not display your happiness to people on social media through sharing your pictures of the food you eat or sharing your holiday pictures, etc. When you show your joy, you bring their eyes to yourself. The Prophet[P] *said,* *"Resort to secrecy for the fulfilment and success of your needs, for, verily, everyone who has a blessing is envied."* **Tabarani.**

- The Prophet[P] also *said,* "When night falls, then keep your children close to you, for the devil spread out then." **Bukhari.**

Many people resort to hatred, jealousy, and envy. This is sad. We need to remember and take heed of the words of our beloved Prophet[P] when he *said, "Verily, my nation will be afflicted by the disease of other nations."* They said, *"O Messenger of Allah, what is the disease of other nations?"* The Prophet[P] said, *"Insolence, arrogance, accumulation of wealth, competition in worldly gains, mutual hatred and envy until there will be wrongdoing and then killing."* **Albani.**

We need to protect ourselves from the evil *jinn* and mankind by having strong faith in Allah[SWT], seeking refuge with Him, beseeching Him, and reciting the supplications for protection regularly.

May Allah[SWT] grant us the *taufiq* to understand this greatly misunderstood topic and grant us protection from the evil eye. May He give us the ability to put total trust in Him alone and use the means through *ruqya* to protect us from the evil eye and *hasad.* Aameen.

A Glossary of Arabic Terms

Adhan   Call to prayer. This happens five times a day before each
                   congregational prayer.

Akhirah   Everlasting life after death - the hereafter.

Akhlaq   Conduct, manners, character, attitudes and ethics.

Allah   The Islamic name for God in the Arabic language. Used in
                   preference to the word God, this Arabic term is singular, has no
                   plural, nor is associated with masculine, feminine or neuter
                   characteristics.

Allahu Akbar   Allah is the greatest.

Abu Dawood   One of the scholars who compiled the six collections of hadith and
                   was famous for his book Sunan Abu Dawud.

Ahmad   Compiler of the Hadith and the traditions of the Prophet
                   Muḥammad pbuh. He was a Muslim theologian, and jurist.

AS   AS means "Alayhis Salaam" (Peace be upon Him), appears after the
                   names of all the archangels (such as Jibreel, Mikaeel, and others)
                   and all the prophets except for the Prophet Muhammad.

Barakah   Blessings.

Dhikr   Remembrance of Allah SWT in one's heart or be reciting His names
                   or sections from the Quran.

Deen   Way of life; the Islamic religion and its practices.

Dua   Varying forms of personal prayer and supplication.

Fatwa   The legal ruling of a knowledgeable Muslim scholar and jurist,
                   based on the Quran, Hadith and Islamic Shariah.

Hadith	The sayings of the Prophet Muhammad pbuh, as recounted by his household, and companions. These are a major source of Islamic law. The hadith were collected and recorded by Imams, Bukhari, Muslim, Tirmidhi, Abu Dawood, Ibni Majah, Ahmad etc.
Hajj	Annual pilgrimage to Makkah, which each Muslim must undertake at least once in a lifetime if they are in good health and the wealth.
Halal	Permissible.
Haram	Unlawful.
Ibadah	All acts of worship. Any permissible action performed with the intention to obey Allah.
Iblees	The Jinn who defied Allah SWT by refusing to bow to Adam and later became the tempter to deviate all human beings to evil; also known as Shaytan.
Eid-ul-Fitr	Celebration of breaking the fast on the day after Ramadan ends. A holiday and feast for thanking Allah SWT and celebrating a happy occasion.
Eid-ul-Adha	Celebration of the sacrifice, commemorating Prophet Ibrahim's willingness to sacrifice his son Ismail. Occurs during the Hajj period.
Fitra	Original and natural disposition; innate nature. They way Allah SWT created us.
Huququl Allah	The Rights of Allah.
Huqul Ibad	The Rights of Allah's creation.
Ibn Taymiyah	One of Islam's most forceful theologians, from the Hanbali school of thought, sought the return of the Islamic religion to its sources: the Quran and the Sunnah.
Imaan	Faith.
Istighfar	Seeking Allah's forgiveness.

Jahannam	Hell, the punishment for those who are judged to be evil.
Jannah	Paradise, the reward for those who are judged to be good.
Jibreel	Gabriel. The angel who delivered Allah's messages to His Prophets.
Jihad	Personal individual struggle against evil in the way of Allah. It can also be collective defence of the Muslim community.
Jinn	Being created by Allah SWT from fire.
Jummah	Weekly communal salah (prayer) and attendance at the khutbah (sermon) performed shortly after midday on Fridays.
Kabah	A cube-shaped structure in the centre of the grand mosque in Makkah. The first house built for the worship of the One True God.
Khutbah	Sermon or Speech on special occasions such as the Jummah and Eid prayers.
Kufr	Rejection of faith. Covering of truth. A *kafir* is someone who reject the truth. Someone who has consciously chosen to forget/deny/turn away from the reality of their existence after the truth has been presented to them.
Masjid	Place of prostration. The Mosque.
Muadhin	Caller to prayer; the Adhan.
Muhammad	Name of the last and final Prophet pbuh - peace be upon him.
Mumin	Faithful believer and an observant Muslim who wholeheartedly submits to Allah's guidance.
Muslim	One who claims to have accepted Islam by professing the Shahadah – the declaration of faith; and believes in the five pillars of Islam.
Nafs	The individual self or soul in Islam.

Pbuh	Abbreviation for – peace and blessings upon him. This supplication is made whenever the name of Prophet Muhammad and other Prophets are mentioned.
Qadar	Allah's complete and final control over the fulfilment of events or destiny. Preordainment.
Qiblah	Direction which Muslim's face when performing salah - towards the *Kabah* in Mecca Saudi Arabia.
Quran	That which is read or recited. The Divine Book revealed to the Prophet Muhammad pbuh. Allah's final revelation to humankind.
RA	"Radhi Allahu anhu" male or ""Radhi Allahu anha" female - May Allah be pleased with him/her. Written after the name of a companion of the Prophet male or female.
Ramadan	This is in the ninth month of the Islamic calendar, during which fasting is required from before dawn until sunset, as ordered by Allah SWT in the Quran.
Sadaqah	Voluntary payment or good action for charitable purposes.
Sahih Bukhari	This is the title of the books of Hadith compiled by Muhammad ibn Ismail al-Bukhari, a Sunni scholar. The collection is described as *Sahih* - which means authentic.
Sahih Muslim	This is title of the books of Hadith compiled by Abul Husayn Muslim ibn al-Hajjaj, a Sunni scholar. The collection is described as *Sahih* - authentic.
Salah	Prescribed communication with, and worship of, Allah, performed under specific conditions, in the manner taught by the Prophet Muhammad pbuh,.and recited in the Arabic language. The five daily times of salah are fixed by Allah.
Seerah	Biography of the conduct and the example of the Prophet Muhammad pbuh.
Shariah	Islamic law based upon the Quran and Sunnah.

Shaytan	Known to be the devil – *Iblees* and his soldiers. They Rebellious and they encourage the believers to disobey Allah.
Shirk	Associating partners with Allah.
Sunnah	These are practices, customs and traditions of Prophet Muhammad pbuh. This is found in both Hadith and in the Prophet's, autobiography known as *Sirah*.
SWT	These letters are mentioned after Allah's name. the abbreviation is to mean – "Subhanahu Wa Talala" translated to mean "May He be praised and exalted."
Taufiq	The ability and opportunity to achieve success. Asking Allah SWT for this.
Taqwa	An intense awareness of the presence of Allah. Someone who is conscious of Allah.
Tawheed	Belief in the Oneness of Allah SWT- absolute monotheism as practiced in Islam.
Tirmidhi	A collection of hadith compiled by Imam Abu Isa Muhammad at-Tirmidhi.
Ulama	Scholars of Islamic law and jurisprudence - singular *Alim*.
Ummah	Community. World-wide community of Muslims, the nation of Islam.
Zakat	Charitable donations to help the purification of wealth by payment of an annual welfare due of 2.5% on the wealth one possesses. An obligatory act of worship.

References/suggested reading

Amira Ayad, 2008. *Healing Body & Soul* – International Islamic Publishing House.

Al-Imam Abu Zakariya Yahya bin Sharafi An-Nawawi, translated by Mahomed Mahomedy, 2017. *Riyad as-Salihin, Gardens of the Righteous* – Zam Zam Pubishers.

Abdul Wahid Hamid, 1990. *Islam the Natural Way* – Muslim Education & Literary Services, London.

A.I. Akram, 2007. *Khalid Bin Al-Waleed: A Biographical Study of one of the Greatest Military Generals in History* – Maktabah Booksellers and Publishers.

Abu Ammaar Yasir Qadhi, 2003. *Dua, The Weapon of the Believer, a treatise on the status and etiquette of dua in Islam* - Al-Hidaayah Publishing and Distribution Ltd.

AAhad M. Osman-Gani, 2011. *Spirituality in Management from Islamic Perspectives* - International Islamic University Malaysia,

Asim Khan & Toyris Miah, 2022. *The Simple Seerah:* Three Parts – The Simple Seerah Ltd.

Dr Muhammad Ali Al-Hashimi, 2007. *The Ideal Muslim Society* – International Islamic Publishing House.

Dr Muhammad Muhsin Khan, 1994. *Summarised Sahih Al-Bukhari* – Islamic University of Madinah: Dar-us-Salaam Publications.

Dr Ilona Boniwell, 2016. *Positive Psychology* – Icon Books Ltd.

Dr Musharraf Hussain, 2019. *The Majestic Quran: A Plain English Translation* – Invitation Publishing.

Dr. Muhammad Abd Al-Rahaman Al-Arifi, 2008. *Enjoy Your Life, the art of interacting with people as deduced from a study of the Prophet's pbuh life* - Maktaba Dar-us-Salaam.

Dr Muhammad Abdul Bari, 2005. *Race, Religion & Muslim Identity in Britain* – Renaissance Press.

Ebrahim et al. *Economic Development Report* - University of Durham

Ibn Qayyim Al-Jawziyya, 2002. *The Way to Patience & Gratitude* – Umm al-Qura Publishing.

Imam Ibn Qayyim Al-Jauziyah, 2003. *Healing with the Medicine of the Prophet pbuh* - Maktaba Dar-us-Salaam.

Jeffery Lang, 2009. Losing My Religion: A call for Help – Amana publications.

Hamza Anreas Tzortzis, 2019. *The Divine Reality: God, Islam & the Mirage of Atheism* - Lion Rock Publishing.

Imran Hosein, 2017. *Methodology for study of the Quran* – Imran Hosein Publications.

Ibn al-Jawzi, 2013. *Seeds of Admonishment and Reform* – Dar as-Sunnah Publishers.

Imam Ghazzali Translated by Fazlul Karim, 1993. *Ihya Ulum-Id-Din: Revival of Religious Learning* – Darul-Ishaat Publishing.

John Adair, 2010. *The Leadership of Muhammad* - Kogan Page Limited.

Jurgen Wolff, 2008. *Focus: The Power of Targeted Thinking* – Pearson Education Limited.

Ken A. Verni, 2015, *Every Day Mindfulness* – Dorling Kindersley Limited.

Kabir Edmund Helminski, 1992. *Living Presence, A Sufi Way to Mindfulness & the Essential Self* – Penguin Putman Inc.

Muhammad Idrees Kaandhelwi, 2020. *Seeratul Musafafa, Biography of the Chosen Messenger of Allah, Nabi Muhammad Mustafa* – Zam Zam Publishers.

Muhammad Ali Al-Hashimi, 2005. The Ideal Muslim: The True Personality of the Muslim as Defined in the Quran and Sunnah – International Islamic Publishing House.

Mufti Muhammad Taqi Usmani, 2018. *The Meaning of the Noble Quran* – Makraba Ma'ariful Quran – Kharachi; Quranic Studies Publishers.

Martin Lings, 1991. *Muhammad, his life based on the earliest sources* – The Islamic Text Society.

Malik Badri, 2013. *Abu Zayd Al-Balkhi's Sustenance of the Soul, The Cognitive Behaviour Therapy of a Ninth Century Physician* – The International Institute of Islamic Thought.

Michael A. Singer, 2007. *The Untethered Soul: The Journey beyond yourself* – New Harbinger Publications and Noetic Books.

Muhammad Saleem Dhorat, 2019. *Inspirations Volume 1* – Islamic Dawah Academy.

Muhammad Saalih Al-Munajjid 2014. *Interactions of the Greatest Leader, The Prophet's Dealings with Different People* – Zad Publishing.

Omar Khayyam Sheikh, 2013. *Strategies of Prophet Muhammad pbuh* – Maktaba Dar-us-Salaam.

Prof. Dr. Abdul Karim Bakkar, 2014. *Change or Lose, An Islamic Vision for the Principles & Methods for Personal Change* – Dakwah Corner Publications.

Prof. Muhammad Zulfiqar, 2006. *Prayer According to the Sunnah* - Maktaba Dar-us-Salaam.

Robin Sharma, 2008. *Leadership Wisdom: the 8 Rituals of Visionary Leaders* – Jaico Publishing House.

Shaykh Salih Al-Jafari. *Light for the Seeker* – Beacon Books and Media Ltd.

Steve Zaffron & Dave Logon, 2009. *The three laws of Performance* – Jossey Bass Publishing.

Syed Sulaiman Nadwi, translated by Dr Rizwan Uddin Ahmad, 1999. *Ethics in Islam* – Darul-Ishaat Publishing.

S. E. Al-Djazairi, 2007. *The Myth of Muslim Barbarism and its Aims* – Bayt Al-Hikma Press.

Umar S. Al-Ashqar, 2003. *Belief in Allah, In the Light of the Quran and Sunnah* - International Islamic Publishing House.

Umar S. Al-Ashqar, 2003. *The World of the Noble Angels, In Light of the Quran and Sunnah* - International Islamic Publishing House.

Umar S. Al-Ashqar, 2005. *The World of the Jinn & Devils, In Light of the Quran and Sunnah* - International Islamic Publishing House.

Umar S. Al-Ashqar, 2003. *The Minor Resurrection: What happens After Death, In Light of the Quran and Sunnah* - International Islamic Publishing House.

Dr Yasir Qadhi, 2024. *The Sirah of the Prophet* – The Islamic Foundation.

Book 2 entitled "Nurturing the Soul" will cover:

Printed in Dunstable, United Kingdom